John Dewey
and the
Artful Life

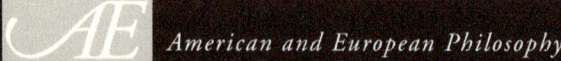
American and European Philosophy

GENERAL EDITORS: CHARLES E. SCOTT AND JOHN J. STUHR
ASSOCIATE EDITOR: SUSAN M. SCHOENBOHM

Devoted to the contemporary development of American and European philosophy in the pragmatic and Continental traditions, AMERICAN AND EUROPEAN PHILOSOPHY gives expression to uniquely American thought that deepens and advances these traditions and that arises from their mutual encounters. The series will focus on new interpretations of philosophers and philosophical movements within these traditions, original contributions to European or American thought, and issues that arise through the mutual influence of American and European philosophers.

EDITORIAL ADVISORY BOARD

BETTINA BERGO, Worcester Polytechnic Institute • ROBERT BERNASCONI, The Pennsylvania State University • PEG BIRMINGHAM, DePaul University • JUDITH BUTLER, University of California at Berkeley • EDWARD CASEY, SUNY at Stony Brook • VINCENT COLAPIETRO, The Pennsylvania State University • SIMON CRITCHLEY, The New School University • FRANÇOISE DASTUR, Université de Paris XII • PAUL DAVIES, University of Sussex • MIGUEL DE BEISTEGUI, University of Warwick • GÜNTER FIGAL, Universität Tübingen (Eberhard-Karls-Universität) • RUSSELL GOODMAN, University of New Mexico • DAVID HOY, Cowell College • MARK JOHNSON, University of Oregon • DAVID FARRELL KRELL, DePaul University • JOHN LACHS, Vanderbilt University • JOHN LYSAKER, Emory University • LADELLE MCWHORTER, University of Richmond • KRZYSZTOF MICHALSKI, Boston University • JEAN-LUC NANCY, Université de Strasbourg 11 (Université des Sciences Humaines) • KELLY OLIVER, Vanderbilt University • STEFAN GEORGIEV POPOV, University of Sofia • SANDRA ROSENTHAL, Loyola University • HANS RUIN, Stockholm University • DENNIS SCHMIDT, The Pennsylvania State University • CHARLENE SEIGFRIED, Purdue University • SHANNON SULLIVAN, The Pennsylvania State University • JOHN SALLIS, Boston College • RICHARD SHUSTERMAN, Florida Atlantic University • ALEJANDRO VALLEGA, California State University, Stanislaus • GIANTERESIO VATTIMO, Università degli Studi di Torino • FRANCO VOLPI, Università degli Studi di Padova • CYNTHIA WILETT, Emory University • DAVID WOOD, Vanderbilt University

David Farrell Krell, *The Purest of Bastards: Works of Mourning, Art, and Affirmation in the Thought of Jacques Derrida*

Bruce Wilshire, *The Primal Roots of American Philosophy: Pragmatism, Phenomenology, and Native American Thought*

Robert E. Innis, *Pragmatism and the Forms of Sense: Language, Perception, Technics*

John T. Lysaker, *You Must Change Your Life: Poetry, Philosophy, and the Birth of Sense*

Alejandro A. Vallega, *Heidegger and the Issue of Space: Thinking on Exilic Grounds*

Scott F. Scribner, *Matters of Spirit: J. G. Fichte and the Technological Imagination*

Scott R. Stroud

John Dewey and the Artful Life

Pragmatism, Aesthetics, and Morality

The Pennsylvania State University Press
University Park, Pennsylvania

Library of Congress Cataloging-in-Publication Data

Stroud, Scott R.
  John Dewey and the artful life : pragmatism, aesthetics, and morality / Scott R. Stroud.
       p.   cm.—(American and European philosophy ; no. 7)
  Summary: "Examines the relationship between art and morality discussed in the writings of American pragmatist John Dewey. Argues that there is a clear connection between the experience of art and the project of moral cultivation"
  —Provided by publisher.
  Includes bibliographical references (p.   ) and index.
  ISBN 978-0-271-05007-2 (cloth : alk. paper)
  ISBN 978-0-271-05008-9 (pbk : alk. paper)
  1. Dewey, John, 1859–1952.
  2. Art and morals.
  I. Title.
  B945.D44S79   2011
  191—dc22
  2011011264

Copyright © 2011 The Pennsylvania State University
All rights reserved
Printed in the United States of America
Published by The Pennsylvania State University Press,
University Park, PA 16802-1003

The Pennsylvania State University Press is a member of the Association of American University Presses.

It is the policy of The Pennsylvania State University Press to use acid-free paper. Publications on uncoated stock satisfy the minimum requirements of American National Standard for Information Sciences—Permanence of Paper for Printed Library Material, ANSI Z39.48–1992.

For Talia
WITHOUT WHOM NOT

Contents

Acknowledgments		ix
1	The Problems of Art and Life	1
2	The Value of Aesthetic Experience	12
3	Dewey on Experience, Value, and Ends	35
4	Aesthetic Experience and the Experience of Moral Cultivation	58
5	Reflection and Moral Value in Aesthetic Experience	93
6	Orientational Meliorism and the Quest for the Artful Life	136
7	Practicing the Art of Living: The Case of Artful Communication	168
8	Beginning to Live the Artful Life	193
	Notes	207
	Bibliography	217
	Index	225

Acknowledgments

Like any complex work of art or argument, this book finds itself placed in a causal web that implicates many people. Whatever value it may possess was surely enabled by the help of many of my colleagues, friends, family members, students, and teachers. I thank my excellent mentors, Richard Shusterman and Paul Guyer, for their inspiration and guidance in pragmatism, aesthetics, and the art of being a great scholar. I only hope to someday come close to following their examples in argument and action. This work has benefited from other wonderful teachers and academic guides, from all the points in my maturation as an academic: Paul C. Taylor, Joseph Margolis, Shelley Wilcox, Rita Manning, Tom Leddy, Eleanor Wittrup, and Jim Heffernan. My colleagues in philosophy and communication, Roger Ames, Douglas Anderson, Gregory Pappas, John Gibson, William Keith, Paul Stob, Nathan Crick, Robert Danisch, Chris Russill, Peter Simonson, Crispin Sartwell, Larry Hickman, and many others are to be thanked for helping me refine my reading of Dewey. The individuals at The Pennsylvania State University Press must be thanked for their professionalism. Patrick Alexander, John Stuhr, and my anonymous reviewers have been particularly helpful to me as this book came into its final form. I have been blessed by supportive colleagues in communication studies at the University of Texas at Austin and in philosophy at the University of Texas-Pan American. I particularly wish to thank Barry Brummett, Richard Cherwitz, and Greg Gilson for their help, in small and large ways, in this project. This work has also benefited from the comments of my graduate students at Texas, including Danee Pye, Robert L. Mack, Roy Christopher, Matt Morris, and Joseph McGlynn.

I have had the good fortune to test some of the fundamental ideas of this book in earlier publications. I would like to thank Rodopi Publishers for permission to include a significantly revised version of this essay as part of chapter 4: "Constructing a Deweyan Theory of Moral Cultivation," *Contemporary Pragmatism* 3 (2006): 99–116. Thanks to Purdue University Press for permission to include a revised and extended version of this article in the extensive argument of chapter 5: "Dewey on Art as Evocative Communication," *Education and Culture* 23 (2007): 6–26. Finally, Pennsylvania State University Press is to be thanked for permission to include revised and extended versions of these two articles as portions of chapters 6 and 7: "Pragmatism and Orientation," *Journal of Speculative Philosophy* 20 (2006): 287–307, and "John Dewey and the Question of Artful Communication," *Philosophy and Rhetoric* 41 (2008): 153–83. This book has benefited from the comments that these earlier expositions of my ideas have provoked, and I thank all those who have helped me refine my ideas into more fully formed positions.

The relationships undergirding projects like the present one are not only academic in nature. Many friends and family members must be thanked. All of my family, those still living and those now deceased, have helped me to become the sort of person that I am. The love and support of my parents, Sandra and Herman Stroud, has always been plentiful, and I cannot imagine undertaking the writing of this book without that foundation. They cannot be adequately thanked for what they have done and continue to do as caring parents. Last, but certainly not least, I must thank my wife and muse, Natalie Stroud. Talia has been there since this project was a mere thought barely expressed in words, and her support will be the key to my future efforts to go beyond this project. Her example in personal and academic matters gives me hope that my ruminations about artful living do apply to life.

1

The Problems of Art and Life

Many people complain about the lack of beauty in everyday life. On a cold winter day in Washington, D.C., the world-renowned violinist Joshua Bell tried to do something about it. In the middle of the morning rush hour, he stood, unannounced, in a corner of a bustling metro station and played some of the greatest compositions the Western world has produced. Not only did he play great music, but he also used a legendary instrument to do so—his 1713 Stradivarius, rumored to have been purchased for $3.5 million. What was his purpose in pretending to be a common street musician? Bell wanted to see how people focused on hurrying to work would react to an unexpected encounter with art. During his 43-minute performance, 1,097 people passed by and heard his masterful playing; only 7 stopped and listened for more than a minute. Twenty-seven people paused long enough to throw some change into his violin case. A performer who typically commands $1,000 a minute for his performances earned around $32 that morning in the station.

Many commuters, driven by their hurried schedule or shielded by the music of their own iPods, passed by and failed to notice him. The only people who seemed to be interested in him and absorbed in the sounds he was creating were children—as they were dragged to daycare by a rushing parent who seemed to have no time to listen to this street musician. Experts and ordinary people alike later judged this experiment to bring great art into the subway to be an extremely discouraging sign for integrating art into everyday life.[1]

What sense is to be made of this experiment? Does it really show that our modern selves have become so numbed by the burdens of work, the sounds of corporatized music on personal players, and our frequently ugly surroundings that real art stands no chance of making headway into our lives? One may feel a vague suspicion that this experiment leaves out another way of thinking through the problems of an anesthetic, fragmented, and hurried life. Must the only way to get art back into everyday life involve the tradition-bound classical masters of music or painting? Think of the individual listening to popular music on his iPod. Surely such a person missed the opportunity to hear a great, albeit incognito, violinist during his subway commute. But is this something to bemoan in and of itself? Reframe the situation, and perhaps one can see the way I want to approach the question of integrating art into daily life—is there a significant difference between the person absorbed in his popular music while riding the subway and the person worrying about the upcoming meeting at work? The former does seem engaged and absorbed in what he is listening to and what he is doing, whereas the latter seems distracted and focused on distant matters. I submit that the former is integrating art into the activities of living, more so than the latter—and that both people need not attend to the world-class violinist to bring art into life.

What I am getting at here is the question of how to integrate art into the practical, goal-driven pursuits that we take to be particularly important. These pursuits obviously include the activities of everyday living, as well as the never-ending task of improving what we do, how we do it, and who we are. Does art have an important role to play in a project of living the best life we possibly can live? Does aesthetic experience have any real connection to issues of moral value and moral improvement? What sort of life would we lead if the experiment I described was conclusive, and our lives were bereft of art? If the term "art" can be taken to be a process of careful and skillful *creation*, what can we say about the ways we create our lives and our everyday experiences? Could we do this in an artful fashion, in a fashion that has a close connection to that quality of experience we tie to the notion of aesthetic experience? If one can skillfully do things that render more of one's experience aesthetic in quality, then such activity can be called artful.[2] This is what I mean by artful living, and the purpose of this study is to use Dewey's thought as a way to illustrate its plausibility.

In other words, I intend to explore the concept of aesthetic experience and what it means for our prospects for moral cultivation. Aesthetic experience has had a fairly long and contentious history in the Western intellectual tradition. Following Kant and Hegel, a human's interaction with nature or art frequently has been conceptualized as separate from issues of practical activity or moral value. Kant's criteria of disinterestedness in the judgment of taste, combined with similar trends in Schopenhauer's asceticism and Hegel's subordination of artistic truth to other forms of consciousness, led many philosophers in the nineteenth and twentieth centuries to insist on the separation of art from the moral.[3] This move, of course, became problematic insofar as it raised the obvious question of the value of art. The removal of aesthetic experience from issues of morality and practice cuts off justificatory paths that lead to the practical, since allowing them to remain united would admit that the value of art is indeed tied to nonartistic practical matters. If the value of art came from its moral efficacy, then morality would have something to say about aesthetic values. In addition, if the value of art is tied closely to the achievement of moral ends, one could imagine a situation in which art would *not* be valuable since other (nonartistic) means could be marshaled to achieve such a desired effect.

The problem that must be resolved is the issue of how art relates to *moral value*, specifically the gaining or refining of values that are beneficial in a normative sense. In other words, I want to examine how art can be seen as a way of moral cultivation. Moral cultivation can be understood in a simple sense as analogous to moral improvement or betterment. How does art help people become more moral or virtuous? This way of phrasing the question raises the specter of art losing its intrinsic value, the same worry that motivated writers in the twentieth-century traditions of aesthetic experience and aesthetic attitude. If art is effective at moral improvement, a goal for which other means can be employed to reach, then art seems like just another method or tool that can be selected or ignored for the purpose of moral improvement pending judgments of efficacy, desirability of moral improvement, etc. This is the worry that is enunciated by those wishing to do justice to the *aesthetic* value of art, a value that is supposedly unique to art and the experiences it spawns. Is the value of Joshua Bell's violin playing in the subway solely registered by its ability to entertain? Or to improve the lives and characters of the subway goers? If it is valued only insofar as it has such practical effects, then it seems that it loses such value with its palpable failure to reach the majority of the commuters who rushed by the performance. And if it could produce such effects, one might wonder if another violinist could do the same at less cost. This is the problem of connecting art to moral improvement: the artistry seems to lose its immediate value and worth.

This book attempts to see if there is a way to solve or *dis*solve these problems. The analysis in the following chapters will challenge the relevance and usefulness of two commonly held distinctions: between the intrinsic and instrumental value of an art object, and between what is internal to and external to an art object in content and meaning. In challenging these distinctions, new ways of conceiving of the relationship between artistic value and moral value become evident. A key thinker uniquely positioned to motivate such a reevaluation of the value of art is John Dewey. Dewey not only offers a way of rethinking value and ends/means relationships, but he also places the experience of art at the pinnacle of his systematic thought. Indeed, in *Art as Experience* (1934) he posits that the experience of art is an exemplar of consummatory experience (what he calls "*an* experience") in general. Thus, Dewey seems to be a profitable starting place for an examination of art and its moral value. The problem that Dewey's account must solve, of course, is the relationship of aesthetic experience to moral cultivation. A key move that Dewey wants to make in his aesthetic theory is intimated in his analysis of the lay of the land in *Experience and Nature* (1925), where he states the options available for aesthetic theories: "There are substantially but two alternatives. Either art is a continuation, by means of intelligent selection and arrangement, of natural tendencies of natural events; or art is a peculiar addition to nature springing from something dwelling exclusively within the breast of man, what name be given to the latter" (291). Dewey wants to select the former alternative as the most defensible starting point for a theory of the aesthetic.

Dewey's approach is diametrically opposed to most standard accounts. A typical example might be that of Berys Gaut, who starts from the position that "the notion of the aesthetic has its primary application to works of art, and its application to natural objects is derivative from this primary application."[4] For Dewey, art and the aesthetic are to be part of the continuum that includes normal, everyday experience. The aesthetic does not primarily or exclusively denote rarified cultural practices and experiences such as that of fine art. The challenge is how to elucidate what makes this quality of experience so different (while being related in key ways) from other types of experience. The other type of experience that this study will focus on is that of moral activity and improvement, or moral cultivation.

What motivates Dewey's work in aesthetics is connected to this division of the possible ways of theorizing about art. Dewey is opposed to the sterilized notion of art, which he dubs the "museum conception" of fine art. Such a view, still prevalent today, indicates that art is far removed from ordinary life and even sequestered in the hermitic confines of museums—places of pure observation. Such a notion of the point of art and its value is often connected to Dewey's rejected reading of art as a peculiar addition to nature, specifically its removal in kind from the affairs of nature and daily activity. According to Dewey, art is a part of the natural range of experiences, and art is a vital part of the full human life. To take such an excellent experience out of ordinary life is to do violence both to life and to the art objects being preserved from the reach of human activity. His aesthetic theory attempts to naturalize talk of aesthetic experience, all the while doing justice to its importance in adding value to human life and activity. Dewey's definition of art will be less of what Richard Shusterman calls a "wrapper definition" that attempts to cover the entire extension of a concept, and more of an evaluative characterization of what the best forms of art aspire to be like.[5] My analysis in the following chapters will attempt to link aesthetic experience to moral cultivation in Dewey's aesthetic theory. Dewey was not very specific on this point, but I believe he left enough clues for a useful account to be created out of his theory of aesthetic experience. Thus, in contrast to detailed historical accounts of Dewey's aesthetic theory, my account will use Dewey and his ideas to construct something that directly engages today's problem of relating art and experience. If anyone would be favorably disposed to such a pragmatic appropriation of concepts, moves, and themes to answer contemporary challenges, it would be Dewey.

At various places, Dewey's work provides us with tantalizing clues to his *real* project—the task of making more of life aesthetic or artful. Of course, he tethers the aesthetic quality of experience to experiences in general (once they hit a certain qualitative high point, what he calls "*an* experience"), yet he continues to focus most of his analysis in his aesthetic work on traditional artistic practices (e.g., painting, sculpture, dance, etc.). I want to develop the idea that more (if not all) of life's everyday activities could be rendered as artful or aesthetic, and I will explore this theme in the context of his developed aesthetic theory in the following chapters. For now it will be helpful to illustrate his wide, albeit undeveloped, approach to matters of art and everyday activity with a passage from an early work, *Outlines of a Critical Theory of Ethics* (1891): "If the necessary part played in conduct by artistic cultivation is not so plain, it is largely because 'Art' has been made such an unreal Fetich—a sort of superfine and extraneous polish to be acquired only by specially cultivated people. In reality, living is itself the supreme art; it requires fineness of touch; skill and thoroughness of workmanship; susceptible response and delicate adjustment to a situation apart from reflective analysis; instinctive perception of the proper harmonies of act and act, of man and man" (316). Here we see an early version of his later critique against the division of art from life, of the aesthetic from "normal" activity. We also see the notion of *artful* living. I will argue that Dewey's work holds the resources to not only provide a satisfactory and interesting reading of how aesthetic experience relates to moral value and cultivation, but also of how one can cultivate the sort of approach to life that can render more of it artful.

The argument I will make for how one can cultivate an artful approach to life is straightforward. Many readings of the relation between the aesthetic and the moral err in simple ways by presupposing certain foundations for such a relationship between art and morality. Dewey gives us a way to reconceptualize ends/means and experience in such a way as to locate the moral value of aesthetic experience *in* the experience of absorption itself, as well as *in* the experience of reflective activity brought about by some art object. The endpoint of Dewey's moral theory is a progressive adjustment or growth of an individual in light of some concrete situation, and aesthetic experience exemplifies such an absorptive attending to one's concrete situation. This experiential reading lets us make sense of art's moral value and provides the foundation for a more expansive reading of aesthetic experience not related to traditional artistic practices. The key (but not the only) part to aesthetic experience is the orientation of the subject involved, which allows for a program of altering or improving the quality of our experience by altering our orientations and deep-seated habits. More of our concrete, everyday experience (such as communication or work activity) can be made more aesthetic (more unified, consummatory, and meaningful), and thus can be considered artful living.

I will start at the dispute that motivates this overall project—the relationship between aesthetic experience and moral value. Chapter 2 will introduce the problem and set the stage for a Deweyan analysis of aesthetic experience. I will examine some major ways the separation of aesthetic value (taken here in the same way as artistic value) from moral value is evidenced in writers in the modern tradition. I will explore the debates that played out over the aesthetic value/practical value issue in some theories of the aesthetic attitude and with theorists of the intrinsic value of art. For the former, I take as representative the work of Jerome Stolnitz, whose reading of aesthetic experience strongly separates it from moral activity in both value and attitude. I also consider the theories of Malcolm Budd on the intrinsic value of art objects, as well as the noncognitivist position taken by theorists who argue against a truth value in literary art. Both of these latter positions extend the internal/external distinction of the art object's properties from the aesthetic attitude camp, and add to it the separateness *in kind* of aesthetic value. In the case of Budd, instrumental value has no place in aesthetic experience, and does not deal with attention to artistic qualities. For the literary noncognitivists, the value of an artwork must be within the work itself, and cannot be replaceable in an instrumental sense.

These thinkers, along with many of the other advocates and critics of the aesthetic experience tradition, miss the Deweyan reading that has ends/means and intrinsic/extrinsic value on a continuum, not as mutually exclusive. They point out some important characteristics of what can be called aesthetic experience, but their insistence on reified dualisms leaves out the consideration of a Deweyan alternative reading. The important point is to find a way to talk about the special degree of quality in aesthetic experience without making this value a special kind of value (viz., intrinsic), or reducing talk of this value to the production of products or effects (making it an instrumental value). Due to their fear of the latter, proponents of the intrinsic value of art and aesthetic experience believe that theirs is the only way to fully incorporate the phenomena and value of artistic activity. This, however, can be seen as an illusion based on the way they conceptualize the problem.

An important pragmatist strategy is often the *dis*solving of seemingly intractable problems, and this is the sort of solution I will offer in chapter 3. There, I build a Deweyan account of aesthetic experience that I call "experiential." I explore a variety of working distinctions Dewey makes concerning experience and reflection, intrinsic and instrumental value, and ends and means. Some experiences for Dewey are immediately had, whereas others have a certain puzzling quality about them that forces one to reflect on what is valued, what one should do, etc. Both immediate experience and reflection, however, can be seen as experiences that a subject undergoes. In chapter 3, I will discuss a Deweyan notion of intrinsic value that does justice to its immediately experienced value, as well as to its more instrumental and reflective phases. The point of my argument is to show that value does not reside *in* the object in a strong ontological sense, and that experiencing an art object can have both sorts of value. I will eventually argue that aesthetic experience is morally cultivating on both levels, so I illustrate how Dewey connects means and ends in activity, both of the immediately meaningful kind and that characterized by reflective consideration of events and situations not directly present to the observer. Both sorts of experience can be approached by a subject in a way that separates means from ends, or in a way that unifies means and ends, activities and desired goals. It is the latter attitude or orientation that will feature prominently in the subsequent chapters.

What should any activity that is related to moral development aim for? Chapter 4 considers aesthetic experience in its immediacy to an experiencing subject, as well as its relation to the goal of moral development. In order to argue that such aesthetic experience is morally cultivating or valuable, a theory of moral improvement and value must be advanced. Thus, I begin this chapter by constructing an account of moral cultivation of the self based in Dewey's early work on ethics—his *Outlines of a Critical Theory of Ethics* and *The Study of Ethics*. These works are an important part of his drift away from idealism and they hold a common theme to his later pragmatism—that of the constant and ongoing adjustment of individual to environment. Attentiveness to the situation is integrally connected to character and moral activity, and I will explore these linkages. After giving such a reading of moral value and cultivation of self, I will argue that aesthetic experience is morally cultivating because it *is* an experience of such attentiveness to situations. I do not claim that this *ends* moral improvement, but instead that it is an instance of the activity and end of moral cultivation—progressive adjustment to or growth in one's surrounding situation. In the case of art objects, I flesh out Dewey's account of rhythm as a key feature that makes attention to an art object attention to a present situation. I conclude the chapter by widening my scope and drawing on Crispin Sartwell's analysis to argue that more than just art objects can be experienced aesthetically. Dewey only hints at such a possibility in his aesthetic work (by focusing on conventional artistic practices almost exclusively after chapter 3 of *Art as Experience*), but the preceding analysis shows that what is moral about conduct is a certain *way* of attending to whatever present situation one is in (such as not being focused on a remote goal), and thus, in not making the present a mere means to a distant end. Aesthetic experience is the attention to and absorption in the rich present, and such a present can be that of viewing art objects or of participating in any other sort of activity. What is important is the *way* that activity proceeds. This is moral cultivation, and this is how aesthetic experience can be immediately valuable.

Before I develop the position that more of life can be rendered artful in a wide sense, I must consider the case of art objects traditionally conceived. Chapter 5 will approach the morally edifying aspects of the aesthetic encounter with art objects from its reflective phase. I will approach this phase of experience in three ways. First, I will examine how art can be used to impel audiences to think. Dewey called art the most universal form of communication, and I will construct an account of how he could have meant that. Art objects, exemplary objects of aesthetic experience, can be used to convey points *about* experience *through* experience. Thus, art can show individuals *how* certain value schemes feel, how behaviors affect people, etc.—in other words, art can force the reflective instatement (creation) of moral values. Second, I will discuss the auditor's activity of interpreting works of art and their possible meaning. Dewey walks the fine line between authorial intentionalism and auditor constructivism, so I will attempt to find the Deweyan middle ground that takes advantage of the thrust of both of these opposing positions. Criticism is a reflective orientation of the auditor that is sensitive to possible meaning as well as to the critic's own role in the construction of meaning. Thus, aesthetic experience has the reflective value of encouraging further reflection on the materials of the present (viz., the art object). Third, I will argue that deliberation, or the imaginative enactment of various possible lines of conduct in art objects (for instance, in narratives) provides a testing ground for the instatement of values and action strategies by an auditor.

Developing the theme that the key to aesthetic experience lies in the *way* a subject approaches an art object or activity in general, chapter 6 will expand this sort of Deweyan analysis of aesthetic activity to my general project of *orientational meliorism*—the meliorating of one's experience by intelligently adjusting one's deep-seated orientations toward self, others, and the value of an activity. I consider the importance of embodied habits (heuristically labeled here on a continuum running from more mental to more physical) to the activities of life, as well as to the connection between attention and one's mental orientation. Extending the discussion initiated in chapter 3, I argue that the connection between means and ends is largely a subjective artifact of mental orientation, and that one can change how one orients oneself toward these constituents of activity. Thus, one can literally reimagine the value of one's activity and its connection to larger projects in such a way that it is not rendered mere drudgery or as a mere means to an end. The promise of Deweyan pragmatism is that it can give you ways to make more of your life artful or aesthetic. Ways to practice such a regimen of orientational meliorism include both embodied methods (say, meditation or Alexander bodywork) and mental methods (say, cognitive therapy in rethinking how one sees an activity). Both embodied and mental practices attempt to inculcate habits of attending to the present situation that are intelligent, adaptable, and beneficial in making one's individual and relational experience more meaningful. To illustrate the power of this way of meliorating common experiences, I end by examining work activity that many consider to be drudgery. How can one render more of one's work activity aesthetic or artful? This discussion connects my Deweyan reading of aesthetic activity to current research in positive psychology and explores cognitive strategies individuals can use to reimagine their work experience to make it possess the unity and quality of the aesthetic.

Chapter 7 explores an important practical application of the experiential reading of aesthetic experience developed in the preceding chapters. I connect this expansive reading of aesthetic experience to the challenge of making our everyday communicative activity artful or aesthetic. Such activity is often done blindly, routinely, and for instrumental purposes; my Deweyan take on aesthetic activity, however, entails that such communicative activity can be enhanced by mindful attention to its particular details. I will examine some of the reasons why Dewey's reading of the expressive in art would seem to preclude everyday communication from being truly artful or expressive in the same way museum pieces are. This will turn out not to be the case if one focuses on the connection between aesthetic experience, expression, and the orientation of a subject toward activity. I end this chapter by exploring some ways that everyday, mundane communication can be made to possess the intrinsic absorption that Dewey finds so characteristic of artistic activity. Chapter 8 considers some common objections to the account that has been developed in the preceding chapters, and provides various responses to such objections.

There is a way to approach art and activity that will render them more unified, meaningful, and ultimately more satisfying, both in one's solitary projects and in one's relations to others in a community. This theme is evident in Dewey's work, but is not fully explicated or developed in light of contemporary concerns in aesthetics. The promise of Dewey's aesthetics is not merely in providing an airtight definition of art or a theoretical reading of the relationship between art and moral value. Instead, Dewey theorizes to meliorate or improve lived experience. The insight of Dewey's work on art is that what makes art *aesthetic* is not any particular property of that particular human practice, but rather its tendency to encourage the sort of absorptive, engaged attention to the rich present that is so often lost in today's fragmented world. The way to substantially improve our experience is not by merely waiting for the material setup of the world to change, but instead lies in the intelligent altering of our deep-seated habits (orientations) toward activity and toward other individuals. The purpose of this book is not to end debate on the relationship between art and morality, but instead to explore ways that Deweyan thought can guide us in our attempts to meliorate our orientations toward life in order to foster and recover the sense of enthralled absorption in the activities in which we are engaged. Life is always lived in some present, and it is here that the battle of life is fought; one can come armed with habits that foster engagement with that present, or one can bring in ways of viewing the here and now (be it an art object or a work task) as a mere means to achieve something in the remote future. Both of these approaches will affect and tone the quality of lived, transactive experience. Dewey's point, which I will explore at length in this work, is that the former approach is constitutive of artful living.

2

The Value of Aesthetic Experience

Art may be the object of criminal activity, but one rarely sees art being used to fight crime. Yet this is just what Mexico City did in 2004. After consulting with officials in New York and Tokyo, Mexico City's administration decided that the way to reduce crime on its crowded subway system was not by hiring more officers, but rather with a program that would distribute seven million free books to subway riders over a two-year period. The director of the subway system, Javier Garza, was optimistic about such an employment of art: "We are convinced that when people read, people change." Many officials believed such a plan would work; the Japanese, who have tried similar plans in Tokyo, think that books foster a sense of community among subway riders. Others are skeptical about the efficacy of such a plan; one official, in regard to Mexico's book distribution program, exclaimed: "Now we'll have an equal number of delinquents, but well-educated."[1] Who is correct? Even if the empirical data could be massaged to give an unequivocal answer to the program's efficacy, how could we explain the success of artistic means in reducing criminal activity? What is foregrounded by this example is the larger issue of whether art can positively affect behavior—does it improve individuals morally? Behind this question lies another: what would such a successful employment of art as a crime-reduction tool do for its value? Is art only valuable insofar as it continues to reduce criminal behaviors? In other words, should we care about such a link to moral improvement if it comes at the cost of rendering the aesthetic experience of artworks secondary to some nonartistic end (such as safety)?

These are the natural questions that may be asked about such experiments, and they are the sort of questions that will be encouraged by a certain way of looking at aesthetic experience in the Western tradition of philosophical aesthetics. We must attend to this general issue of the relation of moral improvement and the experiencing of art objects, and I will do this from the starting point of aesthetic experience. As a concept, aesthetic experience has been the subject of much scrutiny in the twentieth century. As with anything that receives much positive attention, it has also received its share of harsh criticism. Theories of art that include the term "aesthetic experience" in their conceptual repertoire are quite rare today, partly because of the withering assault on the concept carried out from both the analytic and continental traditions. While the term "aesthetic experience" as a concept may be vague, this by no means entails that it is inherently useless.[2] Before I can argue that Dewey's employment of the term "aesthetic experience" is a useful way to think about aesthetic events that transpire between an auditor and an art object, I must give some indication of how the tradition following Dewey went down the wrong path in conceptualizing aesthetic experience.[3] This is useful insofar as pragmatist aesthetics and analytic aesthetics have been relatively sequestered from each other in their respective literatures. Such a story will also explain why aesthetic value has largely been separated from any meaningful contact with what can be termed "moral value," a key component in any scheme of moral cultivation.

I will begin by demonstrating how works in aesthetics after Dewey have *conceptualized* aesthetic experience as radically separate from moral activity, as well as how they have *evaluated* the value of art as different in kind from the types of value resident in moral activity. For the first task, I take as representative Jerome Stolnitz's analysis of aesthetic experience and its causal precursor, the aesthetic attitude, although I will make reference to an earlier theory of "distanced" aesthetic perception given by Edward Bullough.[4] In the following section, I will detail how aesthetic experience has been evaluated as possessing a distinct kind of value from other objects and events (especially in practical matters). This is a natural implication of conceiving the aesthetic experience as totally removed from practical concerns (an example of which would be moral activity). I will explore this removal in two ways: first, by exploring the contemporary evaluation of literature's cognitive merits as a case study in internalizing the value of an artwork (and its experience), and second, by looking at a general account of intrinsic value provided by Malcolm Budd.[5] The point of examining these issues regarding aesthetic experience is to see if there are ways to improve how we discuss a concept that, as Dewey rightly notes, must always be tied in some manner to the improvement of our actual experience. I will conclude this chapter by pointing out what the aesthetic attitude theory of Stolnitz and the intrinsic value tradition have right, and by noting how they could be further improved by redefining the nature of the debate—in this case, by not taking the internal/external or intrinsic/extrinsic distinctions in such a reified manner.

Conceptualizing Aesthetic Experience

Many theorists have insisted on a strong division between art and the matters of everyday life. In part, this was a reaction to the use and misuse of art in the service of religious and propagandistic employments. The way to protect art, according to such a view, is to absolutely separate it from practical matters. Artists are not to be evaluated based on their contribution to society's income, resources, education, etc., but merely by their production of quality artworks. The audience is not to ask the wrong questions of art, but instead must appreciate art for art's sake. One can then see the reason why Clive Bell would make such extreme declarations as: "For, to appreciate a work of art we need bring with us nothing from life, no knowledge of its ideas and affairs, no familiarity with its emotions. Art transports us from the world of man's activity to a world of aesthetic exaltation."[6] For theorists such as Bell, the world of art was totally separate from the world of practical affairs, and expertise in the latter granted one no privilege in the former. While I will not explore Bell's formalist theory here, it is easy to see how his sentiments can be extended to other readings of aesthetic experience. This experience of the work of art, it is said, is radically separate from moral experience. For example, Archie Bahm notes that aesthetic experiences have the important quality of being complete in themselves, whereas moral experiences have a fundamental incompleteness about them.[7] Aesthetic experience, according to Bahm, is different *in kind* from moral experience. The question is, however, how does one go about conceiving of aesthetic experience as so different from ordinary (practical) experience?

One of the earliest answers to this challenge was given by Edward Bullough at the beginning of the twentieth century. Bullough, drawing on psychological investigations as well as phenomenological data, argued that the key characteristic of aesthetic experience was "psychical distance."[8] For Bullough, the observers had to be distanced enough from their affects ("affectations") so that they did not attempt to act on the fiction presented in the work of art. However, they could not be so distanced that the work of art had no effect on them. The example given by Bullough is of sea fog in which an individual is mired. If he or she is appropriately distanced, the fog will produce a very moving experience in that individual. Being appropriately distanced in this situation means that one is not overcome by focusing on the risk that the fog poses to one's vessel, or, on the other hand, that one is not focused on the fog at all. Caught up in one's attention to the fog and abstracting from its practical consequences, one's imagination runs free and the experience is quite powerful. Bullough's point is that the fog and its practical consequences are fairly determinate; what is changeable, however, is the outlook or "aesthetic consciousness" that the observer brings to the situation. It is this outlook that could be underdistanced (too concerned with practical consequences of the object) or overdistanced (not attendant to the object in its aesthetic details in any significant measure). The right amount of distance, according to Bullough, is "the *utmost decrease of Distance without its disappearance.*"[9] Such a state will allow for maximum engagement with the artwork, but with the absolute minimum of *practical* consideration. The observer will attend to the features of the work of art, but not as features that hold importance because of their practical significance. The term "distance" implies a personal relationship between the observer and the object, albeit one that focuses on the aesthetic object itself. This consciousness, for Bullough, is the hallmark of the aesthetic experience.

A more extended account of the outlook required for aesthetic experience is given by Jerome Stolnitz in *Aesthetics and Philosophy of Art Criticism*. Stolnitz begins by noting the lack of success that traditional theories of art and the aesthetic have enjoyed, largely due to their overemphasis on one characteristic of art objects. This opens such theories to attack by counterexamples that involve art objects without that one characteristic, as well as the general criticism that art (and life) is never as simple as the theory posits. Instead, Stolnitz proposes that the aesthetic (a concept that includes the perception of art objects) be defined in reference not to objective properties, but instead by reference to the subjective state of the auditor. Such an approach should be able to capture what is unique about our interaction with aesthetic objects and be general enough to deal with the myriad counterexamples that give so much trouble to traditional "essentialist" theories of the aesthetic. In giving such an account, Stolnitz thinks he will be able to do justice to the intrinsic interest people find in the aesthetic experience.

Like Bullough before him, Stolnitz believes that the solution to the puzzle of aesthetic experience lies in the subject's experience of the aesthetic object, and not in any specific qualities of the object itself. The observer's perception of the object, according to Stolnitz, is a function of his or her attitude. The term "attitude" in this sense is defined by Stolnitz as a "way of directing and controlling our perception," according to the interests and purposes we may have (32). Thus, the Native American scout *sees* different things in his perception of the forest path because of his interests and purposes (largely connected to tracking). An attitude also prepares one for action of some sort; the scout notices certain markings largely for the purpose of tracking, and this perception is guided by the potential activity of employing these marks in future pursuit of game. In terms of the larger picture of aesthetic experience, what Stolnitz is setting up is twofold. Attitudes inherently involve some sort of forward-looking purpose, and attitudes are always involved in our experience of the world. A certain mix of purpose will make up that particular attitude that is conducive for one to have an aesthetic experience. Stolnitz calls such a subjective state the "aesthetic attitude."

Before describing the aesthetic attitude, it is helpful to describe the alternative state, which Stolnitz calls the "attitude of practical perception." This is the attitude commonly taken by individuals, and it involves seeing objects in the world largely in terms of their helping or hindering certain purposes (33). Instead of concentrating on the object in itself, the subject looks more at the connections between this object and other aspects of the world, such as desired states or outcomes she or he would like to see actualized. For example, a real estate developer stares longingly at a pristine mountain lake and is enthralled—he or she wonders how many condos could be sold on the far side to make up for the costs involved in developing in such a remote location. Stolnitz (among others) would not consider such experience to be aesthetic, largely because of the integral involvement of nonaesthetic aspects—the practical interest and connection of the object of perception to other (nonpresent) states of affairs. While such practical attitudes are important, they do not capture the uniquely aesthetic experience that occupies a part of our experience in this world. Stolnitz points out that when one takes an object from a practical point of view, what one is doing is looking at the object largely in terms of its conditions of origin and the consequences it may affect, and not at the object as it is in itself (35). Practical perception considers the object in its interrelations with other objects and states of affairs, whereas aesthetic perception focuses solely on the object itself.

It is this alternate attitude of aesthetic perception that Stolnitz describes as the aesthetic attitude. Stolnitz defines this concept as "disinterested and sympathetic attention to and contemplation of any object of awareness whatever, for its own sake alone" (35). There are at least three important aspects to this attitude that is associated with aesthetic experience. The first is the disinterested criterion for the aesthetic attitude. Stolnitz finds that a key difference between the aesthetic and the practical attitude is that the latter is quite interested. Of course, even the aesthetic attitude involves purpose, since this is a defining hallmark of all attitudes taken by humans. What is noticeable about practical attitudes is that the interest an individual takes in some purpose lies quite far from the actual experience itself. Thus, my purpose in noticing the economic value of a particular painting lies removed from the here and now of perceiving it—it lies down the road when I am attempting to sell it. What Stolnitz prizes in aesthetic experience is that its purpose is internally focused, and is thus disinterested. On Stolnitz's account, no attitude could really be uninterested, since all attitudes and orientations focus on some purpose that shapes and focuses perception. Attitudes are therefore interested (in a practical sense) or disinterested (focused solely on the object and not its relations to other states or objects). The interest in the former stretches beyond the act of perception, whereas the purpose involved in the latter is relatively truncated to the act and object of perception itself.

Another important quality of the aesthetic attitude according to Stolnitz is "sympathetic" attention and contemplation. This is related to the disinterested quality, but in a more positive fashion. Instead of the aesthetic attitude being merely a lack of interest in an object's connection to other objects and states of affairs, it is also focused on apprehending the object in a way directed by the object itself. Thus, the disinterested portion of the attitude screens out extraneous motivations, and the sympathetic portion provides what determines the unfolding of the aesthetic experience—the object itself. Stolnitz characterizes such a sympathetic outlook as allowing one's experience to be guided by the object, as well as on the terms of the object itself. An example of this would be a member of one religious tradition reading a text from a different religion on its own terms, and not merely as a misguided text. The religious, moral, and practical beliefs are left out of this reading experience so as to allow the text to be experienced as it is—or, as Stolnitz puts it, "aesthetically." The aesthetic attitude, comprised of attention and contemplative engagement with an object while guided by these features just noted, is what enables the aesthetic experience. Aesthetic experience is the total experience that one who is approaching an object with the aesthetic attitude undergoes. One final implication of this conceptualization to note is that Stolnitz explicitly claims that *any* object can be aesthetically experienced, as the determinative feature of the experience that allows it to be aesthetic is the attitude of the subject, not some determinate feature of the object (39).

In extending his theory of the aesthetic to cover our experience of art, Stolnitz faces the same challenge that Kant did in his *Critique of the Power of Judgment*. Art involves concepts (and hence purposes and cognitive connections external to the object), but the onus of an aesthetically motivated auditor is to remain disinterested while perceiving such human-made objects. How is one to maintain such a state with the conceptual baggage that comes with art? Two problems are posed to Stolnitz's account by such conceptual and historical material. First, can one hold the aesthetic attitude toward art objects given their conceptual connections to other states and objects (a historical author, genre, purposes, etc.)? This point led Kant to be skeptical of the purity of artistic work, and instead to privilege nature in his accounts of the beautiful and the sublime. Second, even if one can attend in such a way, how much conceptual material is too much for the holding of a disinterested state? Stolnitz wants to maintain that such a disinterested state is able to be actualized even though all attitudes humans hold involve purpose to some extent. His answer to the second challenge will be to delineate how much external connection is allowed before one becomes interested in the object qua practical object. Stolnitz does this by providing a criterion for when such external knowledge as memories, historical information about the art object, and its relation to other genres renders the experience something other than aesthetic experience. Following Bullough, Stolnitz wants the criterion to be one internal to the experience of the art object itself—he tries to maintain

Bullough's point that external associations (with other objects and/or experiences) are legitimate when they increase the aesthetic experience of the object itself through magnifying the significance of one of its aesthetic qualities. For example, one is not attending in an aesthetic fashion when one sees the color red in a painting and then remembers the same shade of red in one's grandmother's card room. Instead, if one's association of anger with the color red is in line with the overall painting, then such an association has been helpful in riveting one's attention to the aesthetic features of the object (in this case, the color red and the role it plays in the overall painting) and in increasing the overall aesthetic experience of the object.

Regarding the conceptual baggage of knowledge about the work of art, Stolnitz proposes three criteria for judging when it is harmful to aesthetic experience (58). First, such knowledge about the object is not harmful when it does not destroy the aesthetic experience. One can imagine that this serves as a negative criterion to delineate disinterested attention from interested attention—aesthetic experience will be detrimentally affected when knowledge renders the attitude (and hence the experience) of the auditor practical. Second, the knowledge about the object is helpful when it pertains to the expressive qualities of the object qua aesthetic object. Thus, knowing that some painter uses a perspective to color his or her paintings in a certain way would help one in experiencing the expressive qualities of a particular painting by this artist. Third, such knowledge is helpful when it increases the quality of the aesthetic response of the auditor. Conceivably, the way it does this is by not interfering with the enabling attitude (per the first criterion) and by amplifying the aesthetic properties and their expressiveness (per the second criterion). What Stolnitz is trying to emphasize with this account is that aesthetic experience must be internal to the auditor-art object interaction in some important manner. Knowledge about an object is harmful because it tends to draw the auditor's attention away from the immediate interaction and toward alternate connections with other objects and states of affairs. Stolnitz puts this in a very straightforward manner when he states: "The cardinal rule in aesthetic experience—focus attention solely on the object itself" (60). Knowledge about the object tends to be knowledge *outside* of the aesthetic object, and thus outside of the experience of this object. As will be seen in the following section, this has important implications for theorizing about the (separate) value of aesthetic experience.

Before I move to the discussion of aesthetic experience and its value, it is useful to examine some criticisms of this type of aesthetic attitude account.

Stolnitz is largely concerned with separating aesthetic experience (and its associated attitude) from practical experience. In doing so, he implicitly appeals to a fairly closed notion of the art work and what can be called internal to the auditor-art object interaction. This point was seen above in his discussion of knowledge about the art object. This same assumption will be seen in one of the major critics of the aesthetic attitude theory, George Dickie. Dickie's main position is that "aesthetic attitude" is no longer a useful concept, and really denotes merely a mythical state.[10] He wants to maintain that what one *really* means when one talks about the aesthetic attitude is attention, and nothing more. Thus, Dickie's account of aesthetic experience (and its accompanying attitude) is what Noël Carroll has called the "deflationary account," since it reduces the aesthetic attitude and aesthetic experience merely to attention to the art object itself (as opposed to a special kind of attention to the art object).[11]

Dickie's critique of the aesthetic attitude follows a simple plan. First of all, he considers the notions of interested/disinterested as applied to attention. Do these denote special kinds of attention? Dickie believes that they do not. For instance, if one looks at a painting and thinks about its resemblance to one's grandfather, then one is not paying attention to the painting in an interested way—one is not paying attention to the painting at all. Dickie wants to maintain that the true choice is between attention/inattention to the work of art, not a special kind of attention to the work of art. One who watches a play while concerned with its revenue potential is attending to the financial impacts of the play, but is not attending to the play itself. Dickie uses the same criticism against Bullough's concept of distance in aesthetic experience. What Bullough calls "being distanced" is not really a different state of consciousness, but instead merely denotes that the individual is paying attention to the art object, the sea fog, and so on, and not something else (its impact on them financially, or in terms of safe seagoing). Dickie concludes that the aesthetic attitude is really just close attention to an art object.[12] This point is echoed in Noël Carroll's analysis of aesthetic experience and aesthetic attitude as merely a combination of "design appreciation" and the "detection of aesthetic properties" in regard to an art object.[13] The former refers to appreciating an object's design and form in light of the purpose it was intended to fulfill, and the latter refers to an observer's attention to aesthetic properties of a work (such as expressive qualities). Carroll and Dickie's ultimate point is that aesthetic attitude theories such as Stolnitz's account merely give an impressive name to something that is either trivial (Dickie's label) or truistic (Mary Mothersill's term).[14]

What is important to note is that Dickie's (and Carroll's) criticism relies on a fairly rigid internal/external split as to what is in the art object and outside of it. If one can have such a firm notion of what the properties of the art object are, then one can class the aesthetic attitude as mere attention *to* the art object, and disregard the motives behind the auditor's interaction with the art object. This may be problematic, as Virgil Aldrich notes, since this assumes a "groomed" concept of the art object that will most likely include properties determined by mere stipulation, and not by any firm ontology of the artwork.[15] What are the aesthetic properties of the art object, and how are they determined? This is a difficult question to answer, and such an answer will not be attempted here. I will discuss the usefulness of the aesthetic attitude concept at the end of this chapter, but the point I will stress here is that both Stolnitz and his critics assume a fairly concretized and determinable boundary between the artwork and extraneous matters—practical interests, other states of affairs, other objects, knowledge about the work that is separate from what is in the work, etc. I will argue at the end of this chapter and in the following chapters that this internal/external dichotomy that is so important to locating aesthetic experience (and its associated subjective orientations) is not a useful way to start such an account, and that insisting on the absolute separation of the aesthetic from the practical (a cause of the insistence on internal/external aspects of the experience of art objects) is misleading. One specific way that such an insistence is misleading is in the value that art objects and their experience have. Positing aesthetic experience as separate in kind from other types of experience seems to surely lead to separating the kinds of value each type of experience has, and the actual attempts at this will now be discussed.

Evaluating the Value of Aesthetic Experience

Related to the categorical separation of the aesthetic experience from practical experience is the further separation of the value of aesthetic experience from the value given to other sorts of activity. I will illustrate how this point has played out in the works of some contemporary writers in two ways. First, I will briefly introduce how the problem has been stated in regard to one specific issue, the cognitive value of the experience of reading literature. The point of this illustration will be to highlight how the division of what is interior to the work and what is exterior easily becomes mapped onto issues of value regarding the experience of reading the work. Second, I will analyze a contemporary global account of aesthetic value as separate in kind from other sorts of value to illustrate the attraction of this way of conceptualizing the value of art objects.

The debate in the philosophy of literature that deals with the cognitive value of literature is usually cashed out in the Western world as the *truth* value of literature. I am not sure this is the best way to begin the discussion, as it seems that *fictional* texts would prima facie resist this question as a starting point.[16] This is how many have framed the debate, however, so I will take the issue on those terms here. The question is whether the concept of truth has any place in discussions about the experience of literature and its value.[17] The way this question has been approached is for participants to give a truth or no truth account. Of particular interest here are those in the latter camp, as they wholeheartedly tend to subscribe to two premises: first, that material can easily and determinately be classed as internal or external to the art object, and second, that the cognitive value of the experience of literature must come *solely* and *uniquely* from the material internal to the literary work. Thus, not only is the experience of reading literature separate from other activities in its object (viz., the material within the work), but its value lies clearly noted *within* the work itself. The no truth answer accordingly argues that literature's value is not cognitive, since what is gained within the direct experience of a work and its contents is not cognitive.

Three common arguments for the no truth position are labeled the "no argument argument," the "no evidence argument," and the "banality argument."[18] The first argues that literature, by virtue of its textual contents, does not clearly *argue* or assert any determinate proposition. Thus, *Hamlet* is not arguing for any given claim about how to treat usurping relatives, but is instead merely telling a story about fictional characters. The second argument claims that even if there are arguments in literature, the experience of reading the text gives no real evidence for their claims. The reason given for this is simple—the author makes up the evidence, which is highly selective to start with, given the story's constructed nature. The third argument is of more interest because its defenders appear to link it to a unique aesthetic experience of literature separate from cognitive activity. The banality argument claims that any truths found in literature are not really significant, and are usually trivial or banal. Why this is a problem, of course, is that such a truth account of literature entails that the value of literature is also banal or trivial. The suppressed premise is that the cognitive value of literature must be something that is *unique* to literature and the experience of reading it. If these truths can be found elsewhere, and their presentation in literature is quite banal, then such an account of literature's value must be severely mistaken.

One proponent of the banality argument is Jerome Stolnitz.[19] He argues quite forcefully that literature holds no truths, cognitive or otherwise. To argue for this point, he attempts to distill truths from novels and illustrates how such a process either ends up with a paraphrase of the story ("person x killed person y and found that pride was their downfall") or with a general, banal everyday truth ("pride is the downfall of many ambitious individuals"). The first is meaningless because of its lack of connections to outside states of affairs (outside of the content of the story), and thus fails to be cognitive. If one tries to connect the storyline to external events via a general truth, Stolnitz maintains that this reduces the cognitive value of the literary work to banality. His reasoning behind such a claim is simple—why did one need the complex, aesthetically sophisticated art object to convey this simple truth that can be found in other ways? For instance, Napoleon's biography can tell you the same truth as the paraphrase one derives from Oedipus's story.

Underlying this type of argument is the same worry that motivates Peter Lamarque and Stein Olsen's critique of the truth position.[20] That position must find or locate cognitive value *in* the artwork itself, and cannot draw from resources external to the work-auditor interaction, or it risks making the literary object superfluous. If the same message can be gained through history or psychology, why is a fictionalized account required? The problem, of course, is then for truth account proponents to navigate this challenge and its main obstacle: locating general, nomothetic truth in a particular, fictional story without rendering it noncognitive (not connected to external events) or too general and banal (not uniquely connected to that which is *in* the literary object). Lamarque puts this challenge quite succinctly when he discusses moral lessons that are said to reside in particular fictional works: "Either the moral lesson is too close to the work, tied too specifically to the characters and incidents in the work, in which case it cannot function as an independent generalizable moral principle, or the moral lesson is too detached, too loosely connected to the specifics of the work to be perceived as part of the literary context or meaning that the work expresses."[21] Like Stolnitz, Lamarque is employing a theory/art object split in an attempt to show the futility of locating cognitive truths within the literary object and its experience by a reader. Either the truths are general enough to be used by moral theory and are hence nonparticular in terms of being removed from what is in the story itself, or they remain at the level of the particular literary story. If the former is the case, they render the truths commonplace (since they are so abstracted from particulars) or they fail to do justice to the literary text (since their disconnection with the details of the story renders them available through other means). If the latter is the case, it is hard to see this as knowledge, as it would only apply to people in that particular story *in* the literary object. Since no reader *is* Othello with all of his problems, *Othello* and its storyline cannot offer one specific advice within the story. This skepticism about applicable knowledge within the rich artwork pushes Lamarque to argue for art's uselessness; he claims elsewhere that "to value a work for its own sake is to value it for what it is in itself, not for the realization of some ulterior ends or for how I might use it to benefit myself personally."[22]

What all of this highlights is that the remnants of the same priorities at work in Stolnitz's aesthetic attitude theory now inhabit contemporary debates on literary experience. The challenge to find the cognitive value *in* the literary art object and its experience by an auditor is maintained largely due to the same reasons Stolnitz and Dickie held in their positions: that a conception of what is in the work and outside of the work can clearly be maintained, and that one can easily keep one's attention on what is inside of the work. Thus, the value of literature as literature must come from appreciating it as it is, and not from importing external material into its interpretation. This concern causes Lamarque and Olsen at one point to criticize Martha Nussbaum and Hilary Putnam not for finding a cognitive value in literature, but for finding a cognitive value in literature *"under an ethical interpretation."*[23] Their readings of the novels in question are fine, but are said to highlight the moral value of these novels as an adjunct to moral philosophy; they are not a reading of the novels' cognitive value on their own literary merits. Within the literary work itself (say, James's *The Golden Bowl*), there is not moral philosophy on the general level; instead, what is *in* the story is merely that—a specific story.

Like the aesthetic attitude theory, no truth advocates in the debate over the value of literary practice focus sharply on the auditor, the auditor's focus on the work, and what the work internally has to offer for consumption. Indeed, T. J. Diffey follows Stolnitz's noncognitivist account, but modifies it in a telling way; he claims that "to learn from a work of art, that is, to move from what is shown in the world of the work to an assertion of what obtains in the world, requires a refusal of the aesthetic stance."[24] Why is this nonaesthetic stance helpful in making cognitive connections that constitute knowledge? Simply because it "constitutes a further move and out of the work . . . to assert of the text, 'and this is how it is.'"[25] Again, notice the attempt to locate value inside or outside the work; Diffey's point is that the cognitive value one may find in literature is not really *in* literature, but is instead added to it from an attitude that connects the literary object to external states of affairs for practical purposes. In Stolnitz's terms, this would be the donning of a practical attitude toward the literary object. The challenge that all of these participants agree to is that the literary cognitivist must find his or her cognitive value of literature in the work, or as David Novitz puts it, must find "a message *in* a literary work of art . . . [that] derives from, but is not about, the content of the work."[26] Extending the internal/external split in the aesthetic attitude debate, the example of the dispute over the cognitive value of literature illustrates how this division can transfer into issues of value and where it must be found in the experience of an art object.

A general theory of art's intrinsic value is given by Malcolm Budd in *Values of Art: Pictures, Poetry, and Music*. This work can serve as an exemplar of the moves I believe a Deweyan approach to aesthetic experience will resist; not only does Budd continue the emphasis on aesthetic activity as different in kind from other sorts of activity, but he also makes a strong case for the value of this activity as different in kind from the value of other activities. It will be useful to lay out Budd's general position on artistic value before I segue into an alternative way of approaching the value(s) of aesthetic experience. Budd begins his account by focusing on the general value of art as an institution and asks, what is the value of art? Budd answers that artistic value is the value of a work of art *as* a work of art (2). This value will be cashed out in terms of the interaction between the art object and the auditor, or as Budd puts it, in "the experience the work of art offers" (4). This experience is quite cognitive on Budd's account, as he indicates that it entails the "full" understanding of the work with an awareness of all relevant aesthetic properties of that work. Like the writers mentioned earlier in this section, Budd appears to hold a strong and determinate internal/external division in regard to what can be attended to in the aesthetic experience. Artistic value is *intrinsic* in this account because it is caused or constituted by awareness solely to what is *in* the work of art (the work's aesthetic properties, etc.). The value of this experience is not connected to other objects, purposes, or states of affairs, since these would render the artwork's value merely *instrumental*.

More needs to be said concerning Budd's intrinsic/instrumental division in value. The vital point is whether or not the experience is the primary focus in the analysis and attribution of value. Budd notes that "intrinsic value" is opposed to "instrumental value"; the latter means "the value, from whatever point of view, of the actual effects of the experience of the work on people or the effects that would be produced if people were to experience the work" (5).[27] Instead, the intrinsic value of a work relates *solely* to the unique contents of a work of art, all of which (according to Budd) are understood and comprehended in an aesthetic experience of that work. Thus, the internal realm of the work of art is linked to a special type of value—intrinsic value. Other ways of approaching the artwork on this account emphasize practical purposes, linkages to other states of affairs, and ultimately focus on the *effects* of the interaction with the work of art. Budd wants to do justice to the interaction itself, and his notion of intrinsic value attempts to do just this. The reasons he gives in his text against instrumental readings of artistic values are a bit more expansive than this simple position. First, he argues that these effects of an art object are too varied and subject-dependent to be part of "artistic value," a value that should be constant across experiencing subjects. Second, Budd argues that our judgments of artistic value and our judgments of the likely effects of art are dissimilar in that the former are strongly held (by subjects) and the latter are quite variable in terms of accurate response prediction. Third, our predictions of responses to works of art are generally not well established empirically. These three reasons seem similar to the object-centered account Carroll gives of aesthetic experience as merely design appreciation and aesthetic property detection.[28] If the subjective response is too ambiguous and varied, focusing on the object and its (assumed) unchanging properties gives one's conception of aesthetic experience the standardization that one may believe it needs. Of course, this assumes that one wants such certainty and fixity in conceptualizing and capturing all instances of aesthetic experience. Budd stays away from instrumental value largely because of these reasons—it is too changing, fleeting, and uncertain to be accorded the special kind of value that is designated by the label "artistic."

Similar concerns give Berys Gaut a reason to exclude effects from his (different) account of art's moral value: "The question of the causal effects of (some) artworks on actual audiences who view or listen to them is an empirical issue, answerable only by carefully controlled psychological and sociological investigations." Even if such effects could be empirically verified, Gaut claims that they could be due to "radical misunderstandings of the artwork, or of the audiences' abnormal psychology . . . or of fortuitous features of a work's context of reception."[29] Like Budd, the idea of what is of value in art (whether moral or artistic) is taken to reside within the work itself. Budd's fourth reason for avoiding an instrumental reading of the work of art is similar to the criterion appealed to in the literary cognitivism debates discussed above—instrumental value (focused on the achieving of certain effects) is in principle detachable from the work of art, and thus does not do justice to what is unique about *that* work of art. This is a version of the "multiple realizability" argument—if a goal can be achieved in another way, why use the circuitous route of the work of art? Budd's position is that there is something uniquely valuable about an auditor's interaction with a work of art, and that cannot be the realization of certain effects, as one can always find other ways to realize these without artistic effort.

In *Values of Art*, Budd does nod toward some effects of art being part of the experience itself, such as enlivening one's consciousness, increasing psychological awareness, enhancing awareness of social conditions, etc., but it is unclear how far he can sustain this argument given his commitment to a strong instrumental/intrinsic value divide (7). In responding to those who give art's value in terms of its communicative ability, Budd argues that this would render art as only *one* means to this message's transmission (12). Budd's insistence on a special kind of value had by art objects precludes saying merely that art communicates these ideas at a different level of effectiveness than regular means of communication. Instead, he must maintain that the realization of this end in other ways renders the communicative value separate *in kind* from the artistic value of a work of art. Thus, it is hard to see how Budd can maintain that some of the *effects* of aesthetic experience are part of its intrinsic value. This is especially true when one considers the types of effects he wants to claim are *part* of the experience. For instance, the effects of "the invigoration of one's consciousness" or a "refined awareness of human psychology or political or social structures" that he notes as "part of" the aesthetic experience can surely be gained through extra-artistic ways (7). Budd cannot reply that art achieves these results with a different *degree* of effectiveness, since he argued against the communicative position that artistic value is different in *kind* from other means of realizing certain effects. He seems committed to the position that artistic value is value merely in the experience of a work of art (as he puts it, in understanding all of its aesthetic properties), and that this value is not to be tainted by reference to effects or states of affairs external to the art object and its experience by an attentive subject. Indeed, Budd displays this commitment when he defends against the hierarchy objection—he explicitly claims that artistic and nonartistic values are separate *types* of value, but that one is not elevated above the other (8).

Toward a Pragmatist Notion of Aesthetic Experience

What can be learned from these previous attempts at conceptualizing and evaluating aesthetic experience? I believe that one can begin to see some of the problems in the framing of the debate through the positing of recurrent dualisms between internal/external aspects to an artwork and intrinsic/instrumental value. The account of aesthetic experience I will begin to give in the next chapter will start in a way that Dewey often begins—by not accepting such reified dualisms as the unavoidable starting point for solutions. Frequently our solutions come in the form of *dis*solutions when the problem is properly formulated. Thus, I will conclude this chapter by highlighting what I believe is of value to my constructive enterprise in this study, as well as what must be abandoned or thought of in a different way.

One of the aspects I find extremely important to any notion of aesthetic experience is the concept of attitude. Attitude does seem to hold a vital position in describing how humans interact with each other, as it often holds a very influential and causal role in creating certain realities. William James referred to this in his essay "The Will to Believe," where he argues that in important cases human belief creates the reality to which it refers or is about.[30] If everyone *believed* that resistance to a train robber was hazardous and ineffective, any efforts at such resistance *would* be ineffective, as the belief held by those involved would have already created the situation in which resistance is piecemeal and fragmented. This general point can be supported in our own reports of everyday activity; often our interactions with people turn out in a predictable fashion that is highly correlated with the attitudes we have going into the interaction (of cautious suspicion, of friendliness, of hope, etc.). James's point was closely related to Stolnitz's theory in its emphasis on the importance of the attitude of the auditor in aesthetic experience, as this is a key element to creating a rewarding interaction. Indeed, if one does not attend to an artwork at all, then no aesthetic experience will transpire. Dickie and Carroll can agree to this point quite easily.[31]

The question is, how do attitudes figure into how we experience an art object? To simply view attitudes as motives for attention to an object or to something else misses the point that Stolnitz and others see as evident—there are different ways of seeing the same object and its properties, and not all of them are easily dismissible as a case of "attending to non-art object *x*." Virgil Aldrich refers to the seeing of snowflakes in two distinct ways, either as the object of focus (in front of a distant lamp) or as objects before the object focused on (the lamp itself).[32] Both are ways of seeing and experiencing the snowflakes, and it is not obvious that one is *really* the way of attending *merely* to the snowflakes. What seems to change is something in the subject.

Indeed, a major point of Dewey's aesthetics (and general philosophy of experience) is to find a way to reflect on experience so as to *improve* future lived experience. One way both to mark experience for reflection and to improve the quality of immediate experience will be through the sort of attitude one takes toward it, and this point will be expounded in the following chapters dealing with Dewey's aesthetic theory. My account will not rest content with the provision of a universal and static pronouncement of what such an aesthetic attitude must consist of. Disinterestedness seems important in some contexts, but not in others. Indeed, Dickie and Carroll make a good point when they highlight that the appropriate way to respond to some art (say, political) will be to do so in an involved, interested fashion. The pragmatists themselves will be the last to say that aesthetic experience is the only type of experience without purpose or selectivity on the part of a habit-filled organism. Instead, I will leave it at this simple insight for now—that the way the subject approaches the art object often (if not always) plays a major role in the type of experience had, the quality of such experience, and the content of such experience (such as what aesthetic properties are observed, etc.). From another perspective, the experiences one has often change the attitudes one takes toward objects and experiences, thus rendering the interaction much more fluid and bidirectional than proponents and critics often postulate.

Another characteristic of aesthetic experience *both* sides have right is its *immediate value* to the auditor. By this I do not mean the *intrinsic value* of the experience (as defined by its modern proponents), but instead the value and enjoyment the felt experience of the art object can and often does bring. Many art objects do hold such an immediate pleasure, and Dewey's account will make much of this. Of course, some art is designed to shock and repulse,[33] but three things may be said about these cases. First, attempts have been made to fit such cases of fragmentation into a pragmatist account of aesthetic experience.[34] Second, it is hard to imagine that art as an institution would get the importance it now has if such fragmentary and disjointed aesthetic objects were the norm.[35] Instead, it seems more likely that they are possible merely because of the sound foundation that pleasurable and powerful art objects have provided through the history of art as an institutional activity in whatever culture one is discussing. Third, one can still describe the effect of such terrifying or fragmentary art objects as immediate, since they make an obvious and noticeable dent in the way one approaches the world. Indeed, portions of modern avant-garde art can be seen as shock therapy to jolt its viewers out of their habitual responses and into an *attitude* more reflective on the content and meaning of art itself.

The point I am trying to make here in a general fashion (and that I will make in a more specific fashion with my analysis of Dewey) is that aesthetic experience does seem significant because it is extremely hard not to notice it. Dickie and Carroll are right that it involves a sort of attention, and wrong in thinking that this ends the story; instead, the *experience* that is brought on by attending to certain aspects of the art object in certain ways (with certain attitudes) is distinct and significant, and should be analyzed further with the goal of improving its meaning in our lives. One important way to do this is to further connect it to moral cultivation, an important goal for pragmatists such as John Dewey. Dickie and Carroll also may be mistaken in what one is paying attention to in the aesthetic experience—limiting the term "aesthetic experience" to the experience of the object may miss the point that significant improvement or meaning is to be gained from *attention paid to the experience itself*. What is needed is an analysis of aesthetic *experience*, including its connection to subjective orientations (attitudes), both immediate and reflective. Such an analysis will be forthcoming in the following chapters, but now it is enough to note the *immediacy* and *qualitative uniqueness* of aesthetic experience as part of what makes it so valuable and striking.

The more important points to address before moving to my constructive account of aesthetic experience will be the hardened dualisms that are endemic to discussions of aesthetic experience. I will first address the internal/external distinction, and then follow with a discussion of the intrinsic/instrumental value distinction. In reference to the first distinction, two things are troubling. First, it posits aesthetic experience as different *in kind* from other sorts of experience, and second, it leads proponents to accept that the separateness of aesthetic experience (from other types of experience) entails the separateness of its value. With respect to the first troubling component of the internal/external distinction, it is difficult to maintain that aesthetic experience is absolutely different in kind from other types of experience (such as moral experience).

Most of the proponents of this view (and even its opponents) try to maintain this position by assuming a clear distinction between what is *in* the work (properties of paint used, certain notes played, specific story lines, etc.) and what is *outside* of it (one's beliefs and values, one's projects, etc.). Stolnitz maintains this position to analyze the concepts of aesthetic attention and sympathetic contemplation, and to answer worries about how much external matter can be brought in before the aesthetic experience is ruined (that is, rendered nonaesthetic). Dickie even relies on a stronger notion of a groomed art object in his deflation of the aesthetic attitude to mere attention to what comprises the art object. This, of course, assumes an easily identifiable set of properties and qualities that comprise the art object and that can be used to individuate it from other objects or states of affairs. The opponents of a cognitivist account of literary value begin with the challenge to locate such value *in* the work of literature, and not to tether it to other objects and other states of affairs. Two questions emerge—is the object of aesthetic experience really so distinct as to allow for principled distinctions of internal and external predication, and does this really cause the stark difference in kind among aesthetic and nonaesthetic experiences?

The answer I would like to advance to both questions is no. As for the first, much debate has focused on precisely this question in the realm of interpretation. Some scholars take a realist line on interpretation, arguing that our interpretations more or less capture what properties the object really has. Others take a constructivist stance and find that interpretation is really the imputation of qualities onto and into the art object, and that these properties are not primarily there in any deep sense. I do not want to wade too deeply into these waters, but I believe it is safe to say that both sides would reject the clean distinction that Dickie and others make in the most deflationary accounts of aesthetic attention. The range of properties of any decent art object seems quite extended, and often integrally linked to cultures of production and reception for their being noticed. Additionally, different sets of these properties could be noticed by different auditors, and this could affect different experiences of that object. It is not readily evident that one is attending to the work and the other is not in such a case. It is difficult to see a principled, determinate way to exhaustively delineate what is inside the work from what is outside.[36] Thus, aesthetic attention is not merely a case of attending to the relevant features of an art object.

The second question dealt with the difference in kind between aesthetic and nonaesthetic experiences. Two lines of response can be given to this distinction. The first is the one that is encouraged by John Dewey's overall melioristic tendencies—one can always see if a different way of approaching the issue would help one gain insight into the phenomena and to improve future experiences of this sort. Can we transform nonaesthetic experience into aesthetic experience? This will be the strategy of this book in the following chapters. The more confrontational move would be to show why a reified split is on the wrong track. I would insist that individuals show me how such experience is truly separate in kind and not in degree from nonaesthetic experience. Indeed, its most vigorous opponents give in at a certain point and maintain that in real life such experiences are more often than not mixed. For instance, Archie Bahm indicates that life is both moral and aesthetic at the same time, and Stolnitz admits a "mixing" point in many instances of "concrete experience."[37]

What do such admissions gain them? Nothing that is not taken away by the larger concession that *disinterestedness* and *interestedness*, or focus on instrumentality, vary only in degree, not kind. If this is so, then the aesthetic attitude is not clearly demarcated from the practical attitude, and theories such as those given by Stolnitz fail to distinguish the very phenomena they want so desperately to analyze. When does a certain experience truly become disinterested? If one maintains that this hard distinction between attitude types is a necessary and sufficient criterion (along with the other parts of Stolnitz's definition), then one must be able to give a clear answer to the boundary query. If one does not insist on the separation of aesthetic experience from moral experience (the kind of nonaesthetic experience I am most interested in), then one does not need to provide such a demarcation. One can merely indicate the ways that a certain experience tends toward having more of this quality and less of another quality. This is the Deweyan move, and it can be seen as motivated by the failure of accounts such as those discussed above to clearly demarcate what is aesthetic experience from what is nonaesthetic experience. One obvious step toward the linkage of aesthetic and moral value in my project will be the challenging and abandoning of such limiting presuppositions as the strong separation of aesthetic activity from moral activity in kind and essence. The question to be answered in the following chapters will be simple—can one find a way to do justice to the immediately felt quality of the aesthetic experience without holding that it entails its own (separate) sort of value (in other words, that it can legitimately be connected with moral value)?

The reified dualism between intrinsic and instrumental value also must be challenged. In the following chapters, I will begin to construct an account of value that resists the temptation to find a final or unconditioned value in anything—that was a point on which Dewey was adamant. Here I will offer some reasons why the hard and fast division between these *kinds* of values seems like a suspect point from which to start any discussion of aesthetic experience and its value. First, a primary reason should be its prima facie sequestering of aesthetic value from moral value. This seems to be a classic case of one's terminological boundaries causing the problems one attempts to solve with such conceptual implements. Of course, proponents like Budd lean toward the intrinsic value of art and aesthetic experience because they insist on doing justice to the unique experience of art. I believe that one can recognize the immediacy of aesthetic experience, its unique phenomenological feel, as well as its connection with other sorts of experience and value (namely, moral value). Intrinsic value, as a concept, implies that it is a sort of value that is beyond conditions, and it is hard to see how any artistic product or experience can hold such a final value.[38] Coleridge's poetry is valuable, but only given certain cultures of production and reception needed to produce it, understand it, and appreciate its power. Without these historical conditions, its value is far from final or independent.[39] The solution that one must offer to do justice to art as well as to recognize its connection with other sorts of activities will be found if one avoids the extremes in the readings advocating intrinsic value. The key is to find a way to talk about the special degree of quality in aesthetic experience without making this value a special kind of value (viz., intrinsic value), or reducing talk of this value to the production of products or effects (instrumental value). Due to their fear of the latter, proponents of intrinsic value for art and aesthetic experience believe the former is the only way to fully incorporate the phenomena and value of artistic activity. This move, however, is caused by the way they conceptualize the problem.

One sees clearly in Budd that instrumental value is ascribed to something when it is seen as *a causally productive source of certain effects.* I refer again to Budd's characterization of instrumental value, as it is very telling of the shift away from experience and toward the causal production of results. He describes instrumental value as "*the value,* from whatever point of view, *of the actual effects of the experience* of the work on people or the effects that would be produced if people were to experience the work."[40] Notice that the point of view is focused not on the experience, but on the creation of certain outcomes or effects. This way of looking at art obviously fails to account for what it is like *to undergo* that experience. This conception, however, in no way justifies a leap to the position that the value of art is separate *in kind* from moral matters and states of affairs. Even Monroe Beardsley may fall prey to this functional approach to art's value, skipping over what is experienced in the actual experience in favor of describing actualized effects such as calming tensions, refining perception, and developing imagination.[41] This leaves something out—namely, that one's experience of art is not of developing of imagination, calming tensions, etc., but is of a certain invigorated *experience* closely tied to some particular art object. The focus should be on the *experience* of art and its value, and not on the *effects* of that experience as related to other, equally ordinary, ways of achieving those effects.

In the following chapters, I will use Dewey's aesthetics as a starting point to give a reading of aesthetic experience that I believe does justice to the uniqueness of aesthetic experience while connecting it to matters of moral improvement. While one can give what I will call a *causal account* of aesthetic experience and its value in producing morally valuable effects (increasing imagination, calming tensions, etc.), I will emphasize an *experiential account* that focuses on the experience of art objects themselves and what this experience tells us or shows us about moral improvement and value. The latter way of thinking about aesthetic experience and its value(s) maintains quite strongly the first-person standpoint, and always acknowledges that the experience of the art object is crucial to discussing its value. This is in stark contrast to the causal account, as it simply replaces the lived experience with a conceptual *x* that connects to certain desired consequences. Thus, aesthetic experience is described as valuable as it produces a given range of effects, but the emphasis is not on the feel of the experience and how this uniquely relates to these effects. Instead, the reading of aesthetic experience I will now provide will break out of the parameters established by reducing a first-person aesthetic experience to a causal view of induced effects, and shift to an analysis that sees the experience itself *as* the effect, and *as* already connected in an intimate way to moral experience and improvement.

3

Dewey on Experience, Value, and Ends

The experience of the aesthetic is taken by most scholars to be a particularly valuable occasion. Yet, the devil is in the details when it comes to describing this value. To build an account of aesthetic experience that does justice to its immediate value and enjoyment by an auditor, one can profitably turn to the work of John Dewey. Dewey sets out to defend the qualitative feel of ordinary experience as it is prior to discursive dissection by analysts. He also has a great regard for the intellectual adaptations of humans, and his thought consequently tries to do justice to the critical or reflective phase of human experience as well. What Dewey does not do, however, is give certain aspects of experience a reified ontological or normative status. This is the fault, I have argued, of the scholars discussed in the previous chapter who hold a "groomed" conception of the art object, as well as those who argue that the experience of art has a value that is different in kind from the value accorded to other experiences. Both of these positions take certain ways of *analyzing* aesthetic experience to be *the way* that the experience actually is. This is the root of what I have called the causal approach to aesthetic experience and the problems such an approach poses for accounts of aesthetic value. Looking at aesthetic experience from an external perspective of causal effects naturally leaves it bereft of what makes it so important in schemes such as Dewey's—its experienced, qualitative feel for the one experiencing it. The experiential approach I find in Dewey will do justice to this immediately experienced aspect of aesthetic experience, and also will provide a theoretical grounding for readings of its value.

To proceed with such an account, I turn to Dewey's analysis of experience, specifically in its primary and secondary phases. This will prepare the way for a focus on the experiencing subject in aesthetic experience, and will lead naturally into a discussion of value and valuation in Dewey's work. Using Dewey, I will demonstrate how one can do justice to the immediacy of aesthetic experience without making its value intrinsic in an ontological sense (separate in kind from other sorts of value). Both the discussion of experience in its main phases and of value/valuation leads to the final portion of this chapter, in which I attempt to show how a causal approach relies on a strong separation of means and ends, a problem that Dewey finds endemic in modern society. His aesthetics is an attempt to meliorate such a problem through redescription and prescription, and I will illustrate how his thought shows that ends and means are not separated in objects and activities. My analysis becomes a key part of an experiential reading of aesthetic experience, since it allows one to account for causal factors noted by reflection that are simultaneous with its experiential, qualitative aspects.

Primary and Secondary Experience

In *Experience and Nature* (1925), Dewey argues that experience is not something that is separate from nature, but is instead *in* and *of* nature. Objects are as they are experienced, and nature is inconceivable outside of experience. There have been some interesting debates as to the extent of the metaphysics presented in *Experience and Nature*,[1] but I will sidestep that issue to focus on how Dewey can be seen as accommodating both the holistic, qualitative, experiential side to experience as well as the analyzed and intellectual side. Dewey abhorred strong dualisms, but his insistence on continuities in nature often led him to postulate what one can call working distinctions. One such distinction, highlighting the sort of emphasis that can be seen in the major types of experience, is made when he divides experience into primary experience and reflective experience. These types are not absolutely separate, as they meld into each other in life and reinforce the qualitative feel of each other. Dewey, however, thought it important to advance this general distinction to highlight differing qualities or emphases in experience. Primary experience is described by Dewey as "gross, macroscopic, crude subject matters" (15). Dewey does not intend to demean or debase experience; he uses such terms because the point of primary experience is to denote that which is prior to linguistic description and analysis—experience as it is before problems and indeterminacies lead one to analyze it for certain purposes. Experience simply is what it is experienced as. Once one has an incentive to analyze the experienced subject matter, one moves to the secondary sort of experience—what Dewey calls "reflection"—by which he means the conscious separation and creation of "refined, derived objects" by focusing on their connections to other events and consequences for possible events (15).

Reflection looks at objects not as they are, but instead focuses its efforts on certain aspects of the experienced situations to ascertain their causal powers or linkages to other states of affairs that one has experienced and/or wants to experience in the future. Primary experience is the default mode of experience for Dewey, since he finds that the human organism is naturally oriented toward action. Given this demeanor, experience is not overtly dissected as to what is not present; instead, the human organism acts and undergoes *in* the presence of the environment as well as its own forces and impulses.

Only when the organism's impulses are stymied is there an impetus to stop and examine the causal factors involved in the current situation in light of creating situations that one has benefited from in the past. This activity is the intelligent, reflective examination of a situation, and can be seen in its highest form in the method of scientific inquiry. Science, as an institutionalized method of inquiry, systematically attempts, according to Dewey, to "discover those properties and relations of things in virtue of which they are capable of being used as instrumentalities; physical science makes claim to disclose not the inner nature of things but only those connections of things with one another that determine outcomes and hence can be used as means" (6). Science as reflection is the overt cutting up of the elements of experience in a purposive way that aims at increasing our intelligent command over situations; by focusing on only a few of the present aspects of experience, and connecting them to conditions and consequences that are not present (namely, ones that have served as causes in the past, or are desired in future situations), humans can create and control the unfolding of such situations. Reflective activity, however, is different from the unanalyzed experience of situations. As Dewey notes after giving a description of scientific inquiry, "the *intrinsic* nature of events is revealed in experience as the immediately felt qualities of things" (6). In an earlier important essay, "The Postulate of Immediate Empiricism," events are said to be what they are experienced as. Take a part of a situation, such as a horse. Different people will experience this aspect of the situation *as* a different thing. A horse seller will not see the concept "horse" with added adjectival descriptions applied to a certain patch of brown in one's visual field, but will directly experience this part of the situation as a wonderful financial prospect; a child will obviously experience the horse differently than does the horse seller. Dewey's point is that no cognitive work is required of any of these individuals. They experience the situation (including what one can label a "horse") without having to consciously apply individuated concepts. Alternatively, if one takes the propositional aspects derived from reflection (statements about parts of the situation) as primary, one robs experience of its qualitative dimension.

Other problems arise from taking the objects of reflection as descriptive of the experience as had by an experiencing subject. The "intellectual fallacy," as Dewey labels it in *Experience and Nature*, is problematic: "When intellectual experience and its material are taken to be primary, the cord that binds experience and nature is cut" (29). The problem is now connecting such discursive propositions and concepts to the world of nature. A continuity is maintained, according to Dewey, if one holds that primary experience is nonreflective (or noncognitive) and that certain aspects of a situation (its quality of indeterminateness) can lead one to reflect on it in a certain special way involving purposely individuated concepts and connections to other situations and events. Thus, "any experienced subject-matter whatever may *become* an object of reflection and cognitive inspection" (30). It becomes this way when there is sufficient impetus for a person to make it so; in much of everyday life, however, habits and situations work out so that reflection is not required. For Dewey there is a strong reason to distinguish between primary experience in its immediacy and reflective experience—the former emphasizes the immediate feel of a situation, and only sometimes does it lead to the mediated consideration of parts of that experienced whole for certain purposes.

One must not hold that these are absolutely rigid *kinds* of experience, as reflection is also an experience. Additionally, reflective activity creates the habits and the meanings that later influence or infuse immediate experience with meaning, a point Dewey makes in *Human Nature and Conduct* (1922), as well as *Art as Experience* (1934). James Scott Johnston has criticized Richard Shusterman's analysis of Dewey on immediate experience (specifically his reading of aesthetic experience) largely on this point: "The qualities of an experience cannot be disconnected from the meanings that those qualities usher. Qualities compel inquiry into them."[2] Shusterman (rightly) notes the influence that reflective inquiry has on qualities as experienced, namely, that it informs/forms the meanings that are later taken as immediate, or that are later immediately enjoyed in the case of aesthetic experience.[3] I believe that Johnston's critique overreaches, however, in strongly claiming that "qualities beget inquiry."[4] The evidence he adduces for this claim is that "prior meanings, formed in earlier reflections into the subject matter, play a (strong) role in the having of a further (in this case, consummatory), experience."[5] The problem, as I see it, is that this does not entail the conclusion that qualities *always* lead one to the state of reflective inquiry into causal conditions and consequences of particular parts of a situation. What his reasoning leads to is that reflection can form meanings that are later important parts of immediate experience (say, of a sculpture). Dewey's point is that the meaning of "horse" for those individuals had become habitual and, as such, did not require reflective inquiry or effort to use; instead, the meaning was there in the experience.

Shusterman has argued a similar point in his analysis of interpretation when he claims that everyday uses of language are immediately understood (without interpretation), such as the beach-going utterance of "surf's up."[6] Only when someone uses that phrase in a perplexing context (i.e., as a greeting in a department store in Ohio) is interpretation required. What one is then doing is reflecting upon the past uses of this phrase, the possible intentions of the speaker (perhaps aided by other observations of his or her actions), and consideration of possible meanings/uses of the phrase in that situation. One is no longer immediately experiencing the phrase as meaningful, but as perplexing; this in turn is what leads to the activity of inquiry. Inquiry is not directly connected, however, to successful situations of immediate understanding of language, or of experience in general (say, at the horse stables). What brings on such reflection is some sort of problem or barrier to one's impulses or habitual patterns of interacting with an environment (including linguistic habits of meaning). Only then is Johnston correct in claiming that qualities lead to inquiry. It does not affect my claim that he (along with Shusterman) points out that reflection can lead to qualities being experienced in a certain way; indeed, if reflection were not efficacious in this manner, there would be no purpose to such controlled, purposive inquiry brought on by barriers to impulse in the environment. The main point I want to make is that not all experience has to be *reflective* experience, nor need it lead to reflective activity. That some (important) experience is reflective and leads to immediate experience of a certain sort does not conflict with this claim.

Shusterman also brings up the insightful point that reflection itself can be seen as immediate experience in an important way. He points out that "not only can prior reflection prepare the way for immediate enjoyment but reflection itself offers its own aesthetic pleasures of immediacy. We can enjoy the process of reasoning, speculating, interpreting in a direct or immediate way without postponing our satisfaction to a subsequent appreciation of the results of our reflective process."[7] What is being claimed here is twofold. First, reflection can be taken as an immediate (aesthetic) experience, and second, this itself can serve as material for future reflective activity (although this step is not needed for the immediate enjoyment of reflection in the first place). The first claim is the one I want to focus on here, as it illustrates an important connection between Dewey's notions of primary and secondary (or reflective) experience. Reflective experience can be seen as immediate (and hence, a primary) experience in that it is open to immediate enjoyment, has a qualitative feel to it that distinguishes it from other experiences (including other reflective activity), and is itself informed by past experience in terms of meaning.

One may ask, does this render defunct the distinction between immediate experience and reflective experience? Shusterman himself provides the start of an answer to this worry by noting that in a very important way, some sort of immediate experience is logically and temporally prior to reflection, since the latter is spurred on by the feel of the former experience and reflects on the matter of that experience.[8] It is reflection on *something*, and that something is the experience that serves as the cause of the reflective activity (since not everything is reflected upon, given Dewey's assumption of the primacy of action in human experience) as well as what is being examined for some purpose (to improve future experience). In reflection, the hallmark activity is that of breaking experience into distinct concepts that are cognitive in the sense of being consciously connected to other states of affairs. This is an experience in itself, but it is not the whole of human experience, nor is it identical with what is being analyzed with such concepts. Dewey recognizes this limitation of cognitive components to experience, and points out that "the cognitive is never all-inclusive; that is, when the material of a prior non-cognitive experience is the object of knowledge, it and the act of knowing are themselves included within a new and wider non-cognitive experience—and *this* situation can never be transcended."[9]

The act of reflection is itself an experience with its own qualitative feel, and only parts of that activity are reflective in the sense of consisting in mediated thought (viz., conceptual connections to nonpresent situations and objects). Part of it is reflective, just as part of a "normal" immediate experience *becomes* reflective when it is picked out for cognitive scrutiny and inquiry. The whole of experience, however, is never reflective, but is qualitative. This is Dewey's point, and it is a point that is lost when philosophers knowingly or unknowingly adopt the causal approach to understanding aesthetic experience. As pointed out in the previous chapter, such an approach reads aesthetic experience as another mere causal element in a sequence of causes and conditions, a reflective move that leads to the quality of the aesthetic experience being seen as replaceable, or as inadequately described in favor of an emphasis on its connection to other (nonpresent) effects.

Dewey's notions of primary (immediate) and secondary (reflective) experience are transferred into his discussion of aesthetics and value as "appreciation" and "criticism." More will be said about these modes of aesthetic experience in the next two chapters, but it is important here to emphasize their parallels in Dewey's account of experience. Appreciation (taste) is described by Dewey as an immediate enjoyment of some object or situation, such as when someone sees and enjoys a beautiful painting. Dewey's point, of course, is that such immediate appreciation is a precursor to critical reflection on the painting, and is determined (in part) by past critical experience. An example of this dialectic is given by Shusterman when he describes how an appreciation of French poetry is conditioned by training in language, poetic tradition, literature, and so on.[10] One also can see how the immediate experience (appreciation) of such poetry will shape and direct future critical inquiry. The important aspect to this situation is that criticism, like reflection, should not be confused with the felt experience of life—in this case, of the art object one is appreciating. Built into this notion of appreciation is not merely enjoyment, but also a notion of value. Something in experience is enjoyed, and one can seek this out in future experiences. In Dewey's terms, it can be seen as a held "value."

Dewey on Intrinsic and Instrumental Value

The standing challenge at the end of chapter 2 was to find an account that did justice to the immediate value of aesthetic experience, while not estranging this type of experience from other sorts of experience. This chapter will answer this challenge by building on the analysis of experience just given. Accounts such as Budd's and those of the noncognitivists err when they place a reified value on art as the only alternative to seeing the work of art as a mere causal means that achieves something that can be actualized by other means. Dewey's reading of experience does justice to the ultimate qualitative feel of experience while allowing for a variety of ways of analyzing experience for reflective purposes. In terms of value, I will argue in this section that the aesthetic experience can have *both* an immediate value *and* an instrumental value. Thus, the immediacy and quality of aesthetic experience are accounted for from the perspective of aesthetic experience *as* an experience of a subject.

Dewey discusses the concept of intrinsic value under the heading of "immediate value," and he does this for a reason. According to Dewey, immediate value is closely connected to the qualitative feel of immediate experience. To see how this is so, we look to Dewey's account of value. Value is a difficult concept because it denotes a *way* of prizing or acting toward something, and it can also refer to a process of justifying such prizing. As Dewey notes in the essay "The Logic of Judgments of Practice" (1915), "the *experience* of a good and the *judgment* that something is a value of a certain kind and amount have been almost inextricably confused" (23). The former is a "direct, active, non-cognitive experience of goods and bads" (26), and this can be what I have called above an immediate value. Such a value is shown when one takes delight in something directly, as when one hears a favorite song or reads a poem that accords with his or her preferences. One does not need to establish that such things are good or valued; they just are valued or experienced as good.[11] After the fact one may label the enjoyment or prizing a "value," but that does not motivate the actual experience of the object or situation in question. Take an individual who walks about on the street and avoids mud puddles. Dewey would say that even though the individual has not gone through an elaborate and reflective process justifying such behavior, the person immediately *acts as if* he or she valued staying dry.[12] Although this is a rather pedestrian example, it makes the point that Dewey wants to make in his ethics and his aesthetics—much of our confrontation with the world is in the form of habits, and these include what can be called values and the activity of valuing. Only in certain cases do humans *evaluate* or *valuate*—create and justify some value in reference to other possible or actual values.

In Dewey's essay, "Valuation and Experimental Knowledge" (1922), this theme is continued, albeit with more explicit reference to a held, immediate value being ultimately intrinsic. Such a held value can be approached as instrumental to other effects or states of affairs, but this does not deny its present immediate valuing or prizing by the agent. The important point he maintains in this article is that the value can be already held, or it can be the product of a reflective, critical process of deliberation and justification. The former describes the same immediacy Dewey refers to in his 1915 work on judgments of practice, and dovetails with his reading of immediate experience in *Experience and Nature*. Again, part of the immediacy of the values can be the meaning habitually had in some situation, and such reactions to the environment can include the quality of emotion *in* the situation or the perception of relations immediately *in* the situation. One sees one's national flag and has some immediate meaning attached to it, as well as perceives it in an emotional fashion (it is a *powerful* symbol, an *angry* sight, etc.). Such immediate values serve as the material for future experiences of value, and also for future critical reflection over the comparative weight or worth of this value.

Dewey notes that this other, reflective use of value or of judgment of value comes about when one's values are put into conflict or doubt because of some aspect of the situation. In other words, the indeterminacy of the situation leads one to deliberate or evaluate, or as Dewey puts it at one point, to "instate" a value. This is a conscious, reflective process that is spurred on by indeterminacy in immediate experience, and this process can take at least two forms. First, one can deliberate over what value should be privileged in a situation involving the conflict of two or more held values. In such a situation, action may be overdetermined by the values one holds, and one may have to pare down the values upon which one will act. One is reflectively creating a hierarchy of values, and this occurs in light of considered causes and consequences of holding such values. The second form that this reflective evaluation can take is the justification of one's held value; perhaps a value comes into conflict with some part of a situation, and one is led to consider if one should really prize that object as much as one does. In such a situation, one comes to a critically reached justification for one's holding of such a value, a different situation than the former mere holding of the value without reflective justification. Through such reflective evaluation, values are either adopted, ranked, or justified, but all are changed from the previous state of mere valuing by the act of going through this reflective process. The process then becomes part of the newly held value, and future situations involving this value will now be packed with the added meaning of this reflective process once undergone. This new value may become enshrined in habit and become a new, but still immediate value, and may need to be reflectively analyzed again due to future indeterminate situations.

At this point, it is possible to argue that a notion of intrinsic value is available within Dewey that would do justice to the immediacy of aesthetic experience without making it a separate kind of value in some strong sense. When Dewey explicitly links this notion of immediate good to intrinsic value in his 1942 essay, "The Ambiguity of 'Intrinsic Good,'" he is careful to note that the *immediacy* of value is what is intrinsic, and not some sort of value that has an essentialist primacy. He wants to delineate the essential versus existential uses of intrinsic value. The former indicates that the value at hand is part of the nature of the object, and does not vary based upon changes of condition. What Dewey has in mind here is G. E. Moore's famous test of intrinsic good, which abstracts from all the particulars of a given situation to see if good still remains attached to the object. If it does, then the quality of good is intrinsic to the object in a strong sense as part of its nature, or, as Dewey adds, its essence.[13] This claim is questionable, according to Dewey, largely because it entails the added metaphysical attachment of unchanging essences that must then ground this attribution of value, which seems as questionable as saying the quality of "white" is *in* a baseball in a strong sense, viz., that it does not change even if the conditions of light, sensory apparatus, etc. change. Instead of such an essential notion of value, Dewey recommends a notion of intrinsic value that is existential. By existential he does not mean that the value exists apart from the experience of a subject, but instead that the value *qua* quality belongs to that object in experience. When one sees a white paper, it is experienced as white. Whiteness is intrinsic to the object, *in those conditions*. The same applies for value. As Dewey notes, "*all* qualities whatever are 'intrinsic' to the things they qualify at the time and place of the occurrence of the latter."[14] Since one such quality is the immediate liking or prizing (i.e., valuing) of some object or part of a situation, values can be intrinsic.

With such a notion of intrinsic value that emphasizes the connection of immediate value to one's reaction to a situation, one is in a position to challenge the assumptions of the chapter 2 accounts. There, the contrast was largely between a notion of intrinsic value and extrinsic value, and was tied closely to a closed view of what is inside the artwork and what is outside. One sees in Dewey an alternative approach that does not contrast intrinsic value to extrinsic value, but rather focuses on the immediacy of reaction to the art object. Preempting critics who want to essentialize the notion of intrinsic value to avoid nonnecessary connections of object and value, Dewey argues that "the contrast in question is to be regarded not as a contrast between something good only in an 'extrinsic' or accidental sense and that which is good because of an eternal and universal nature, but as a contrast between a good which is *immediately* such and one determined as good upon *reflection* covering an extensive number of existing cases."[15]

The move Dewey is positioning against is the same one we saw in the chapter 2 discussions over moral value hinging directly on what is *in* the object. The noncognitivists in the debate over literature and its moral value make such a move when they argue that certain positions render literature and its experience expendable, or as one means of many available. In such a case, the value attached to such a practice would be conditional and accidental—conditional on achieving such a result, and accidental because other means could be devised to affect such a change in the subject. If one sees that it is possible to conceive of intrinsic value as *immediate* value experienced in the situation, then one need not be forced to argue with essentialist presuppositions. The immediate value of art is tied to what it is *experienced* as, and what one can call its instrumental value can be the *same* experience considered in light of its conditions and consequences as connected to other states of affairs.

Such an account of value has the obvious advantage of not setting intrinsic and instrumental value as opposing, mutually exclusive qualities that attach to the object in a noncontextual fashion. The object can have both depending on *how one orients oneself toward it.* Dewey argues just this point, stating that "while the distinction between instrumental and final goods is a necessary intellectual distinction, we must avoid converting it into either a logical disjunction or an existential separation. Existentially, the most immediate good or liking is after all part of a course of events. As such it has consequences for future immediate goods and ills."[16] The difference between these sorts of value is not something about the object, but is merely dependent upon perspective or attitude. Seen one way, the valued object's immediacy is highlighted; seen another way, its connection to other goods (i.e., desired states of affairs not present) is highlighted. In *Democracy and Education* (1916), this connection between intrinsic and instrumental value is emphasized as really a matter of perspective (247). In discussing the relation of these two sorts of value, Dewey notes the immediacy of intrinsic value, and points out that this immediacy renders it incomparable to other objects of value: "They are invaluable; and if a thing is invaluable, it is neither more nor less so than any other invaluable" (ibid.). Notice that Dewey is not saying that this *object* has this sort of value that is incomparable to all other (types) of objects. He is merely saying that *as experienced*, this object has a quality that is not comparable to other (nonpresent) objects. It is immediately enjoyable and captivating, and that is *in the present;* all other comparisons and possibilities are not readily there in the present.

Some situations arise, however, when objects of value conflict or force one to choose (say, an instance of conflict between one's love of cheesesteaks and one's dislike of the heartburn that inevitably follows). Now one must evaluate and determine which value should be acted upon, held with justification, etc. Dewey describes this way of looking at intrinsic values (and the objects they are attached to) as "evaluation," which "establishes an order of preference, a greater and less, better and worse. Things judged or passed upon have to be estimated in relation to some third thing, some further end. With respect to that, they are means, or instrumental values" (247). The same object and qualities are looked at, but now with the widened perspective of a nonpresent situation or object (in the example, the likely state of indigestion and its undesirability). The focus still includes the present (viz., the qualities of the object at hand), but also draws on its connection to situations more remote. This is the hallmark of reflective activity for Dewey, and valuation follows this pattern of widening the present's connection to conditions and consequences. The difference between instrumental and intrinsic value is simply the scope or perspective with which the qualities of a present situation are considered.

The question, however, now becomes, does the conversion of the qualities of the object into means connected to future states of affairs via evaluation render them no longer *intrinsic*? The shadow of the chapter 2 accounts of intrinsic value loom large here, as one hears the challenges of instrumental values being *mere* means and thus *replaceable* or nonessential to the desired end. How can something retain any notion of intrinsic value once it is converted to an instrumental value? I suggest that this conundrum arises only when one hypostatizes the value of the experience of an object into the object itself. If one instead sees these values as characteristic labels of emphasis of a subject's orientation, then one can see how an object can be taken as immediately valuable or as instrumentally valuable. In addition, I want to argue that the object can be taken as *both* immediately valuable and as valuable for other states of affairs. To build toward such an account, however, it is necessary that I expose a certain assumption of the accounts that would oppose the linking of intrinsic and instrumental value in such a way—namely, that ends and means are distinct, inherently separate concepts. If ends and means can be closely linked, then there is room for what I consider to be the ultimate fruit of the experiential approach—the realization that attention to the immediate experience of art can tell one something about the moral cultivation of the individual.

Dewey on Means and Ends

How one sees the structure of the world is often dependent upon how one analyzes it into conceptual parts. The conceptual tools that are employed are almost always a function of their effectiveness in use *and* of the tradition in which one is mired. Dewey holds this view, and consequently gives genealogical analyses of many concepts to explain why they are held and how another way of approaching the problem they address is available. One such genealogy he discusses deals with the current separation of means and ends in analyses of action and value. Why, he asks, are means and ends so often rigidly separated? Separation leads to such dilemmas as: does the end justify the means? Another related problem it creates is: which is more valuable, the end or the means? Both of these questions presuppose that means and ends *are* separate in some real sense, and that we must then deal with this "fact" about the world. Dewey wants to argue that there is another (more productive) way to conceptualize the relationship between means and ends, and to start such an account he gives a genealogical reading of why Western philosophy so often reifies a separation between ends and means.

The problem, according to Dewey, begins in ancient Greece with the separation of ends and means in human form. In *Experience and Nature*, he argues: "For the Greek community was marked by a sharp separation of servile workers and free men of leisure, which meant a division between acquaintance with matters of fact and contemplative appreciation, between unintelligent practice and unpractical intelligence, between affairs of change and efficiency—or instrumentality—and of rest and enclosure—finality" (80). Thus, the structure of society and its assignment of tasks were reproduced and given value in a society's philosophical analyses. Means and instrumentalities were separate in human form from those who thought about final ends in nature and human conduct, and this led to systems of thought that devalued and segregated the values of means and instrumentalities from that of ends. Greek thought wrote this separation of means and ends into its science of nature, and found the point of natural processes in the achievement of teleological purposes. Means were separate from ends in both value and existence.

After the transition to modern mechanistic physics, Dewey finds that ends are transferred from the realm of nature into the realm (albeit more truncated) of conscious mind. The emphasis with the rise of science is on the means by which nature operates, but ends are reserved for conscious human action and are removed from the natural world with the demise of teleology. Science begins to prize causal accounts of events, with an extensive focus on the exact means at work in natural processes. Dewey notes that "causality, however it be defined, consists in the sequential order itself, and not in a last term which as such is irrelevant to causality, although it may, of course be, in addition, an initial term in another sequential order" (84). Ends drop out of this picture of nature, and the real focus of inquiry is said to be the means by which things occur.

Two important things must be noted about modern science. First, means and ends are still rigidly separated. Even though modern science changes the emphasis on ends from the Greek view, ends and means as concepts are still separate—ends just have little explanatory power in the modern vision of the world. Second, this separation of ends and means in modern science has led to the development of a field of applied science that devotes itself solely to the development of means—what we now call (in a loose sense) technology. Technology is a natural consequence of modern mechanistic views of the world, since, writes Dewey, "by its nature technology is concerned with things and acts in their instrumentalities, not in their immediacies. Objects and events figure in work not as fulfillments, realizations, but in behalf of other things of which they are means and predictive signs" (101). Whereas

Greek science separated means and ends based upon social structure, modern science does the same based upon its view of the world; instead of ends and teleology being privileged, however, modern science's focus on causality has led to the development of elaborate forms of instruments that are rigidly separate from ends in the sense of a "fulfillment to activity." Dewey identifies this as a problem with modern thought, and as one that leads to the demeaning of actual ends in nature—namely, the *quality* of one's experience. Dewey notes that the quality of one's experience is the part of ancient teleology that is left out of the modern view of the world. On this point, he argues that "empirically, the existence of objects of direct grasp, possession, use and enjoyment cannot be denied. Empirically, things are poignant, tragic, beautiful, humorous, settled, disturbed, comfortable, annoying, barren, harsh, consoling, splendid, fearful; are such immediately and in their own right and behalf. . . . [E]sthetic quality, immediate, final or self-enclosed, indubitably characterizes natural situations as they empirically occur. . . . *Any* quality as such is final; it is at once initial and terminal; just what it is as it exists" (101). This is the "truth" in the ancient teleological approach for Dewey, and modern science tends to leave out the qualitative feel of experience. An important part of this feel is the valuing of certain parts of the world, which combines emotion and meaning in immediate experience in such a way that differs for people with different projects and purposes, backgrounds and past experiences.

There are ends in nature, and they are the qualities that are directly grasped and in many cases valued. Modern mechanistic approaches to science and the natural world shift the focus away from this (crucial) aspect of first-person experience, and, as such, lead to real effects as to the quality of this experience. Dewey hints at this one-sided focus on the "intellectual or instrumental phase" of things, saying that "in principle the step is taken whenever objects are so reduced from their status of complete objects as to be treated as signs or indications of other objects" (106). This is a hallmark of scientific reduction of quality in the world, and forms the basis for what I have called the "causal approach," since it highlights the focus on causal sequences instead of qualities and subjective consummations of particular experienced sequences. Dewey warns of the harm of such a one-sided approach. "Enter upon this road and the time is sure to come when the appropriate object-of-knowledge is stripped of all that is immediate and qualitative, of all that is final, self-sufficient. Then it becomes an anatomized epitome of just and only those traits which are of indicative of instrumental import" (ibid.). This causal approach, epitomized by mechanistic science, prizes the viewing of objects and events as *causal* entities, and "from the standpoint of causal sequence, or the order with which science is concerned, qualities are superfluous, irrelevant and immaterial" (87). The particularities of causal sequencing are taken as separate and more important than the qualities of certain events, and such a view has little room for the experience of value in the world (or its attainment as a consummation of activity).

Dewey notes that these views that separate means and ends find their way into ordinary experience, leading to the debasement of means as *mere* means ("common labor"). Thus, technology is seen as not being artful, and craft is seen as separate in kind from the practices of art (often called fine art). As Dewey laments in *Art as Experience,* art in such a scheme is locked away from ordinary life in museums, and craft and activity are portrayed as not being aesthetic or artful in their best forms. This separation keeps individuals from enjoying immediate labor, since it is a habit of thought, a way that they look at what they are doing. Dewey notes this effect of orientation by pointing out that "every divorce of end from means diminishes by that much the significance of the activity and tends to reduce it to a drudgery from which one would escape if he could."[17] This divorce occurs not so much in the *type* of activity undertaken, but instead lies mainly in the *attitude* or habit of thought of the acting individual. Since science is held as a paradigm of reflective analysis of situations, objects, and events, the question then becomes, can one find a way to incorporate immediate value in the world in a scheme that avoids this separation in kind and value of means and ends?

The Experiential Approach to Aesthetic Experience

Instead of conceiving of aesthetic experience as a *mere* causal factor in moral development, I propose that one look at it through what I have called the "experiential" approach. Such an approach will do justice to its felt immediacy (its intrinsic value), as well as locate its morally efficacious qualities *within that experience.* This will avoid the problem of conceiving of aesthetic experience as only one (merely causal) means to achieving communication, moral improvement, etc. Instead, something unique about the experience and its qualities will be the morally cultivating factor, an exact something that is not found elsewhere. An important part of my argument will be that the experience of an art object is an experience of moral cultivation, and I will deal with this strong claim more fully in future chapters. What I must do at the conclusion of this chapter is show how the experiential approach that I see in Dewey can unify the notions of ends and means such that the experience of art can be more than a *mere* means to moral cultivation. In order to do this, I will discuss two ways that Dewey unified ends and means in his work. The first is primarily used in his works on aesthetics and deals with the means composing the end. The second way is often found in Dewey's discussion of "ends-in-view," his label for consciously (reflectively) chosen values that guide action in the present. What will be evident in both of these approaches is the value and emphasis they each place on *the present*—the location of *experience* as felt by a subject, as well as the location to which mere means are often consigned.

In *Art as Experience*, means and ends are portrayed as being intimately linked in art objects. Dewey finds that it is an aberration of modern thought that leads to a strong separation of means and ends, practical matters and fine art, culminating in what he calls the "the museum conception of art," which literally separates art from the everyday world of action (12). Instead of removing art from practical matters (including moral improvement), Dewey finds in art the potential for a different situation—art as part of life. The way Dewey wants to go about bringing aesthetic experience back into contact with the activities of life is by emphasizing how art unifies means and ends. Dewey draws a contrast between purely (in terms of emphasis) intellectual activity (such as science) and aesthetic experience. Intellectual activities result in conclusions that have a value that can be detached from the study or line of inquiry that led to them—as Dewey puts it, the conclusion "can be extracted as a formula or as a 'truth,' and can be used in its independent entirety as factor and guide in other inquiries" (61). Thus, a well-done scientific study about political information seeking that finds a conclusion can be easily used *just for that conclusion*. Future use and research builds off of that study in terms of its conclusion, but the study can be seen as separate in an important sense from the outcome or results.

In an art object, there is no conclusion that is as easily detachable from any means. Instead, "in a work of art there is no such single self-sufficient deposit. The end, the terminus, is significant not by itself but as the integration of the parts. It has no other existence" (61). There is no single sentence that can convey the point of *Othello* or Christo's *Gates*; instead, the experience of the whole art object *is* the end that is to be actualized. To believe otherwise would be to commit the "heresy of paraphrase," finding that a plot summary or something similar could create the same effects as experiencing the whole artwork. What Dewey is trying to argue for is the claim that the constituent parts of art (as experienced) are, at the same time, both the means and the end of the artwork. In explaining the notion of "medium," he discusses this point further. "Means," like "media," are "the middle, the intervening, the things through which something now remote is brought to pass." Not all means are media. Some means are *external*, meaning that they are separate from the consequences that they are to affect. This type of means is merely a way of reaching an end that is in this case a cessation of activity once the end has been reached and are "usually of such a sort that others can be substituted for them; the particular ones employed are determined by some extraneous consideration, like cheapness" (201).

Dewey's notion of qualities in immediate experience also entails another notion of ends, however—that of a consummatory end that entails a conclusion and integration of what came before. Media are means that are *internal* to the end they aim to affect; thus, "esthetic effects belong intrinsically to their medium" (201). Change the medium and you have substantially altered the effect or product. Dewey provides the example of a house to illustrate this sort of product of artistic means. The bricks, mortar, windows, etc. are not mere means to create a house; in a very real sense they *are* the house. Pigments, canvas, etc. are not the way to create a separate thing called a painting; they *are* the painting. Such materials are used in such a way that they "express a meaning which is other than that which it [the material used] is in virtue of its bare physical existence: the meaning not of what it physically is, but of what it expresses" (205). The meaning is embodied in the material, hence rendering it a medium of that meaning. The means *are* the end to be affected.[18] These means, as well as the end, are both in experience, and thus are tied closely to the qualitative feel of the art object *in the present*. The qualities of the art object grab an individual, and the ensuing experience of the art object's qualities is an experience of the artwork itself. The art object is not a mere means to an aesthetic experience; experiencing the art object (and its qualities) *is* an aesthetic experience. A vital feature of the experience of art is the heightened sense of immediacy that is also implied in ordinary, nonreflective experience. Art's spontaneity is said by Dewey to indicate the "complete absorption in an orderly development."[19]

I will speak more to what aesthetic experience tells us about experience in general in the next chapter, but I want to highlight this subjective notion of absorption in the immediate qualities presented by the art object. Dewey is noting that it is the experience of the art object in the present that is so powerful, and that it unites the means (its qualities, materials, etc.) with a consummatory end (meaningfully integrating all of the means into the end actualized). The art object would not be so absorbing if this unity and qualitative richness were not present in it, parts and whole. If it were a mere means, one would see the experience of its parts and qualities as a mere mechanistic way to cause some effect; there would not need to be any absorption into *these* means, since they are separate from *that* conclusion or effect. This sort of view of all means as mere means is typical with the causal approach to experience, and can be rendered habitual and internalized as a way to view life and activity. Dewey notes such mechanization in habitual orientation toward activity with a simple example: "One student studies to pass an examination, to get promotion. To another, the means, the activity of learning, is completely one with what results from it. The consequence, instruction, illumination, is one with the process."[20] Both individuals go through the same motions, but the latter *experiences* it as part of the process of education, not as a mere means to be suffered through. This type of orientation toward seeing means and ends as united is part and parcel of the experiential approach to aesthetic experience, and can be rendered habitual through the course of life, just as a causal way of seeing certain processes as separate and distinct from their ends can be internalized. The experiential approach will be able to give a reading of aesthetic experience and its connection to value based in part on this immediacy of experience that lies within the experience of perceiving art objects.

Dewey also unites means and ends together in a more reflective and conscious fashion. In many cases, facets of a situation push individuals to evaluate held values and purposes. This activity is reflective or critical and involves some distancing from the immediate properties of the situation at hand to bring in conditions and consequences not readily present. It is in such reflective activity that Dewey finds that consciously held ends are formed. This notion of ends, however, does not mean that they are separate from means employed in the immediate situation. Dewey loathed such a separation of ideal ends from the concrete specifics of a given situation and thought that such a separation led to insensitivity to the needs of the situation as well as to a devaluing of the activity of the present (viz., the "mere" means). Instead, Dewey argues that these ideal ends can be seen as "ends-in-view." As Gouinlock notes, the end-in-view is different from a value precisely because the former "has been selected by some process of inquiry and reflection," and is a purposive response to a situation and its specific details.[21] Values are often blindly or unknowingly held; ends-in-view are chosen (at some point) and consciously applied to a situation because of their likely efficacy. These can be rendered habitual to a point, but they still retain their added meaning from reflection since they are sensitive to connections among details within a given concrete situation and other nonpresent situations (desired states of affairs, etc.). As Dewey describes ends-in-view in *Human Nature and Conduct,* these "ends are foreseen consequences which arise in the course of activity and which are employed to give activity added meaning and to direct its further course. They are in no sense ends *of* action. In being ends of *deliberation* they are redirecting pivots *in* action" (155). Here we see ends-in-view being described as the product of reflective activity (deliberation among ends and values), and as responsible for giving added meaning to a certain event or object being experienced. Thus, a person experiencing a certain art object in a reflective manner will not just be absorbed in the immediate qualities presented, but will also reflect on the meaning of those qualities *as connected to other events, qualities, or states of affairs.* The reflective activity gives one added meaning and allows one to order or instate values in one's experience.

Additionally, Dewey connects this activity of ends-in-view with that of means—in a very real sense, ends-in-view are *in* the present activity (and are not remote ideals or ends) and are functional as means in that they guide present activity toward some consummation that unites the meaningful action leading up to it. In *Human Nature and Conduct,* Dewey has in mind moral activity, but his emphasis on combining means and ends in activity also illustrates the same point in aesthetic experience. I will discuss this point in later chapters, but for now it is enough to note that the experience of this reflective activity of ends-in-view fulfills the criteria in chapter 2 concerning activity being tied closely to the experience of the art object without assuming that there is a clearly demarcated or groomed art object with internal properties and external relations. In his discussion of art and experience in *Experience and Nature,* Dewey describes an end-in-view as a "constant and cumulative reenactment at each stage of forward movement. It is no longer a terminal point, external to the conditions that have led up to it; it is the continual developing meaning of present tendencies—the very thing as directed we call 'means'" (280). Instead of being a mere means, the activity of the present is transformed by the presence of the end-in-view into movement toward consummation, or a particular desired and projected endpoint. Means and end are combined in this conscious and reflective activity, and "the process is art and its product, no matter at what stage it be taken, is a work of art" (ibid.). The "ideal," to be discussed later, is the transformation of much of our everyday activity into such a work of art—this is the endpoint of making present activity meaningful, intelligent, and ultimately efficacious.

The instated value in an end-in-view guides present activity, be it moral action oriented toward others or thought directed to an art object. Dewey gestures toward this point when he notes that the reified separation of means and ends renders means as drudgery and leads one to view the means of activity as annoying. Instead, he gives the solution in *Human Nature and Conduct*: "It is found in a change of the dispositions which make things either immediately troublesome or tolerable or agreeable" (157). Notice how the solution is a change in *disposition,* just as the problem deals with a disposition that has been rendered habitual concerning the value of means and ends. The only difference is that the solution will be to increase one's reflective sensitivity to the details of situations, and one way of doing that is by paying attention to the present activity *in light of* what one consciously wants to affect.

These reflectively formed ends-in-view are meaningful because they (1) tie one's attention to the details of the present situation, *and* (2) bring in details of situations not present to the here and now. If the former is absent, one is devaluing the means and the present activity, and risks ignoring vital details of the present that are not only immediately valued but also important in longer-term projects (including future desired states of affairs being efficaciously realized). If the latter is absent, then one is not *intelligently* or effectively adapting the current situation to one's project or purposes. When building a house, the end-in-view is held as a constant plan that not only determines what the desired end state is, but is also united with the means (the bricks, etc.). The bricks and the organization (the "form" of the house) unite in the construction; one does not haphazardly build a house, nor does one construct a plan and then ignore it until the house is built. The plan (the end-in-view) is contemporaneous with the use and employment of the materials because it guides their *intelligent* use. If material facts change (say, the soil underlying the future house is of an unexpected sort), then the plan changes and adapts as well. The employment and organization of the materials are then deliberately and consciously changed in light of this end-in-view. What Dewey is opposing is "the subordination of activity to a result outside itself."[22] In the case of immediate experience, means and ends were said to be united in a close fashion; here, in cases of reflective thinking, Dewey feels the need to resist the bifurcation of experienced activity even more.

Even in cases of reflection and cognition, the disposition of the subject toward the activity of the present and the ends-in-view can be either more unified or more disintegrated. In the latter case, means and activity will be subordinated to nonpresent goals or ideals, and *present* activity will be less meaningful and, most likely, less effective (due to the separation from concrete details of the situation). On the other hand, one can cultivate a disposition of reflectively embracing the situation that does not rigidly separate means and end, activity and goal. Part of this involves the realization that the present *is* in a real sense that sort of situation to which the goal refers. Dewey points this out: "What sense is there in increased external control except to increase the intrinsic significance of living? The future that is foreseen is a future that is sometime to be a present. Is the value of *that* present also to be postponed to a future date, and so on indefinitely? Or, if the food we are struggling to attain in the future is one to be actually realized when that future becomes present, why should not the food of *this* present be equally precious?"[23] Goals are always of some present, and in pursuing a remote ideal the tendency is to ignore the present here and now. Cognition and reflective activity should not become so abstract that they totally remove one from the qualities of the present, *including the qualities of the present as given meaning through reflection.* The experiential approach that I will detail in the next few chapters will attempt to do justice to our cognitive experience of art objects, as much of art does challenge its auditors to think and reflect. Dewey understands this quality and is insistent in general on doing justice to the present—be it in immediate experience or in reflective activity as experienced. This involves a commitment to the present; as Dewey notes in reference to a person's orientation toward his activity, "control of future living, such as it may turn out to be, is wholly dependent upon taking his present activity, seriously and devotedly, as an end, not a means."[24] Thus, reflecting on a situation and its connections to what one has decided to consciously value (in other words, the formation of an end-in-view) ought to unite activity and goal *in* one's present activity and not render one's attention remote and on faraway states of affairs. Dewey shows yet again that a rigid separation of ends and means is not necessary, and not necessarily desirable.

At this point, we have two directions in which the experiential account can proceed. In the following chapters, I will detail aesthetic experience as immediate experience and, more important, as immediate experience of moral value. On the account given above, intrinsic value means attention to and absorption in the immediate qualities of a situation, and I will argue that some important qualities of aesthetic experience are qualities of moral experience and moral cultivation. Moral uses of art in this sense will not be external or instrumental in the sense of using some experience as a mere means to an effect; instead, the experience of an artwork *is* an experience of morally important and beneficial matters. Following this, I will analyze the reflective experience of art objects and discuss how this experience can be morally cultivating. Using Dewey's analysis of reflection and ends-in-view, I will argue that such experience is not the mere causal production of moral improvement, but is closely tied in its qualities to the end desired. In these ways the experiential approach hopes to avoid the concerns noted in chapter 2, all the while doing justice to the immediacy, qualitative feel, and importance of aesthetic experience.

4

Aesthetic Experience and the Experience of Moral Cultivation

In the previous chapter, I detailed a theory of value based in the work of John Dewey that attempted to do justice to the immediacy and power of the sort of value that is attributed to the aesthetic. A vital part of that account focused on Dewey's insistence on the fundamental connection between means and ends in action. This chapter will extend the Deweyan reading of value with the addition of the experiential perspective of the subject that figures so prominently in aesthetic experience.

Aesthetic experience is a special or unique (in degree) experience of some object or event, and the Western tradition has usually made it a response to the fine art object. This leads to the dilemmas noted in chapter 2 involving the radical separation of aesthetic value from moral value. Dewey's aesthetics resists this move, however, noting that such a result is a consequence of the accidental separation of art from life, and not a feature of art itself. What is of importance is the way that we interact with the art object, an emphasis that seems prima facie transferable to moral activity because it deals with the *how* of activity instead of the specific *what* of activity. Although Dewey discusses art objects as the content of aesthetic experience, he often intimates the grand vision of aesthetic experience as integrally connectable to any facet of life. At an often-overlooked part of *Art as Experience,* Dewey (elaborating on an example from Max Eastman) notes the difference in the experience of different men crossing the Hudson River into New York City by ferryboat. One man sees this portion of his commute as drudgery, and cannot wait for it to end; he notes "landmarks by which to judge progress toward his destination." Another man sees "the scene formed by the buildings . . . as colored and lighted volumes in relation to one another, to the sky and to the river. He is now seeing esthetically." This person perceives an interconnected whole, a "perceptual whole, constituted by related parts. No one single figure, aspect, or quality is picked out as a means to some further external result which is desired, nor as a sign of an inference that may be drawn" (140–41). Two points of importance are found here. First, one sees the continuation of the previous chapter's connection of means and ends—seeing the skyline aesthetically is distinct from seeing parts of the skyline as merely indicative of progress to the remote end of work. Second, the same situation or object can be experienced in a variety of ways. A certain way of experiencing an object with a certain sort of *attention* and *absorption* characterizes what Dewey labels "aesthetic experience." The question now becomes, can such a way of experiencing a situation or object (be it a work of art or a nonintentional skyline) be morally valuable or cultivating? In other words, is such an experience *merely* aesthetic, or does it connect in some close way to moral betterment?

The answer I will give in this chapter is that aesthetic experience does connect to moral improvement. In order to argue this point, I will build a notion of moral cultivation from Dewey that holds a place of importance for attentiveness to situations and relationships. Attentiveness denotes a first-person sense of experience, so I will base my account on Dewey's earlier ethical works, with their first-person focus on the individual and how one orients one's attentiveness to activity. In later chapters, I will bring in Dewey's later work as a complement to this focus, demonstrating that the same sort of attentive adjustment is evident in his description of growth as a moral end for individuals. In the final portion of this chapter, I will argue that the immediacy of art not only involves its integration of means and ends, but also its focusing of personal attention in that particular situation. I draw on accounts of Dewey's aesthetics that highlight the importance of absorption in activity to argue a point that I intimated in the previous chapter—that aesthetic experience *is* an experience of moral cultivation insofar as it *is* an experience of attention to one's situation and the relationships in which one is embedded.

Dewey and Moral Cultivation

Before I can argue that aesthetic experience is morally cultivating, I must enunciate a notion of moral cultivation within Dewey's thought. In doing so, I will be elucidating what is of moral value, or what is conducive to the type of personal development that ought to be desired. Moral cultivation is not a concept employed in many Western ethical theories, largely because their authors often overlook or undervalue the developmental aspects of moral activity; instead, they favor criterial matters of moral judgment.[1] One often sees this concept employed in discussions of ethical systems of China, India, and Japan. For instance, Philip J. Ivanhoe examines the early Confucian tradition and finds three types of cultivation models—the acquisition, development, and reformation models of moral cultivation.[2] These correspond to the approaches of Confucius, Mengzi (Mencius), and Xunzi, respectively. All of these assume some sort of subject (viz., the person or agent), and assume that there is some sort of goal to moral development. This is the point to which cultivation contributes, and it is the reason why the theories are often called *self*-cultivation theories. The "self" portion refers less to the agent of cultivation and more immediately to the object of cultivation, although we shall see in chapter 6 of this study how self-initiative and activity have a role to play in such cultivation approaches. In the developmental model, the key point is the encouragement of latent tendencies within the self to fully flower, whereas in the reformation model, potentially harmful forces in the agent are reformed in such a way that they are conducive to moral selfhood. The acquisition model shies away from a commitment to the existence of original inclinations to good or bad in the agent, but it does insist on certain formations as the endpoint of self-development. In all of these accounts, it seems as if the self is going somewhere, namely, to a state that it does not currently occupy.

This presents an immediate problem to any sort of Deweyan notion of moral cultivation. Dewey was strongly against any separation between ideal and real, especially in the moral realm. In addition to the reasons adduced in chapter 3 concerning the connection of means and ends, Dewey also thought that ideals being separate from current situations would lead to either a lack of action in the here and now (as the ideal does not connect to the concrete particulars of the given situation), or a moral fatalism, since it is often posited as a corollary of idealism that the real can never reach the ideal.[3] This is the sort of critique Dewey leveled against the self-realization theory of Thomas Hill Green in his article "Green's Theory of the Moral Motive" (1892). There, he argues that Green's contrast between the concrete self of activity and the ideal self leaves one "conscious of an ideal which sets itself negatively over against every attempt to realize itself, thus condemning us to continued dissatisfaction" (162–63). If the ideal is truly separate from the concrete, the problem of actually reaching the ideal becomes apparent. Dewey found that a theory such as Green's so differentiated the ideal that the real could never reach it. It appears that such a problem may exist for any account of moral cultivation—what is the ideal, and is it truly separate from the concrete details of the moral situation in which an agent finds himself? Is there truly a fixed goal that is to be reached or achieved in the act of cultivation? Dewey would seem to say that no such final consummation exists and that the project of morality is ongoing, without certain beginning or end.[4]

One can rebuild a notion of moral cultivation in Dewey that does not fall prey to the separation of means/ends or real/ideal. Such an account can be based in his early ethical writings concerning what he calls "self-realization." Realizing one's self can take two forms—one can discover what one already is, or one can become something that one is not at that instance. Dewey takes the former approach in his early writings, relying on the importance of expanding our understanding of our desires and ourselves. This attention to our character and its output into action then relates to the present self we will be in some future occasion—an approach that is remarkably different from notions, such as that of Green's, that postulate some sort of movement from a present self toward some future self. In those accounts, attention is on the future and not the present, whereas absorption in the present is a vital part to ethical development for Dewey. While Dewey's move away from idealism after 1904 does result in substantive changes of emphasis in his philosophy of experience, basic themes remain—including the idealized immediate meaning that assumes such a prevalent role in his 1934 *Art as Experience*. This connection is so obvious that pragmatists such as Stephen Pepper and idealists such as Benedetto Croce would quickly criticize that later work as being irreconcilably idealist. Although others have explored the grounds of this accusation,[5] I will avoid that controversy here and construct one possible reading of the moral efficacy of Dewey's aesthetic theory based on a dominant theme in his early works—that of attention to the present. I am not convinced that this theme, or its related end-state (albeit temporary) of progressive present adaptation, disappears in Dewey's later "naturalistic" work. In the next chapter, I will draw heavily from Dewey's later work to make additional points on the relation of aesthetic activity to moral cultivation.

Dewey's analysis of ethics and moral activity came on the heels of *Psychology* (1887). While this work was quite idealist in the neo-Hegelian sense, Dewey began what he later called a slow "drifting" from Hegelianism around 1890, which culminated with his stated break in 1904.[6] Along the path of moving away from idealism in its Hegelian form, Dewey wrote two works on moral philosophy that explore a notion of self-cultivation and that do not rely as heavily upon Hegelian commitments as do his earlier works. He holds two points in common with these earlier commitments—first, that in one way of seeing things, the self is "finished" and existent in the present situation, and second, that there is a reciprocal relationship between agents and their environment (viz., the world in which they are embedded). Both of these commitments lead, as I hope to show, to a notion of self-cultivation that prizes a progressive adaptation of the self and its capacities to its specific, concrete place in the social environment, as well as to an insistence that a key part of this adaptation is attention to the present activities of the acting self.

Dewey insists in his early works that the self is not a separate entity above and beyond the embodied agent, but is instead integrally tied to the concrete situation in which it finds itself. This is a common theme in *Outlines of a Critical Theory of Ethics* (1891) and *The Study of Ethics* (1894), two works that are often overlooked in commentaries on Dewey's ethical thought. I will use these two texts as a fairly unified presentation of what can be reconstructed as Dewey's early ethics, even though I acknowledge differences in their particular details. For instance, Jennifer Welchman's precise study of Dewey's early ethical thought notes some divergence between *Outlines of a Critical Theory of Ethics* and *The Study of Ethics*, particularly with the concept of will as used in analyzing individual action.[7] My purpose here has less to do with the history of philosophy and more to do with a constructive endeavor to use the resources in Dewey's early work to propose a solution to a perennial problem in relating art to morality. It is with this caveat in mind that I will now begin to provide a notion of moral cultivation from these two works.

While not from Dewey's naturalistic writings, both of these texts base their analysis on a reading of human activity and selfhood in light of an embodied creature in a surrounding environment. Thus, *Outlines of a Critical Theory of Ethics* points to the general division of "specific capacity" and "specific environment" as vital to a workable notion of individuality. This notion of individuality has both a descriptive angle (viz., how humans find themselves situated in the world) and a normative angle (viz., how to best optimize or balance these factors of capacity and environment). The term "specific capacity" is said to mean "special disposition, temperament, gifts, bent, or inclination." These can be seen as "internal" elements in that they are based largely *in* one's character, even though Dewey would acknowledge that they are formed and reformed in relation to external (objective) conditions. One must not mistake Dewey's working distinctions for reified dualisms. The other side to the human situation is the "specific environment," or the "station, situation, limitations, surroundings, opportunities, etc." in which a human finds himself situated (301). Thus, an agent may be prone to fits of anger and could be in a social station that promotes this trait; conversely, an individual with a passive nature may find himself in a society that prizes aggression and may not advance as far in its ranks because of this mismatch between specific capacity and specific environment.

The connection between these two factors is what Dewey calls "function," or the "active relation established between the power of doing, on one side, and something to be done[,] on the other" (303). The individual has certain pushes to alter the environment and the environment (including the social setting) holds certain resistances and limits that affect the agent's desire and ability to act in certain ways. Notice how the specific environment that individuals find themselves in conditions their capacities and their development—individuals in a society that does not prize artistic creativity may never discover their abilities to draw, paint, and so forth. Function as union combines these two factors into their own unique combination—one's concrete capacities join with one's concrete social situation (station, cultural surroundings, etc.) to form one activity or process. Like the analysis of means/ends in chapter 3, this process does not truly produce a product, but instead melts into other processes. There does not seem to be an end to the merging of one's internal capacities and drives with one's social station and its requirements. Instead, it seems that this is a process, or as Dewey puts it, an activity that continues with ongoing modifications in the specifics of the two general factors (capacity and environment).

In *The Study of Ethics,* Dewey talks less of capacity, but uses a term similar in meaning—"impulse." Dewey begins by separating ethics into psychological and social perspectives, and it is fairly clear that he focuses more on the former (234). The use of the term "impulse" seems fairly consonant with the term "specific capacity" insofar as they both indicate an inner push that originates, at least within the confines of a delineated situation, from within the agent and its character. Thus, impulse covers those drives that have evolved connected to the maintenance of life, as well as those drives arising from one's existence in a social situation. The important point about impulse is that, due to its lack of meaning, it is not clearly distinguished from other such drives—a characteristic tailing left by reflective or conscious mediation for Dewey. Impulses have results, and the nature of the human organism is such that it notices these results in light of the originating impulse. To use one of Dewey's examples, a child sees a lump of sugar and puts it in its mouth. The *meaning* of a lump of sugar has now been expanded as the results of this experience reflect back upon the original impulse to eat the sugar. Afterwards, the child sees the eating of sugar as closely connected to a pleasant sweet taste, whereas before such a meaning was absent. According to Dewey's early work, the impulse leading up to the act of eating the sugar has been *idealized*—a particular concrete situation and impulses to activity have gained a meaning and connection to other states (past and future consequences) that are not present in the act itself. The act has become meaningful. What was formerly called "specific capacity" of an agent now segues into a more biological idiom of "impulse," but the import is the same. The agent pushes against the environment, which consequently resists, leading the agent into reflective or mediating activities that imbue the present activity with more meaning. What Dewey called "function," he now describes by the nature of mediated impulse in light of environmental conditions. The important connecting point for both discussions is the interaction between the subject and the environment and the impetus this provides for meaning-making activity. This mediation serves as an overlay to the activity then, as well as in the future.

In *The Study of Ethics,* mediated impulses become a conscious guide to conduct (i.e., one now knows that a certain act *means* such and such). This system of impulses is what Dewey refers to as "character," and it has an impact on specific activity in three ways (240). First, impulse can be so completely mediated that it is transformed into an engrained habit of activity. The meaning of drinking coagulated milk could be so clear and evident that once one has done such an act, its future meaning is evident and readily translatable into action—namely, instead of initiating drinking activities, one cringes when one sees milk of that sort. This is the instantiation of meaning into fairly rigid structures of action, a reading of habit that continues in later works of Dewey's such as *Human Nature and Conduct* and *Ethics*. A second way that such mediation can affect action is by the provision of certain lines/plans of action as connected to a certain impulse. Thus, when a teacher is confronted with a student's excuse as to why he could not meet an assignment deadline, the teacher's reaction is an impulse toward caution that is held within certain lines of meaning—past student tricks, ways that such an excuse could be legitimate, ways to negotiate both of these possibilities in teacher reaction, etc. The teacher does not think of physical violence largely because such an action is outside of the plans connected to this general mediation of impulse (viz., the reaction to student excuses and potential abuse). A third way in which impulse is mediated is through the consideration of specifics—some impulses and the situations that evoke them can acquire such a meaning that attention must be paid to *that* situation's specifics. This could be what Dewey will later discuss as a "habit" of reflection or consideration. Here it is noted as a particular way that impulse can have meaning, and must be distinguished from his more limited notion of habit in the first way discussed previously.

All of these levels of mediation of impulse and its reaction to an environment in the way of concrete activity are called by Dewey "tendencies to action," which, "taken together, constitute 'capacity.'"[8] As in his *Outlines of a Critical Theory of Ethics,* Dewey includes environing factors as well as the internal drives to agent activity. Capacity still survives as "the power of action, whether impulsive, or habitual, or reflective, which an agent has at his disposal."[9] Two main elaborations are made, however, in the notion of capacity. First, Dewey has specified in more detail the ways that an agent is driven to action—including original impulse, previously established habit, or reflective activity. Second, Dewey anticipates his later dialectic of organism-environment by noting that these are both *drives* to action and *enabling* powers of action. Habit, as well as reflective activity, limits *and* allows action; only naive and incomplete definitions of habit portray it as dumb and purely limiting on human capabilities. In both texts, Dewey starts with the potentials of a human agent (capacities) formed in light of environmental factors and highlights their interaction with that environment in activities that the agent undertakes.

The goal of moral activity in such a system is optimally to align human capacity with the resisting and enabling forces in the environment. In *Outlines of a Critical Theory of Ethics,* Dewey highlights this endpoint of moral activity as optimal function, or "the performance by a person of his specific function, this function consisting in an activity which realizes wants and powers with reference to their peculiar surroundings" (304). What is in the background of Dewey's thought here has already been broached in chapter 3—the connection of the ideal with the material of the present situation. Welchman connects this reading to Dewey's challenge of the standard dichotomy between normative and descriptive values: "The moral scientist was (1) to describe and explain just what ideal personal capacities had historically been realized by human agents and (2) to suggest ways ideal personal capacities (and so persons themselves) could be more freely and fully realized."[10] *The Study of Ethics* changes this equation, according to Welchman, by leaving out the need for the moral scientist to know historical forms of realization and to even further minimize any "normative suggestiveness" that (2) proposes. Discussing the endpoint of Dewey's self-realization, she goes as far as to state that "since knowing and expressing the self is our true end, then obviously any science that increases our understanding of ourselves is inherently 'practical.'"[11] While I agree with Welchman's emphasis on the present situation (versus historical forms of realization), I disagree insofar as both texts do appear to contain practical proposals, instead of merely relying on knowing the self. The self can be expressed (and known) in differing degrees, and certain of these can be more unified and whole than others. It is not simply a matter of complete knowledge/expression being whole, as there is a reflectivity built into the capacity-environment distinction that prevents it from going one way. I argue that the environment modifies our capacities to some extent, a claim Dewey makes in his later work on habit and reflection.

The important point I want to emphasize here, however, is that moral cultivation ought to end with the agent being optimally adjusted to his or her environment; this means expressing his or her impulses, habits, and so forth in a sustainable, meaningful, and effective fashion in light of the present situation (environment). Dewey translates this point into the idiom of judgment (and with it, conscious direction of practical activity) by defining right actions as those that "tend to expand, invigorate, harmonize, and in general organize the self."[12] Moral cultivation of the self involves a revealing of that self and its capacities in a certain situation, but it also deals with better or worse ways to *express* impulse in action. Creating a character that expresses impulses that are well adjusted to other impulses and to the agent's environment is vital to moral activity for Dewey, as actions flow from an agent's character, and both are evoked and formed in light of some prevailing environment. Self-expression is the expression of the self we ought to be—the harmonized system of impulses given meaning in light of our present environment.

Why does Dewey call this self-realization or expression? Partly because of his commitment to avoiding a strict removal of ideals from the present situation—including the ideal of what sort of self one ought to become. It is also due to Dewey's insistence on a close relationship between an agent's character and his actions. Largely eschewing notions of will that signal a radical sort of metaphysical libertarianism, Dewey instead ties responsibility and volition to the drives inherent in one's character—a good person is good because he or she does good acts. One's character is formed by one's actions, and one's actions flow from or *express* that character in concrete situations. Agents ought to be concerned with adjusting their selves to their specific environment largely because of this connection between character and action. The correct amount of concern and effort is that which balances the drives of the self (character) with the opportunities and challenges of the environment. This is the endpoint of moral cultivation for Dewey, and is labeled as "goodness," or "progressive adjustment" of conduct to the demands of the environment (including the demands of one's social station).[13]

In such a scheme, what is of *moral value* is that which conduces to this endpoint of progressive adjustment of character to environment. This is obviously a wide notion of moral value, but it is the one that follows from Dewey's commitment to the interconnection of agent and act. Agent and act are not inherently separate, but are both parts of a single activity. Separating act from agent (viz., his or her character) leads to problems with indeterminacy or caprice in willing, or at the very least, a need for an independent faculty of will. Dewey has reasons why these are not palatable options, and closely connects character and action worth. Indeed, he notes in *The Study of Ethics* that "the act, no matter how specific, utters his whole self" (293). The act is an expression of the agent's character, even if a small instantiation of it (e.g., dishonesty in a card game). Conversely, the act reflects back on the creation of character; expression is something that can be controlled to an extent, and this explains why Dewey calls for certain *types* of expression (the sort that increase coordination and wholeness among the system of agent impulses). The endpoint of moral cultivation, progressive adjustment, is not a set of certain actions that are morally worthy or a specific virtue that is mandatory, but instead involves the "development of character, a certain spirit and method in all conduct" (307). Thus, *any* activity can have moral value insofar as *any* activity can affect one's character and can serve as the forming ground of the aforementioned spirit and method of conduct. Like the putative category of moral activities, Dewey holds that there is no delineated realm of moral value (and objects that possess it) because of the wide nature of character and the ways it can be developed. I will now argue that a vital part to this spirit and method of conduct that is so important to developing and developed character is a keen *attention* to the present situation.

To further clarify this discussion of Dewey on moral cultivation, one can schematically state some of the major concepts involved. As has been evidenced previously, the endpoint of moral development is *progressive adjustment* of the internal aspects of an individual (capacities) to her surrounding environment. Since actions are closely tied to character, one can see this adjustment as stemming from a certain sort of *character* that one wants to foster (which in turn leads to more adjusted actions as a natural outpouring of that character). Character differs per individual and concrete environments and capacities, so the most we can say about character is that it involves a certain *way* (spirit or method) of going about action. What I will argue in the remainder of this section is that this way of acting integrally involves *attention to the present situation* (involving the concrete aspects of the agent's capacities and environment). Thus, moral cultivation involves the development of attentiveness to one's present situation. I must now discuss why attention to the present is so important. For Dewey, moral situations are basically unique in their concreteness, and moral principles can only guide action in general, not in its specifics. Why is the subjective orientation of attention so important for moral cultivation, or for adjusting one's capacities to one's environment? To answer this challenge, I will supply two lines of argument—first, attention is vital because the moral situation is fundamentally a present situation, and second, because the ends and implicated goals of moral activity always occupy a present situation.

First, it is clear that Dewey insists on the present nature of moral activity—the moral situation is an immediately present situation that demands activity. It has certain concrete details about it, details that are not likely to be exactly replicated in other situations, and this means that there is no substantive notion of moral ends that transcend the particulars of a present situation. The needs of the situation, composed of the environment and the agent, dictate the ideals of conduct and the available actions. Thus, attention to the concrete details of this function or relation between capacities and environment is needed for a full assessment and response to the situation. Focusing on some distant and abstract moral theory is just that—focusing on something other than the situation in all of its details. Another key part to the situation is the instantiated relationships in which an individual agent finds itself enmeshed. Impulses and available actions are suggested and constrained by the environment, a major part of which is the role one plays relative to others. Thus, a mother has certain obligations to her offspring that others may not even think of; conversely, there are some general considerations that all may think of in virtue of being citizens of the same state (viz., legal rights and their protection). An important part of moral activity is the upholding of these relationships in an intelligent way; thus, attention to these relationships and the actions they seem to suggest is a vital step in being a morally sensitive and caring individual. Attentiveness to the present is a key constituent in upholding one's relational obligations.

One final consideration of the value of the present in moral activity is that it is the locus of preparing for future situations. I have argued previously against strong intellectualist readings of *The Study of Ethics,* particularly those that emphasize too strongly a fixed self that has merely to be expressed. Dewey revolts against such notions of self, and his discussions of self-transformation highlight the changeability of that self that is to be expressed. The self is made aware of its "self" (its specific character) in the act (since the act utters the self), and "character [can] be transformed and developed through this continual mediation" (359). It is the meaning that we see in the present and in response to the present situation that lets us know our character and, more important, lets us cultivate our character. Part of that cultivation involves improving character through acts of attention, and that character itself will create a person who is attentive to his or her actions and situations. The important point is that attentiveness to the present is a vital way to cultivate the self toward the goal of progressive adjustment, and it is also a vital means in the present to do so. Insofar as attention is both a means and an end-in-view, it flows naturally from chapter 3's discussion of Dewey's theory of value.

Another related way in which to defend the importance and moral value of attention to the present is by highlighting the point that the end or goal of moral cultivation and activity is always some *present* situation. In other words, the means of moral activity are also an instantiation of the end of moral activity, since there is no principled difference between present means and present ends—both are part of the continuous life of purposive activity. I have intimated a version of this argument above with the discussion of attention as a means and end to character transformation; here I will emphasize the general point that attention to a situation *is* an instantiation of what is desired in general moral activity. I will do this in two ways. First, attention to a situation entails attention to the details of the self (one's impulses and desires), as well as to the environment (one's station, one's duties, the needs of others). Attention to the situation *is* adjustment to the situation. Attention to some remote ideal or abstract consideration removes attention from the concrete details of the situation, and hence any adaptation is purely coincidental. Sustainable and reliable (progressive) adaptation requires attention, and is constituted largely by attending to the demands of the situation. Thus, attention is a key element to moral cultivation because it is, in a very real sense, an instantiation of the goal that one is attempting to achieve. Dewey makes a similar point in his later moral work—happiness always occupies a present situation, and should not be looked at as something far off.[14] Happiness is a full, unified functioning of the human organism—it is an activity. What makes it progressively adapted is the agent's attention to its development in the present and in the situations after the present.

A second argument for the importance of attention deals with relationships. Dewey always placed great importance on relationships, from his idealist works to his later works.[15] Indeed, it is from such a concern that Steven Fesmire criticizes notions of self-realization in Deweyan thought—for Dewey, Fesmire argues, there is no individual self to cultivate.[16] Raymond D. Boisvert offers a similar criticism, indicating that self-realization schemes seem to place growth apart from social interactions.[17] One must note, however, that even Dewey's early idealist thought prized the social integration and constitution of the individual. Relationships allow for one to exist as an individual, as well as to flourish as a truly developed individual. This latter point is what Dewey is maintaining in his discussions of the ethical postulate in his early work in ethics: "In the realization of individuality there is found also the needed realization of some community of persons of which the individual is a member; and conversely, the agent who duly satisfies the community in which he shares, by that same conduct satisfies himself."[18] This postulate assumes that individuals and communities cannot be ontologically separated, that communities are made up of individuals and an individual will always be relatable to some grouping of other individuals. The more important claim Dewey is making is that the development of the individual *is* the development of the community, and vice versa. Is this defendable? It seems so, if one looks at the goal of community development to be a group of individuals who enjoy their activities out of the worth of these activities themselves. Insofar as this system must be cohesive and sustainable, the moral development of one is dependent upon the moral development of others. Improving one's character is the improvement of the community because (1) the community is closer to its overall realization than it used to be (viz., by at least one agent), and (2) the activities of each agent affect others, so there may be a multiplying effect to self-realization. Notice that since the end state is not certain and static, I am not claiming that the improvement of one individual ends all need for community development. Instead, ends-in-view are constantly changing and meeting the needs of the present situation, so attention to the needs of one's station and capacities is an instantiation of moral development, albeit not the last one that will ever be needed in that community. Attention to the relationships one is involved in is a fundamental part to upholding one's own self-development as well as developing the community. These relationships suggest actions, highlight obligations, and also compose vital parts of the happiness of individuals. Attention to them *in the present* is a vital part of successfully upholding them.

Of course, a version of the hedonistic paradox could be leveled against this sort of defense of moral cultivation as attention to present relationships. It could suggest that if agents pay attention so intently to the here and now, they will not be successful in future situations (through a lack of preparation in connecting the present with these future states, perhaps), or they may fail to uphold the demands of the present. For instance, a father who goes through life consciously trying to be a good father may not turn out to be the best father possible—he may overanalyze mistakes or avoid parentally risky encounters with his son (for instance, coaching a baseball team and assuming a potentially conflicting station with his role of father). In other words, thinking so much about the present may hurt the effectiveness here and at later times that one wants, and would reduce the ease and pleasure with which one navigates through the present situation. I believe that such a critique can be answered easily from Deweyan grounds elucidated in chapter 3. Such an objection rests on a dichotomized understanding of ideals in moral conduct (including relational behavior). What the father is focusing on is not the present, but some remote ideal of fatherhood that must be upheld in the present. This is substantially different from basing a father's actions on and in the concrete details of the situation because a large part of the father's attention is *not on the present situation*—it is on the remote ideal. If the father was truly focused on his impulses, his son's needs, the demands of the specific relationship they are embedded within, etc., it would be much easier to be a good father. Indeed, one may argue that a good father is one who is totally present in the situation—not lacking the time to be present physically, not focused on the demands of work when he is present, and not focused on remote goals not germane to the concrete situation at hand. This is an excellent example, I believe, of what Dewey pictures as a morally cultivated individual—one who is attentive to the situation (both capacities and environment) and attentively adjusts his or her actions to reflect both the situation and his or her character.

This is the concern for the results of activity *in* the activity itself that was brought up in the previous chapter. There, Dewey connected means and ends, intrinsic and extrinsic value for largely theoretical reasons; here, one sees the practical reason for such integration. The present, if viewed in the right way, *is* the end one is continually seeking. One's attitude is vital to such a notion of cultivation and the key part to this attitude is attentiveness to the situation, including one's relationships. Such attentiveness is both a means to further instantiations of desired states (and progressive adjustment in general) as well as the end of moral activity. Situations continue to change, so this end is as final as any moral end gets for Dewey—it is the focus of attention in the present, now and in any of the future presents one may occupy. I have left out a discussion of Dewey's later concept of growth, but it is functionally equivalent to the notion of progressive adjustment I have been elucidating. Both denote a constant mating of organism and environment, and both ideally set up future instances of equilibrium reaching. I will have more to say about the Deweyan notion of growth in chapter 6. But for now it is enough to note that both progressive adjustment and growth signify a tight absorption in or attention to the present situation. Even the goal of happiness will be situationally contextualized in the present. As Dewey puts it in a later work on ethics, "happiness, reasonableness, virtue, perfecting, are on the contrary parts of the present significance of present action. Memory of the past, observation of the present, foresight of the future are indispensable. But they are indispensable *to* a present liberation, an enriching growth of action."[19] It is this aspect of presentness that will be foregrounded by the aesthetic.

Aesthetic Experience as Moral Cultivation

Even in Dewey's early and largely "nonaesthetic" work, aesthetic experience is portrayed as having value in that it contributes to what I have called moral cultivation. Such a relationship is typically couched in broad terms, and, anticipating his *Art as Experience,* is not limited to art pieces typically resident in a museum. Dewey's vision of aesthetic experience is wide, as evidenced in the discussion of the experience of the individuals on their ferry ride to work noted at the start of this chapter. Aesthetic experience is a *way* that experience can be, and Dewey marks this off as the highpoint of experience. Such an apex of experience is both qualitatively unique from other experiences and is not limited to a special range of objects, events, etc. The dominant theme in *Art as Experience* is stated quite succinctly in his earlier *Outlines of a Critical Theory of Ethics*—that aesthetic experience can encompass most of life, and that life becomes the "supreme art" that one is to master. Speaking on this connection of aesthetic experience (as related to artistic production) to the activities of life, he states: "Living itself is the supreme art; it requires fineness of touch; skill and thoroughness of workmanship; susceptible response and delicate adjustment to a situation apart from reflective analysis; instinctive perception of the proper harmonies of act and act, of man and man" (316). Art is important to moral matters largely because it is (commonly) connected to a type of experience that is called "aesthetic." What is this experience in its most rudimentary form? It is attention to a present situation, adjustment and growth in light of that situation, and the harmonious unfolding of that situation with the funding of past experience and present potentials. This is the basic form of what Dewey will describe in the early chapters of *Art as Experience,* and what I will build on momentarily. What I wish to highlight here is that for Dewey, aesthetic experience *is* closely connected to moral matters, and that if one balks at such a suggestion (as the authors discussed in chapter 2 seem to), it may be a result of one's framing of the problem. Dewey notes this much in his early work, pointing out that "if the necessary part played in conduct by artistic cultivation is not so plain, it is largely because 'Art' has been made such an unreal Fetich—a sort of superfine and extraneous polish to be acquired only by specially cultivated people" (316).

Putting aside this current conception of art (and the rarefied notion of aesthetic experience it entails) as only one way experience can be, this final portion of the current chapter will turn to a Deweyan way of describing how aesthetic experience is both an instance of moral cultivation and a preparation for further moral improvement. In other words, I will attempt to show how aesthetic experience is an instance of the endpoint of moral cultivation—attentiveness to a present situation, the fundamental element in progressive adjustment and growth—as well as a way of developing such sensitivities for future situations. To accomplish this task, this section will do two things. First, I will examine one way that aesthetic experience (including that brought about by art objects) *is* an instance of such attentiveness. Second, I will examine the more general connections that such attentiveness in aesthetic experience has to moral matters—in other words, how such a *way* of experiencing life is morally valuable. The former deals with the more traditional delineation of aesthetic experience as experience of art objects; the latter deals with an approach to activity in general that shares the important characteristics of the former and can thus transform the activities of life into aesthetic experiences.

Aesthetic Experience and Rhythm

In order to discuss how aesthetic experience can be morally valuable, it is useful to start where Dewey starts—with aesthetic experience as a continuation of natural tendencies resident in all experience.[20] Aesthetic experience is simply different in degree from other experiences because it holds exemplary levels of what other experiences hint at—connection to other states, integration of past meanings, enjoyable enlivening of the creature, etc. One way of concretizing such an experience is by tying it to the experience of art, a move that has traditionally been made in Western aesthetics. I, like Dewey, want to expand what our notion of art includes, however, from merely static objects removed from everyday life to a notion of art that is integrated with life. Thus, craft and skilled making of all kinds becomes art, just like the skilled production that went into the *Mona Lisa*. This moves the meaning of art toward including what is now labeled "craft" or useful arts as well as the fine arts. Later chapters will even argue that there are ways we can *skillfully make* most activities of our lives aesthetic, and therefore artful. All of these objects can excel at producing what Dewey calls "consummatory experiences" (with high levels of integration and completeness), or they can be rather ordinary experiences. Dewey provides an account of how experience can attain the level of consummatory experience, so I will detail this as well as its connection to the important element of rhythm. Dewey finds that not only music but also life has what can be called rhythm, and that attentiveness to this element in experience (of art objects, say) is attention to morally valuable features of human activity.

In regard to his explanation of experience, Dewey maintains that aesthetic experience (caused, although not exclusively, by the purposive practice of making and sharing art objects) is of the same type as normal experiences, only differing in degree in some of its characteristics. Thus, many of the key traits it has will be shared with all experience. Experience, for Dewey, begins when the living creature is confronted with an environment. Indeed, as Dewey puts it in *Art as Experience*, "life goes on in an environment; not merely *in* it but because of it, through interaction with it" (19). What the organism experiences *is* an environment, and this is a defining characteristic of life. The organism has needs that must be met and the environment holds the resources to fulfill these needs. These needs, such as hunger for food, thirst for water, etc., all denote some sort of lack, or as Dewey describes it, a "temporary absence of adequate adjustment with surroundings" (ibid.). Such impulses from within the organism impel it to reach out into the environment for satisfaction of these needs. The environment, however, is not exactly united in purpose and direction with the animal and is thus not always yielding what the organism requires. This is felt by the organism as a push from the environment, or an "undergoing," as Dewey puts it. The organism, being an organized and self-sustaining system, has its own powers to pursue its needs and their satisfaction, and thus exerts its own influence on the environment. This is the "doing" aspect of the live creature. These two stages or forces, doing and undergoing, eventually result in a type of (temporary) equilibrium or adjustment between the creature and its environment.

At the macro level, this equilibrium is represented by sustainable birth and death rates of a species in the face of a given environment. At the micro level, it is the individual organism's survival or lack thereof in the face of its needs and the environment's reluctance to meet those needs. Of course, not all experience is of this "do or die" sort, but Dewey's point is that this basic structure remains in all experience—that of an embodied organism doing, being faced with undergoing at the hands of something external, and reacting/adapting its doing in light of a resisting force. This is similar to Dewey's reading of capacity/impulse and environment in his early work on ethics, and is taken by him in *Art as Experience* as the basic situation of life and experience of any sort. In a general way, "life grows when a temporary falling out is a transition to a more extensive balance of the energies of the organism with those of the conditions under which it lives" (20). Experience, for Dewey, is therefore closely connected to activity and a qualitative assessment of activity; this point is evident in his moral writings in his use of the term "progressive adjustment" to a specific and changing environment. In his aesthetics, however, Dewey is expanding the point to underlie all living experience in general.

The outcome that is needed for continued life is for the organism to reach some sort of equilibrium with the environment. Barely scraping out of the environment what one needs to sustain a minimal level of life is a sort of equilibrium, but one that will be far from comforting or sustainable of its own accord. Equilibriums reached can be more sustainable in regard to humans by being more meaningful or integrated with other states of affairs (for instance, past situations and future needs). This sort of rich equilibrium is what Dewey describes as a consummatory experience, and it is equivalent to the experience noted as aesthetic.

This basic reading of experience involves at least three characteristics, according to Dewey, and the most optimal levels of experience (viz., consummatory or aesthetic) will hold these characteristics to a high degree. This is what Dewey famously describes as *"an* experience." First, any given experience will display some sort of completeness. Some aspect must be given that makes that experience stand out as a separate experience from other experiences. In much of everyday experience, such completeness is not wholly evident. In what Dewey calls *an* experience, the levels of completeness are noticeable and very important. An experience is set out as being complete in itself; while it is still connected to events before and after, it stands identifiable as a recognizable experience with parts that clearly connect in a complete fashion. Dewey notes this sense of completeness by stating that "every such successive part flows freely, without seam and without unfilled blanks, into what ensues. At the same time there is no sacrifice of the self-identity of the parts" (43). All of the parts seem to work in conjunction, and no part of the experience seems dead or out of place. According to Dewey, art objects have the properties that contribute to such an experience of unity in the viewer. Like the experience of having an exquisite meal in Paris, interacting with a powerful art object results in the subject *feeling* the completeness of the work.

Two points must be noted here. First, Dewey's notion of the aesthetic experience and the work of art is separate from the art object itself. The painting is not the work of art; the latter requires interaction with the viewer to become a work of art. Thus, aesthetic experience is an integral part of something truly being a work of art. The suppressed premise, of course, is that the honorific title of "art" is to be applied to those situations and objects that have value for us. Dewey could have gone with the common notion of art (the museum conception), but he instead begins with the commitment to ordinary value and naturalism in aesthetic theory. He therefore must link what is really art to the interaction with those whom value affects—humans with their interests and needs. The art object, like other environmental forces, challenges the human in its givenness; the human then interacts with the object and what it offers in terms of material for experience, often adding their own interpretation and meaning to it, to produce the work of art through this interactive experience.

The second concern to note is brought up by George Dickie concerning the false jump from properties of objects to properties of experience.[21] Put succinctly, his claim is that the object's property of completeness is no reason to suppose the viewer's experience will be complete. Beardsley responded to this claim in detail,[22] but I shall add my own comment here. I do not think Dewey is mistaken in discussing the experience as being complete, since we can imagine situations in which the qualities of the object are directly related to our states of being. Although a brown object may not cause me or my experience to be brown, a confused or disorganized argument can leave me in a state of confusion. Such a state is usually composed of my mental activity wondering about why the argument was so bad and what exactly the arguer was trying to do. Simply put, *I* am confused because the *argument* was confused. The properties of the argument and its statement are what lead me to the state of confusion. The same can be said of an art object. While "completeness" is not a physical property of the art object, the art object can have its properties arranged in such a way that it is experienced as complete or as less than complete (leaving one full of questions, unfulfilled, etc.). Thus, it is not prima facie objectionable to talk of complete experiences, just as it is not objectionable to talk of states of confusion or clarity concerning an argument, plot, and so forth. For Dewey, then, completeness is a mark of *an* experience, the exemplar of which would be that brought on by an art object.

A second characteristic prominently displayed in integral experiences (*an* experience) is that of uniqueness or distinctness. This type of experience is particularly unified, with all of its parts seemingly identified, in part at least, by their belonging to *this* whole. The individual parts of this experience are significant because of their interactions among one another, and the nature of this interaction is that of a unified, coherent whole that is distinct from other experiences and objects of such experiences. This is a unique interaction that lets the subject know this experience as separate and individuated from other experiences. Thus, a particularly moving aesthetic experience brought on by a unique painting will itself be unique; it will be tethered to that painting, as well as to the concerns, subject matter, etc. drawn from in making that painting latent with meaning for a given audience. A contributing factor to such uniqueness in aesthetic experiences is probably the experience's completeness—it is immediately different from the range of experiences that one has that are not felt as extremely complete in and of themselves. Another factor that accounts for this uniqueness is the next trait of a pervading quality to the experience.

The third trait, which is related to both completeness and uniqueness, is that of an underlying quality to the specific experience. Dewey argues that each experience has some sort of qualitative feel to it, or a certain quality that is specific to that experience. Thus, one sees that experience as unique insofar as one feels its unique quality. Surely this cannot be the only way to individuate actions, as one can tell experiences apart by purpose, objects involved, etc. Being chased by a bear is objectively a different situation from stealing home in a baseball game. I think Dewey's point, however, is this—the two situations noted will have a different qualitative *feel* to them. Some controversy has arisen over the exact role of immediate quality in Dewey's account of experience.[23] My position is that this subject-centered aspect to experience is an irreducible part of experience, and cannot be exhausted by language. Dewey makes this point even in regard to science—in *Experience and Nature*, he describes science as a reflective method to instruct others on how they can have a similar experience with those aspects of reality described in the data (19–20). Even a reflective endeavor involves leading one back to immediate experience. The best explanation I see as to why this is so is simple: immediate experience has an aspect that can be felt, but that cannot be completely captured by language. If it could, reflective talk might take the place of the experience of art (a particularly intense experience). Instead, the Deweyan position is closer to both reflective activity and immediate experience, each having something valuable and irreducible to contribute to human well being and experience (including that of reflective activity). More will be said about overtly reflective values of art in chapter 5.

In *Art as Experience*, Dewey explains this last trait of underlying quality thus: "An experience has a unity that gives it its name, *that* meal, *that* storm, *that* rupture of friendship. The existence of this unity is constituted by a single *quality* that pervades the entire experience in spite of the variation of its constituent parts" (44). As to whether or not this unifying property comes after the experience in the activities of reflection or discourse, Dewey is quite clear: "This unity is neither emotional, practical, nor intellectual, for these terms name distinctions that reflection can make within it [experience]" (44). Dewey is claiming that this quality is something immediate and is internal to one's experience, whereas what is brought up and dissected in reflection is usually external to that which is being reflected upon. Thus, one has a moving, complete, unique experience while reading the poetry of Wordsworth. Later, one examines this instance in reflection. The former felt unity, completeness, etc. can be discussed in reflection, but that is extraneous to the actual experience being analyzed—one need not even reflect on powerful aesthetic experiences, one can just have them.

In general terms, Dewey's reading of experience involves an interaction between organism and environment; the three characteristics of completeness, uniqueness, and pervading quality are brought up in aesthetic experiences. It is in the latter degree (not "kind" in the strong sense) of experience that the human creature feels most alive, due to its interaction with nature (in this case, the art object). As Dewey puts it: "The live animal is fully present, all there, in all of its actions: in its wary glances, its sharp sniffings, its abrupt cocking of ears. . . . What the live creature retains from the past and what it expects from the future operate as directions in the present. The dog is never pedantic nor academic; for these things arise only when the past is severed in consciousness from the present and is set up as a model to copy or a storehouse upon which to draw. The past absorbed into the present carries on; it presses forward" (24). This sort of attention to the present is captured in the aesthetic experience. Indeed, "this absorption is characteristic of esthetic experience; but it is an ideal for all experience, and the ideal is realized in the activity of the scientific inquirer and the professional man when the desires and urgencies of the self are completely engaged in what is objectively done" (285). The absorption of the aesthetic experience contributes to a feeling of completeness in which the organism (in this case, the viewer) notices and feels the unity and wholeness both within the art object (the plot, parts, etc.) and external to the art object (its connections to past and future meaning and experience). Needless to say, the aesthetic experience for Dewey is an extremely powerful and valuable experience. The question now becomes, how does it come to possess these characteristics to such an exemplary degree?

Part of Dewey's answer to this question comes in his analysis of the interrelation of form and matter in the work of art. A key element to the unity and unique/pervading qualitative feel of a particular aesthetic experience comes from what Dewey calls "rhythm." By this term, he does not mean the common notion of rhythm—what he refers to as the view that "identifies rhythm with regularity of recurrence amid changing elements" (168). Rhythm is instead the cumulative variation that develops in an orderly fashion that delineates *an* experience from others, as well as giving that experience its *integrated* quality. What Dewey is highlighting here is that the experience of an art object unfolds in such a way that it is temporal and yet constantly interrelated. Thus, one watches a film and gradually is exposed to the whole object—the sequence of scenes in their given order and totality. More than that, of course, is the "work" that the film does on the viewer—in this case, the cumulative meaning of each present scene in light of what came before and what is to be anticipated based upon the meaning summed up in the present scene.

Dewey emphasizes this aspect of rhythm, pointing out the relation of variation in a work to its ordered development: "This principle, once more, is that of cumulative progression toward the fulfillment of an experience in terms of the integrity of the experience itself—something not to be measured in external terms, though not attainable without the use of external materials, observed or imagined" (169). Dewey is making two important points. First, a work of art is connected to aesthetic experience in such a way that both subject and object are integral parts to it. The order and development of rhythm are not solely in the "external terms" (material) of the art object, but instead require external material to be experienced by a subject that has a past fund of meanings from previous experiences. Once exposed to a given art object, the observer's experience unfolds in a particular way, only partially dictated by the properties of the art object. Thus, a given play may aim for a quick pace through its rapid changes of scenes and events, but such an effect is only realizable with the attentiveness and cooperation of a sensitive auditor. Furthermore, such an individual's experience of the play may be affected by other considerations as well—issues in his or her own life, for example. Whatever occurs, Dewey believes that the experience will have a certain rhythm, a certain meaningful pattern of alternating events spread out over time.

Even the viewing of a painting has a certain temporal or rhythmic development. One is first drawn to certain parts of the work, and then one moves on to take in the rest of the painting in some order. The experience of what the painting means also has a temporal development that can be particularized in various ways—one can develop a deeper meaning as more and more of the painting's details are taken in by one's viewing activity. The second point to note is that this development is cumulative in an extraordinary degree. What comes first is incorporated into what is second, and the meaning of the second (as well as the third event) integrally includes that of the first. One's history includes one's bicycle riding in the third grade, but the immediate meaning of this activity in the eighth grade does not readily incorporate this past instance. A work of art is different in that the climatic scenes are climatic primarily because their meaning is directly informed by the scenes leading up to them. The meaning of the past is summed up and carried forward in the present (viz., the part of the work with which one is presently occupied). After experiencing the whole work, one has a sense of completion, a sense that the presence of the object, while now past, has been of a complete whole, and this is what leads to that event being individuated and called *an* experience.

The element of rhythm in art objects for Dewey is a sign of the deeper experiential process occurring, namely, that of undergoing/doing by an organism in light of a given environment. Rhythm is the quality of art objects that leads to the ordered and affected experience of an auditor. Rhythm in this sense is merely the relationships among parts of the art object, or as Dewey puts it, "esthetic recurrence is that of *relationships* that sum up and carry forward" (171). Parts of an art object are relatively unimportant if they are not *part of* some sort of whole. Thus, what rhythm displays is not the mere units (be it of sound, pigments, words or phrases, characters, etc.), but instead the *relationships* among these, as well as the concurrent developing experience in an attending individual. This development of the relationships through the art object does not have to be standardized—that is what Dewey maligns as the "tom-tom" theory of rhythm. Instead, what is important is some sort of *meaningful* development and interrelation of the parts of the art object. Dewey echoes this point by claiming that "rhythm is rationality among qualities" (174). What makes a certain interrelation of parts or qualities of an art object meaningful or rational? It would have to be dependent upon the *degree* of interpenetration of these elements into the experience of each. In other words, what has come before is now incorporated into the specifics of the present part attended to, and the present also anticipates certain future parts to be attended to. Dewey highlights the connection of this aspect to his organic reading of aesthetic experience: "Esthetic recurrence in short is vital, physiological, functional. Relationships rather than elements recur, and they recur in differing contexts and with different consequences so that each recurrence is novel as well as a reminder. In satisfying an aroused expectancy, it also institutes a new longing, incites a fresh curiosity, establishes a changed suspense. The completeness of the integration of these two offices, opposed as they are in abstract conception, by the *same* means instead of by using one device to arouse energy and another to bring it to rest, measures artistry of production and perception" (174).

The back and forth between organism and environment gets an important boost. It is immediately obvious how one's experience is satisfied in its development, and the variation of experience is had in a meaningful fashion. There is a logic to its development, something that is not always evident in "natural" interactions with the environment. What makes art objects so effective in bringing about aesthetic experience is simply the fact that they are excellent forums for arranging objective materials in such a way that they will lead to similar and meaningful experiences in an auditor. Enjoyment of the fruits of the past and anticipation of future activities are integrated into the present not through the units that are used in an art object, but instead through the interconnection of all the parts of an art object into a whole. This for Dewey is rhythm, and this is a vital part of what makes an experience of an art object aesthetic or integral.

What makes this experience of an art object *morally* valuable? I will argue for such a connection via rhythm in the experience of the art object and attempt to defend the reading of aesthetic experience that I labeled in previous chapters "experiential." One's experience of an art object is an experience having a certain rhythm. This is an instance of attention to the particulars of a situation and therefore is an instance of what it is like to be a morally cultivated individual. Thus, the *experience* of art is also an experience of moral cultivation. In his study of Dewey's aesthetics, Thomas Alexander notes a major moral concern for Dewey—the fact that most of our lives are filled with activity that is not aesthetic or consummatory. Alexander points out that for Dewey, a majority of a person's actions are really of two sorts. First, many actions proceed mechanically from habit, often connected with a focus on some (distant) end. Second, other actions are merely reactive and disorganized, and lack any integration with other surrounding activities.[24] What I would highlight about both of these sorts of action is that they are noncultivated ways for human action to proceed; as indicated in the first section of this chapter, Dewey places much importance on cultivating habits of attention to the present situation.[25] In the former, habitualized action, the agent is not attending to the present situation, and his or her activity can best be described as mechanical. This is the sort of labor that chapter 3 discussed as not being the utmost in fulfilling and rewarding conduct. Indeed, Dewey's work in ethics notes the ethical importance of being attentive to one's present situation and its combination of personal capacities and environmental forces. In the second sort of action, activity is noted by an agent, but it is not paid attention to in its wider present meaning. Thus, one fails to see any connection of one activity to another and any attention to the present is isolated from the flow of life's continuing process of activity. This is as separated and remote as the first sort of action in that the present focus of attention is not the meeting of past and future in the present, but is instead simply on a disconnected (and hence meaningless) present. Aesthetic experience strikes at both sorts of remote and distanced activity through its vivid inclusion of rhythm.

Rhythm is that relation among the parts of an art object (and how they are perceived by an auditor) that both individuates and connects such separate parts. Rhythm *is* the relation among such parts, and such relations are so integrated that the whole is merely the relationships of the parts themselves. Thus, in chapter 3 I discussed Dewey's collapse of artistic means into artistic ends—the pigments do not *cause* the painting, they *are* the painting. The means *are* the end to be achieved and this fact is what makes an artistic means a *medium*. It is not a *mere* means to some disconnected end, it is *the* end itself. The collective group of the parts of an art object (say, the scenes in a play) *is* the art object. What Dewey's concept of rhythm provides is the *quality* that links these parts together in such a way that they do not become mere means to an external end. This is an integral part of rhythm, "for whenever each step forward is at the same time a summing up and fulfillment of what precedes, and every consummation carries expectation tensely forward, there is rhythm."[26]

Rhythm is that quality of an art object that denotes one seeing a present stage in an aesthetic experience as inclusive of what came before it, as well as anticipating what may come next. Dewey notes this connection of the past and future in the present; he states: "What is retained from the past is embedded within what is now perceived and so embedded that, by its compression there, it forces the mind to stretch forward to what is coming. The more there is compressed from the continuous series of prior perceptions, the richer the present perception and the more intense the forward impulsion."[27] This passage demands two remarks. First, notice the same connection of past, present, and future that was found in Dewey's ethical works, as well as in his texts discussing the values of means and ends in activity. Attention to the present is funded by the past and anticipatory in regard to the future; the bottom line is, however, that all of these relations and connections (to past events, future states, etc.) are seen *in the present situation*. Attention is not solely on those remote states, but is instead on the potential and resources of the present, concrete situation. This is where environment and agent capacity meet, and this is the proper locus of experience. Second, this quotation portrays the power of art objects—their purposive compression of meaning into any given present part of the work. This is so evident in art (as opposed to everyday activity) according to Dewey because the art object is created in a purposeful fashion and readily shapes and focuses attention on its parts (as opposed to other possible constituent parts). *Moby Dick* has a particular plot line, characters, and events that make it *that* story. The experience of that story and its rhythmic relations among events and characters will be different from the experience of, say, the film *The Matrix*. Each of these art objects is comprised of its various parts; these parts have a certain relationship among them that make up that work's rhythm, and this rhythm entails certain differences in the experience of the auditor. Both works may be said to cause aesthetic experience, even though the specifics of the experience are different, largely because each experience has the general characteristic of completeness and integration of parts with other parts. Unlike much of life as it is currently experienced, the experience of the art object is one in which the present part attended to culminates what came before it and anticipates what comes next; at the conclusion of the "work" of art, the observer is left with a feeling of a complete whole—the flow of the first parts attended to up to the culminating portion (such as the end of the story, or having seen *the* picture as a whole).

Thus, attending to an art object is an instance of the sort of attention that is morally worthy for Dewey. Attention to the present as a meeting point of past and future is exemplified in what he has called an art object's rhythm, and this attention is an attention to the relationships immediately evident in the present. Thus, one's perception of Captain Hook in J.M. Barrie's novel *Peter and Wendy* initially includes certain scars and missing body parts. At later points, those perceptions are imbued with a relational meaning—namely, previous events and creatures that resulted in having a hook instead of a hand. In the story, attention to Captain Hook is funded with the meaning of what came before, what the reader has learned from previous portions of the narrative. Thus, the missing hand is related to actions of Peter Pan, as well as to actions of the crocodile. The meaning of the character of Captain Hook is dyed with these other (past) events and the reader sees something along these lines when he or she encounters later scenes with Hook. The present is imbued with the stains of the past. *Finding Neverland*, a film about J. M. Barrie's creation of the play *Peter Pan, or The Boy Who Wouldn't Grow Up*, incorporates different parts (episodes and events), and thus contributes to a different experience in the auditor. Thus, one experiences Hook in the later parts of that film not only as losing a hand due to the actions of other characters, but also as being based upon an imaginative reconstruction (by Barrie) of a threatening grandmother of a real-life boy named Peter. Both experiences of each art object work in a similar way, although the particulars of the experience change. What is constant is that the present is a meeting of the past and future, and this is what constitutes the artistry of that object's creation (along with its connected experience by an observer).

The moral value of such an aesthetic experience is that it *is* an experience of the moral endpoint of moral activity and development. R. Keith Sawyer notes that Dewey's reading of aesthetic experience highlights the fact that the process is the product, but he fails to account for the moral value of seeing the process (of the continuously advancing present) as morally valuable.[28] What is vital to notice is that the process is valuable because it is the process that moral cultivation aims at—attention to the merging of past and future, capacity and environment in a conscious present situation experienced by an agent. Dewey notes this educational import of art in terms of life; he states: "The living being is characterized by having a past and a present; having them as possessions of the present, not just externally. And I suggest that it is precisely when we get from an art product the feeling of dealing with a *career*, a history, perceived at a particular point of its development, that we have the impression of life."[29] Like the sort of action we ought to aim for in life, art is a focus on a present funded by a history and anticipating future activities. Aesthetic experience, such as that initiated by attending to an art object, is morally valuable because it is an instance of attention to a present situation with connections to past history and future activity. Dewey captures this value by noting that if art objects reproduce anything, it is not the details of life, but instead must be the energy or flow of the experience of life.[30] The moral value of art is closely tied to the immediacy of meaning and value as experienced, and it is internal to the experience of the art object itself. This is what makes such an account different from the *causal* variety, and instead renders it what I have called an *experiential* account. The morally valuable features of aesthetic experience are internal to that experience, since that experience itself is an instance of moral cultivation.

Jeffrey Petts approaches such a reading of the moral value in Dewey's aesthetics, but falls short of the version I have given with my experiential account. He argues that the value of aesthetic experience is that it reveals value in the world, namely, the various rhythms that humans are subject to as well as the powers of the external environment. He claims, in summary, that "aesthetic experience, then, can be said to be revelatory of real value because it marks an adaptive felt response of humans to their environment, and this adaptability is grounded in human needs."[31] Petts also notes that such a revelation shows that part of the process of adaptation is not within the control of humans, namely, the part that is from the environmental side of the experiential dialectic. While this is a laudable reading of Dewey on value, I believe that Petts's account must be supplemented in two ways. First, he has failed to provide an account of moral value in Dewey's system (viz., how and why is adaptation morally valuable?). I have done so in this chapter, as well as in the third chapter's account of immediate and instated values. My account highlights that it is a certain attitude that is key to morality (the spirit and method to conduct), and this attitude is closely tied to an attention or orientation toward the concrete present. Second, Petts falls prey to the challenges posed in chapter 2 of this work, as his account can be said to be merely causal unless some notion of *what* the experience is about is given. I have tried to provide such an account, noting that rhythm is the interpenetration of the constituent parts to an art object and that these focus attention in such a way as to result in what Dewey labels *an* experience. Merely claiming that the experience of art reveals human needs is not strong enough, nor does it connect the moral value of the experience closely enough to the experience itself. I wish to claim that the experience itself is morally valuable because it is an instance of moral cultivation. This is subtly different from claiming that the experience teaches us about moral action, or reveals some bit of knowledge about the world.

Instead, I believe it is better to say that an aesthetic experience, like the attentive activity featured in Dewey's notions of progressive adjustment and growth, *is* an instance of such an endpoint. The important point, of course, is that it is not the final endpoint. Morality is an expansive process, both in time and range of activities, and an experience of heightened attention within that process is just one step well taken. Morality is a lifelong project and I can now claim that aesthetic experience is a vital part of that project. How large a part can aesthetic experience play if most of our everyday life and activity does not involve art objects? The answer to this question was hinted at in Dewey's example of the ferryboat passengers that opened this chapter—if art objects are special merely because they are very effective at creating the conditions for aesthetic experience, then it is possible that *any* activity could be experienced as aesthetic if conditions and attitudes cooperate to make it so. The question then can be asked, could not the majority of one's life be an aesthetic experience or an artful activity?

Life as Art

What my experiential account of the value of aesthetic experience and Dewey's moral writings seem to point to is the value of experiencing activity in a certain *way*. Can any activity be aesthetically experienced? Dewey would seem to give the prudential answer of "no," largely because certain economic structures leave the individual faced with much activity that is inherently menial or laborious.[32] In his account of the problem and its solution, however, one sees the possibility of any action being aesthetic. Thus, it is *possible* that many or all of life's activities could be classed as consummatory, as evidenced by his example of the ferryboat passengers experiencing the ride and the skyline in different ways. In this final section, I will provide an account of how activity in general can be aesthetic or consummatory, and in so being, how it can be of moral value just like the experience of an art object is. To do so, I will start with one commentator's analysis of how Dewey's account of aesthetic activity can be widened.

Crispin Sartwell has argued that Dewey's work can provide a working definition of art and that this definition can be expanded to cover many activities of life as artistic.[33] Although my project does not address the definitional challenges posed by art, it converges with Sartwell's concern to highlight a *way* that activity can and should precede.[34] Sartwell also notes the role of absorption in aesthetic experience, as well as in the definition of art. Art objects, according to Sartwell, have the characteristic of inducing us to "merge or achieve fusion with them."[35] Art can include many of our everyday activities, as these can be done with a certain absorption in the experience itself. What I have called "attention" is roughly equivalent to Sartwell's notion of absorption in activity. Sartwell also notes the bivalence of experienced situations that I noted in chapter 3. He states: "We may experience paintings in order to cultivate our sensibilities, impress our acquaintances, or augment our collections. But painting can simultaneously be experienced for the sake of experience."[36] In other words, experiences can be both instrumental as well as intrinsically valuable. What I want to argue is that attention to the concrete present situation and its immediate meanings (including relations to past and future) is an instance of what it means to be morally cultivated. Sartwell's account does justice to this way of reading the mechanics of aesthetic experience, but does not go as far as I would like in relating it to a Deweyan theory of moral value. Simply put, why is such absorptive experience valuable?

There are two parts to such an account. First, it maintains that attention must be paid to the present, and second, that the endpoint of moral development is always some present situation. Sartwell provides a good analysis of the first point, noting that such a point is evident in the ancient Hindu religious-philosophical work, the *Bhagavad Gītā*. He argues that Krishna's advocated doctrine of karma yoga, or enlightenment through the path of nonattached action, is important because it suggests that "it is not that we act wholly and always without ends; that would make human action impossible. Rather, we ought to reconstrue the *relation* of means to ends in our actions . . . our action should not be performed *merely* for the sake of the end; the end must not absorb or expunge the means in our deliberation."[37] The protagonist in the *Bhagavad Gītā*, Arjuna, is advised not to value the fruits of action, but to care only about the (duty bound) action itself. This, according to Sartwell, is a corrective to our common and exclusive focus on ends in action: "If we could achieve the end by sheer force of will, if we could realize it without performing the means, we would. [Krishna] asks us, not to renounce all desire and thus all action, but to desire the means as intrinsically valuable as *well* as valuable in service of the end. The means are not to be absorbed in the end; the time and energy devoted to the means are not wasted. Rather, this time and energy are to be *consecrated*."[38] Although there is much more that can be said about the theological and soteriological context of the *Bhagavad Gītā*, one can see a certain value in Sartwell's pragmatic reading.[39] His account emphasizes that means are to be seen as an intrinsically valuable experience and not merely valuable insofar as they reach a desired end. This is a radical point and one that seems far from Dewey's pragmatism, especially in the more simplistic descriptions of it. The point I have tried to make in chapter 3 as well as in the reading of moral cultivation from his work in ethics is that Dewey does place attention (or absorption) to the present activity as a key part to moral action and value. Focus on the present prevents the estrangement of labor from valued activity, as well as focuses individuals on the enjoyment that they have aimed for in past instances. Was not action in the past aiming to produce pleasure and reward, like one's activity now? Why should one now malign the results of those past activities when they finally become present by ignoring them for the next (albeit remote) link in the chain of unfolding experiences? The point we can get from Dewey is that moral value always resides in the present, either the present of today or the present that will be experienced tomorrow.

Art objects are valuable because they are an exemplary instance of what all action ought to aim for—seeing the present means as intrinsically valuable and as interconnected with ends-in-view. Art strikes at the separation of present activity from remote ends by making the means or process the end or product. In art, the subject and the object closely fuse and are integrated because the focus of attention is on the immediate material of the experience. Like Martha Nussbaum's reading of the moral value of literature, Dewey's account can be said to be valuable because it opens the door to the experience of an art object being an experience of moral cultivation. For Nussbaum, the fine and detailed attention one puts into attending to a literary depiction *is* an instance of the attention needed in moral activity, such as that of upholding demands emerging from relationships and specific situations. Simply put, she is arguing that "obtuseness is a moral failing; its opposite can be cultivated."[40] For Nussbaum, one primary way of such cultivation is through the instances of attentiveness in what can be called aesthetic experience. Such an instance of the endpoint of moral cultivation, for Dewey or for Nussbaum, does not end moral growth or striving; as I emphasized in the previous section, it is an instantiation as well as a connection to future states of affairs.

Cannot one attain such an aesthetic focus on the present in the ordinary activities of life? Like the ferryboat passengers, a human can adopt the orientation toward activity that sees it as valuable and as the here and now in which life exists. Activity has an immediate meaning as well as implications for future states of affairs (viz., desired ends). Dewey was well aware that humans can alter and adjust their orientation toward these states, a fact that is noted in a 1939 essay titled "Democratic Ends Need Democratic Methods for Their Realization." In this work, Dewey hints at the point I have been explicitly developing with my experiential account of aesthetic experience—that the value of aesthetic experience is tied to attention to the present as intrinsically and immediately valuable, as well as its connection to other future presents that are aimed for. In discussing the topic of using nondemocratic means to achieve ends that are democratic, he notes that democracy is only created by instantiating a form of it *now*. This is because the *now* reflects our attitudes and values as well as shapes future attitudes and values. It is both an instantiation of the endpoint (democracy) as well as preparation for future instantiations of that endpoint. Those who think the present can be sacrificed (in other words, treated as a mere means to a future goal) are forgetting the *value* of the present in immediate experience. Dewey reminds us that "we must always remember that the dependence of ends upon means is such that the only ultimate result is the result that is attained today, tomorrow, the next day, and day after day, in the succession of years and generations" (368).

The goal of action (the end) always lies in some present, some here and now, and there is no determined final present. One should not make the activity of a given present a *mere* means to some remote end, as this makes it expendable and not equal to what the valued future state is—a present site of experience that can be a source of immediate meaning and value for an experiencing individual. Failure to recognize this equivalence leads not only to the lack of experiential value that the present (now) is capable of, but in all likelihood will foster habits and attitudes that will equally soil the meaning and potential of the future when it too becomes present to the agent. Dewey makes this point in his work on education as well. In *Experience and Education* (1938), he attacks theories of education that make education a mere preparation for something external to it (whether cognitive skills, virtue, etc.): "The ideal of using the present simply to get ready for the future contradicts itself. It omits, and even shuts out, the very condition by which a person can be prepared for his future. We always live at the time we live and not at some other time, and only by extracting at each present time the full meaning of each present experience are we prepared for doing the same thing in the future."[41] It is the *meaning* of the present that is *in* the experience, and that is what ought to be the focus of attention, not some remote end or state. Like Sartwell's rereading of the *Bhagavad Gītā,* the means of the present situation must be accorded the seriousness and attention they deserve, and one's attention should not be focused on remote ideals, ends, and so forth. *That* is progressive adjustment to the present situation and its actual meaning to some degree or another, and is exemplified by the close connection of means and ends in aesthetic experience. The rest of life can be aesthetic insofar as one attends to the activity of the present as if it were an integral part of the end of activity, and a part possessing a value that is not subservient to the value placed upon the end.

One common objection that can be anticipated to this sort of account of aesthetic experience is that it is too wide. It simply lets everything count as art, or as an object that could bring about aesthetic experience. Noël Carroll replies to what he calls the "content oriented account" of aesthetic experience in this way, claiming that "this formula is far too broad to provide a sufficient condition for art status, since virtually every human artifact will present unities, diversities, and/or intensities for apprehension."[42] He goes on to give examples of nonart objects that meet such a definition, such as powerboats, loaves of bread, and telephones. Objections, however, often reveal as much about what the objector is interested in as they do about the weakness of the targeted position. In this case, that is evident. Carroll and others are engaged in the quest for definitions that provide necessary and sufficient conditions for identifying art. This sort of objection also betrays the locus of its power for the objectors—the a priori assumption that some objects in the world are art and other objects are not. The position I am arguing for above (1) does not attempt to define art or use aesthetic experience as necessary and sufficient criteria for such a definition, and (2) explicitly expands aesthetic experience to (potentially) the whole range of human experiences. While Carroll might think it strange to say that a sleek powerboat is beheld in a way similar to a work of art, there is nothing intrinsically objectionable to this position once one considers examples such as that of handmade firearms in the American colonies. Such weapons were made with skill and elaborately decorated; they were useful in procuring food, and were a prized possession. Their use was susceptible to more or less skillful deployment, and one can be absorbed in the activity of using them much as one can be in painting or when admiring a painting. Why ought we to exclude any object from the realm of those things that can be potentially involved in the having of an aesthetic experience? The only reason the pragmatists would allow would be the *usefulness* of such a demarcation, and I hope the track I have taken previously has shown the use and value of such an orientation that a subject can take. Attention to and absorption in the development of activity, be it that of art or life, is what a fully flourishing, growing, and adjusted human must continually strive to attain. This is a purpose higher than that reached by defining certain events in certain ways and it is a move that has much more practical value in how individuals experience the world. Indeed, it is a reading of moral cultivation that can be found in Dewey's ethical writings as well as in his later aesthetic work.

5

Reflection and Moral Value in Aesthetic Experience

If my previous arguments are in any way felicitous, one should see a way that all experience can be experienced as aesthetic. While this includes art objects, it definitely minimized the role that such objects play in aesthetic experience, as many created and natural objects fall outside the conventionally defined realm of art objects. In order to do justice to the power of art objects as meaningful entities prized by their surrounding culture, I will refocus my analysis in this chapter on such intentionally created objects. The question becomes, how can art objects be morally cultivating? I have given one answer in the initial part of chapter 4. The experience of art objects, like other aesthetic experiences, is morally cultivating because it is an instantiation of the endpoint of moral cultivation—attention to a concrete situation given in the present.

In this chapter, however, I want to explore another way to answer this question, a way that is connected to the power of art to challenge held values, dispositions, habits of perception, and so on. Of course, not all art does this. I am content here with focusing on this power to challenge as a significant employment of art objects. In other words, I will focus on the power that art holds to spur reflection on the part of the auditor. Such reflection is of moral value for Dewey because it is also an instance of devoted attention to the present, albeit to new factors and connections to other states (past or future) that have been made present in a deliberator's imagination. One readily notes the aesthetic elements in the definition S. Morris Eames gives of the endpoint of Dewey's thought: "The goal of all philosophical and educational experience for Dewey is a human being who is perceptive, imaginative, apt in memory, and creative in thought."[1] Such a reading of the moral value of deliberation, reflection, and imaginative engagement with an art object will extend the notions offered in chapter 3 concerning the presence of "ends-in-view," as well as the value of attention given in chapter 4.

Such an analysis of the power of art objects must begin with the source of their power—their meaning. Art objects are differentiated from natural objects in that they are (in some way) intentionally created and are imbued with meanings that are the result of the overlay of culture. Joseph Margolis has given a reading of the emergent nature of aesthetic meaning from physical objects in his work, and calls such objects "intentional" due to this added meaning derived from cultural influence.[2] Margolis's characterization of art highlights two important aspects of art objects. First, artworks are uttered or intentional acts imbued with meaningful properties (especially evident when they are linguistic texts such as literature). They are created by humans, who putatively hold purposes and reasons why they created them in a certain way with certain properties. Second, the meaning of a work of art is *determinable*, but not *determinate* or fixed.[3] The properties of a painting are open to many interpretations, but it is hard to see how one interpretation is conclusively *true*. One must provide a standard with which to adjudicate such interpretations, and I would argue that such standards are themselves open to reevaluation. Thus, Margolis's use of the term "intentional" is not identical to common uses of the word "intentional" that tether meaning to an author's actual intention.[4] The basic fact of determinable properties still remains concerning the interpretability of a work of art—there is not a determinate meaning entailed by a given authorial intention. Meaning is a public and culturally inflected affair. Common communicative utterances are chosen by a communicator (a sender) because of their antecedent, public meaning (viz., the fact that a receiver will understand such-and-such as their meaning). This meaning has a range or latitude, but not one specific meaning. Art objects, due to their richness and complexity, have a wide range of acceptable meanings and thus can create a variety of meaningful experiences in a variety of auditors. Art objects are importantly intentional in their use in human-to-human interaction (communication), but they hold a richness in meaning and potential effect on an audience that goes beyond everyday linguistic utterance.

If there is no determinate or true meaning to an art object, how can it function in a way that is morally cultivating? In answering this question, I will extend Richard Shusterman's characterization of art as dramatization.[5] In discussing the power of art, Shusterman likens it to the general form of drama—art unites a vivid and lived subject matter with an intentionally constructed frame or presentation to "re-present" its subject matter to an audience. What such an intentional frame does, I will argue, is to give the subject matter presented the added meaning of not only a cultural background but also something that is *present* to an audience. What has been framed in a particular art object is brought to an audience's attention. Certain experiences are framed in an art object instead of other experiences, which consequentially draws attention to certain details, situations, and configurations of meaningful properties or qualities. This attention is important because it is further attention to the concrete situation one is confronted with—in this case, that which the art object places before an auditor. What I am interested in exploring is how such attention can be tied to reflective activity, an important part to Dewey's readings of moral improvement in both his early and later work.

This chapter will explore the *use* of art objects in evoking reflective or deliberative experience. Such a use can be intentional insofar as an art object is intended by an artist to bring about a certain sort of reflective experience in an auditor, and this will be explicated in the first section of this chapter. In the second section of this chapter, the other way such an art object can be experienced will be considered—the experience (brought on by a certain critical orientation of the auditor) of an art object *as if* it were intended to bring about a certain experience for some sort of point. What I am aiming to do here is to analyze art in its communicative or argumentative function—how art can be used by an artist or by an auditor to force consideration of values, beliefs, and action strategies. Such a consideration *is* deliberation or reflection over what one should do, value, or think, and is consequently of moral value in terms of its active shaping of who one is and how one lives one's life. The final section of this chapter will explore just this connection of art, deliberation, and moral value.

Dewey on the Evocative Function of Art

John Dewey's theory of art has often been characterized as expressive, given its emphasis on an artist's imbuing of a physical object with meaning. Environmental pressures are also noted in *Art as Experience* as the "undergoing" that ex*presses* the energies/emotions out of the artist in the medium of the art object. This is an important aspect of the aesthetic process to highlight, as it is often overlooked how art relates to natural activities and the environment of a living organism in general.[6] What is often lost in this type of reading, however, is that Dewey's characterization of art is more than expressive—it also integrally involves the audience's reception of the art object.[7] Hence expression is coupled with reception in the complete aesthetic situation. The artist's experience of creating the art object is rich, full, and unified (*an* experience, as Dewey calls it); given the optimal circumstances and orientation, the audience's reception of the art object can also attain the heights of being a unified, full, and rich experience. These two aspects are made clear by Dewey in his description of the artistic and the aesthetic processes.[8]

It is this point that comes under attack by the critics of the expressionist theory of art, such as Alan Tormey. Tormey objects to Dewey's theory of the arts in particular because Dewey seems to be committed to what Tormey identifies as the primary fallacy of the expressionist theory—believing that expressive qualities in an object or action entail an expressive act on the part of an agent.[9] Thus, one may have an expression of cruelty on one's face without the intention to express cruelty. In terms of music, one could write a sad composition without having gone through a related emotion of sadness. According to Tormey, this entailment to which the expressionists are committed leads to absurdities such as the "falsifying" of an expressive quality in an art object (say, the sadness of a musical piece) because of the empirically revealed fact that the composer was not sad nor was she intending to express sadness when the act of creating the art object occurred. Both objections, of course, assume that Dewey is attempting to give a descriptive definition of art that covers its entire extension and provides a necessary and sufficient criterion for the application of the label "art." As has been evidenced from previous chapters, Dewey is not engaging in such a pursuit.

Two important points can be said in response to Tormey's argument against Dewey's reading of expression. First, notice how Tormey takes the act of expression as necessarily simple—one expresses one's experience of *sadness* through the composition of a song with sad qualities. Of course, one recognizes that any art object is going to have a multitude of meaning-giving intentional properties, so something seems amiss in critiquing Dewey's theory by assuming it necessarily presupposes a simple and homogenous notion of expressive content (viz., sadness). Instead, the art object is intentional in that it is created and imbued with meaning partially by the actions of the artist, but also because of the crucial contributions of meaning that a common cultural background contributes to the activity of producing and receiving art objects. Thus, Dickens's novels are meaningful and expressive of certain emotions and thoughts largely because of the common meaning of terms, actions, and other such public bearers of significance held by him and his audience (then and now). Of course, there is always a latitude of meaning that a particular item of culture (say, a certain action in a certain situation) has, but its meaning and content is still public in an important sense. The second point to note is that Tormey is discussing expression in light of a faulty inference back to the sender of the expressive act. Even in everyday communication such inferences are not universally held to be warranted. Thus, in regard to artistic expression, it is not unreasonable to say that some artistic acts of expression are actually tied directly to experiences the artist has had *and* that it is useful to think of art *as if* it was tied to a certain experience the artist would like to convey. This is a pragmatist move that slides away from Tormey's descriptive approach to analyzing art and one that moves closer to Dewey's ideal—that of a useful frame with which to approach art objects and to correlatively enhance our experience of them.

What I want to explore in this section is how Dewey's characterization of art includes its rich communicative value, or, using the language of Tormey's critique, when the inference is valid from expressive qualities to an actual expressive experience of an artist. What I am adding to this topic, of course, is the communicative aspect of art in light of a particular audience. This is what makes some expression communicative, and Dewey meant art to fulfill such a demand; indeed, in *Art as Experience* he calls art the "most universal and freest form of communication" (275). If communication seems to imply anything as necessary to its common practice, it would have to be the notion of intention—humans communicate for a purpose, be it to achieve certain results, transform others, and so forth.

How does art fit into the realm of communication, and what specifically makes it the most universal and freest form available? Art can be construed as *evocative* in the sense that it can be employed by an agent (the artist) to evoke a certain experience in an observer. In many cases, the creation of art can be guided by the author (entailing a real intention), but in some cases such activity involves an unclear intention. The important aspect is the orientation an observer takes toward the art object. Certain orientations allow the art object to be understood in a way that would either (1) allow for the artist's actual evocative intentions to be successful, or (2) allow for the observer to experience the art object *as if* its author were trying to evoke a certain experience. I will not offer much defense for the latter point on intention and interpretation in this section, since these tend to develop more in discussions of audience *reflection* (i.e., criticism) on the primary experience involved. I will deal with the issue of hypothetical intentions in the next portion of this chapter. What I will emphasize in this first part of the chapter is the possibility of art objects being used in an evocative way, and why they fulfill a unique purpose in such an employment. To start this argument, I will first briefly examine what Dewey finds as the value of the empirical method he advocates and how it is reflected in his theory of communication. Then I will discuss how art objects can be used communicatively, both from the subjective factors involved (viz., the auditor's orientation toward the art object) and the objective aspects at work (the art object evoking a given experience). Lastly, I will anticipate and answer some objections as to why art is a *unique* form of communication distinct from everyday linguistic behavior.

Empirical Method and Communication

In *Experience and Nature,* Dewey argues strongly for the value of what he calls the "empirical method." Before discussing such a method, however, Dewey lays its foundation with his analysis of experience. An initial misconception that Dewey must overcome is that experience is opposed to nature; instead, experience is *in* and *of* nature. It is a rich process that deals with the obstacles/events of nature as material, as well as the objective conditions for such an experience to occur in the first place. As living organisms in an environment that is not always friendly to their survival, humans experience nature and find that they must reflect on it to enhance their control and use of it. Thus, one can distinguish a division (though not strict and hermetically sealed) between primary experience and reflective/secondary experience. The latter type of experience involves a second-order reflectivity on what one is experiencing/had experienced (primary experiences) and the constituent parts of such experiences. A fallacy to be avoided is the taking of the items of reflection (initiated with conscious purpose) as *the* constituents of the primary experience (25). To employ Dewey's example, one can reflect on a chair as a number of brown patches or as an object to sit on—both are ways of analyzing what is experienced. The chair is not *solely* an instrument for sitting, as many other possible descriptions can be given in reflection. The important point here is that experience is a primary, unanalyzed, integrated totality, and reflection breaks up such a whole for specific purposes.

Dewey is particularly enamored with one method of guiding reflection. He extols the empirical method employed in the sciences because it "is the only method which can do justice to this inclusive integrity of 'experience.' It alone takes this integrated unity as the starting point for philosophic thought" (19). Unlike other modes of philosophical analysis that take the functions found in reflection as the important part of experience, Dewey advocates the method of the sciences because it seems to him to be the best way to usefully ground philosophy (and reflection in general) *in* experience without doing damage *to* experience. What is damaging, of course, is when this description is taken to *be* the experience—for instance, the overly intellectualized and misguided notion that we *experience* "patches of brown in a chairlike shape." The empirical method starts by acknowledging the integrated unity of primary experience and then applies distinctions in reflection, all the while judging these distinctions as to their value in use and consequences for future experience. This is the general orientation of this approach, and one who takes this empirical method to heart thereby incorporates this orientation to the world and reflection upon it. The question then becomes, how does this impact such an individual's reflective activities?

First of all, this method orients one toward empirically testable and fruitful descriptions of experience. In science these are called hypotheses, and the individual comes up with them and empirically explores if they are defendable. Dewey focuses less in *Experience and Nature* on the context of discovery and more on the context of justification, and this suits my purposes in this section. For what he does in discussing the empirical method is to lay out a *procedure* by which one can relate to primary experience in order to create knowledge (which is reflective and involves the noting of meanings guided by purpose). The empirically oriented researcher experiences something of nature's operation, reflects upon it, and then sees fit to transfer this to another (interested) human. This is a clear case of communication, one that often occurs in scientific argument. What Dewey finds as important, though, is that the empirical method directs one to use means of communication not as directly representative of the experience described, but instead as a pointer *to* such an experience. Thus, the empirically minded thinker "state[s] the purpose so that it may be re-experienced, and its value and the pertinency of selection undertaken in its behalf may be tested" (35). This avows the choice of others and empowers them to follow the same procedure in order to *experientially* verify the claims made about the experience by the initial researcher. Such verbal report as given in scientific writing then serves to direct one to a given experience, which one will then reflect upon in a manner similar to that of the initiating partner in this interaction.

What Dewey is doing here is twofold. First, he is tethering reflective enterprises such as science and philosophy to experience, both in the beginning and end of reflection. Second, he is proposing a reading of discourse as persuasive, as action oriented toward changing/transforming the other in an intentional and directed fashion. Thus, one argues for a certain claim about one's experience, and in doing so issues of truth and error are broached. Dewey notes the persuasive and transformative character of such discourse, arguing that "to convince of error as well as to lead to truth is to assist another to see and find something which he hitherto has failed to find and recognize" (35). The empirically oriented argument serves as a linguistic recipe for creating a similar experience, from which the experiencing person is free to come to his or her own conclusions. If the speaker has done his or her job correctly and effectively, the receiver will have a similar experience and confirm the speaker's reflective description/analysis of it.

This is the "miracle" of communication as Dewey describes it. It involves the transformation of external events (both the material of experience and the means of communication) into a real participation and sharing of meaning among individual humans. Through such communicative practices, primary experience qua unified/felt event turns into objects with meanings and reflectively analyzed consequences. In communication, the qualitative immediacy of experience is transformed into publicly accessible symbol systems (such as spoken or written language), which then allows for purposeful reflection on the meaning (e.g., consequences and relationships) implied by the object in its environment. These symbol systems acquire their own objective meaning in that a proficient speaker will recognize the meaning of the word "dog," regardless of who uttered it. Further modifications can be negotiated, but the word has a meaning that grounds such reflection on the full import of the word. The word has a usually intended meaning that both signals a presumptive intent of the speaker and can be reflective of the actual intent of the speaker.

Like experience in general, communication is both the (direct) experience of such meanings as well as the reflective analysis of such meanings and processes. The point I want to emphasize, however, is that communication for Dewey relies on meanings, something reflectively introduced to account for some primary experiences that are inherently nonreflective. Communication uses these meanings as a "method of action, a way of using things as means to a shared consummation, and method is general, though the things to which it is applied are particular" (147). Like the empirical method, communication is a general approach or method to how individuals can most profitably reflect on experience. An integral part to these two methods is the respecting of individual autonomy enough to value one's ability to (1) have the same (relatively speaking) experience as another person and (2) reflect on it to see if the proposed claims (meaningful descriptions of this experience) are the best that can be advanced *given that experience*. The first is upheld by the empirical method (and communication) of tying meaningful statements to replicable/public experiences, and the second is encouraged by the giving of helpful means to experience such a state as that reflected upon.

Art as Evocative Communication

In *Art as Experience,* Dewey puts art at the apex of communication in terms of universality and general reach. He clearly states that "in the end, works of art are the only media of complete and unhindered communication between man and man that can occur in a world full of gulfs and walls that limit community of experience" (110). How are we to analyze such a claim and how can we relate it to his empirically oriented analysis of communication (including scientific communication)? In this section, I will argue that art can be used for communication by evoking a certain experience through the art object. The description of this employment requires an elucidation of (1) the subjective orientations in the receiving individual that enable such a use and (2) the ways art can be experientially used to evoke experience in a communicative fashion. In the following discussion, I assume that the artist *intends* such a use of the art object, although Dewey acknowledges that this is not always the case. The absence of authorial intent, however, is not fatal to such an account. In the next section, I will address the usefulness of a critical orientation of the receiver that takes the art object *as if* a creator was trying to accomplish something through its creation and airing to the public.

Dewey's characterization of art depends on orientations in the artist *and* the audience. Of particular interest to my argument is the orientation that the audience must take. This receiver orientation is crucial, as art's reception as valuable in the public sphere depends on the precondition that the audience attends to it in such a fashion that its uniquely communicative power is available. In general, Dewey extols art for its ability to bring about wholly unified and integrated experiences, a point that commentators readily note.[10] What must be added, of course, is that artists may *use* art to evoke such an experience for a communicative purpose—for instance, to get the audience to see what they saw, feel what they felt, and so on. Or artists may wish to evoke a certain response (experience) in the audience and use the artwork for such ends/effects (note how this clearly distinguishes an *evocative* reading of Dewey's aesthetics from a merely *expressive* reading). In either of these cases, the artist depends on an openness of the audience to the work of art in the first place. This initial condition allows the work of art to be experienced *as a work of art*, not as a potential doorstop, investment, and so forth. Taking Dewey's division between experience and reflection on experience, I will note needed experiential and reflective orientations in the subject that serve as preconditions to the art object being evocative.

What is needed is a subjective orientation of the observer to experience this object as what we call an "artful" object. Such a requirement is minimal, and mostly forms a negative *experiential orientation* toward the object. It screens out direct experiences of an art object as something *totally foreign* to a stylized artwork. As Dewey notes in his essay "The Postulate of Immediate Empiricism," events are what they are experienced as—a horse is experienced differently by a horse seller, a child, and a biologist. What the *experiential orientation* must not include are elements that totally exclude attention to an object in its aesthetic features—form, material, immediate interaction with the auditor, etc. Thus, a doctor who is overly focused on the appearance and health of musculature would not be in the best position to observe what a sculpture of the human frame is trying to convey, simply because the doctor's overemphasis on one aspect of the art object threatens any diversity in the experience intended by the object. Dewey notes this point: "A crowd of visitors steered through a picture-gallery by a guide, with attention called here and there to some high point, does not perceive; only by accident is there even interest in seeing a picture for the sake of subject matter vividly realized."[11] Indeed, in cases of what Dewey calls "perception," the agent is actively engaging the environment with purpose and interest, and it is this basic attention and interest that I argue is an enabling experiential orientation on the part of the subject that allows for art objects to evoke any type of aesthetic experience in the first place. Openness to the object allows the "beholder to *create* his own experience,"[12] and this would be precluded by an excessive emphasis on utility or another aspect of the object.

Just as in communicative situations where one must have the habitual orientation that experiences the communicative utterance *as* understandable and meaningfully intended communication, the art object also must be experienced as some type of intentional art object.[13] Here we need not defend some extraordinary state brought on by an aesthetic attitude. Instead, one merely needs to build upon the base that is provided in chapters 3 and 4 concerning the importance of attention to the present. Again, I think here of Dickie's and Carroll's critique of aesthetic experience and their deflation of it to "mere" attention. Dickie points to an auditor seeing a painting and thinking of his grandmother's resemblance to it. This, he notes, is not attention to the art object. Attention, according to Dickie, is attention and there is nothing special about aesthetic attention. I believe that one can see an important difference in the quality of attention given, however, in terms of its temporal location. Is one attending to what is immediately given in experience (including reflective activity) or is one focusing on remote states of affairs and not on the present object? This is what Melvin Rader and Bertram Jessup hint at in their response to Dickie—while soldiers attend closely to a present situation, it is due to remote, practical ends (outmaneuvering an enemy in battle, taking a series of hills, etc.).[14] Their attention is not on the present situation, but largely on an extraneous matter. Of course, such strategic goals can be utilized as ends-in-view, but then they would be integrally tied to the meaning of the concrete situation. In the case of the art object, attending directly to it and to its present meaning is the *mode* of experience that is connected to aesthetic experience, and this mode ought not to be conflated with a particular *content* of experience.[15] As was the case in chapter 4, we see that attending aesthetically to an object is attending to it in a certain way—attending to it in its immediacy. One's attention can be drawn away for other reasons, political or cultural,[16] but the possibility remains that an experience can be had that is tied to one's close experience of the object and the meanings that are immediately present in it to an observer.

Of more importance to this section is the *reflective orientation* a subject takes toward the art object.[17] The habits individuals have concerning how they reflect on a work of art are an integral aspect to the experience of that work as well as to future experiences, as Dewey notes in his discussion of criticism in *Art as Experience*. Expression, or true communication, must include certain orientations on the part of the communicator and the receiver. For instance, Dewey takes the cry of the newborn infant. Such a wail is merely a discharge of energy on the part of the baby, even though it may be one with survival value. The energy and tension caused by frustrated needs such as hunger rush out in an inarticulate and uncontrolled form. An observer may note that this is a *sign* of hunger in the infant, but surely an observer will not describe it as an intentional and purposeful *symbolic* act of communication. Instead, impulsion must be structured and ordered for it to be a purposeful act of expression, and not just "a boiling over" (67). The speaker must try to manipulate symbols and objects in such a way as to use them meaningfully in expression, and the observer must take the *reflective orientation* that the speaker is trying to do this. This is the empathetic element to communication that Dewey notes in *Experience and Nature*, in which an important part of such interaction is not mere response, but response to a statement as it is meant from the standpoint of the other participant. Indeed, the only way the infant's wails can be *taken* as communicative activity is by the "reflective interpretation on the part of some observer—as the nurse may interpret a sneeze as the sign of an impending cold" (ibid.).

I believe that what Dewey means here is that in such cases of clear impulsive discharge (the wail), it is solely the orientation of the receiver that makes it conceivable *as* communicative or expressive. Face-to-face interaction with another person, however, clearly entails the orientation that the words he or she speaks are to be thought of as communicative utterances. The case of art seems to fall as a middle point between the wail and the conversational sentence, since it is clearly structured by the artist but lacks the immediate human intentionality that is behind a conversational utterance. The author is removed from the art object, yet it is clear that someone purposefully created it with these features for some (unknown/uncertain) reason. The observer in such a situation would seem compelled to take the reflective orientation that such an object is intended to evoke some response in a receiver for some type of reason. While these purposes are indeterminate, one can reflect on the art object in more or less useful ways for both the meaning of this experience and the experiences one has in the presence of other art objects. Not taking this orientation would seem to leave one reflecting on an art object as merely a physical object, not intentionally created by an author for some meaning or purpose. While one cannot know this intention with certainty,[18] it is useful to approach art objects with the orientation toward what experience they may be designed to evoke. This experience is meant to be transformative to the experiencing subject, and the features of the object must be assumed to have been chosen by a purposeful agent for certain ends. The aesthetic experience is one that the observer undergoes, and one seems forced to reflect on the art object instigating it as purposefully designed by some creator. Anything less would seem to compromise one's experience of that object as purposefully created, as well as one's experience of future art objects.

Let us assume the presence of this orientation, as well as the presence of an intention of an author to communicate with her audience. How can art be conceived of as communicative? My basic argument begins with the idea that an artist may want to convey either (1a) a certain experience to an audience or (1b) lead them to reach certain judgments about some experience. (2) The artist cannot directly convey/describe the desired experience through language, or the subject matter she wishes to engage *is* the felt experience of some object, so (3) the artist employs the media of art to *evoke* the experience he or she wants the audience to have or reflect upon in subsequent judgment. This is a clear communicative process of an artist using an uttered artwork to affect the audience in a controlled way that expands its range of experience and possibly its reflection on such experience. Is such a process to be found in Dewey's reading of aesthetic experience and art?

It seems as though Dewey, who only asserts generalities about art's communicative power, does not fully develop this line of thought. It is there, however, especially when one approaches it from his extolling of the empirical method and his description of art's power. First of all, (1a), (1b), and (2) form the core of this argument—that there is some important aspect of experience that is beyond the reach of language. This point, tied closely to Dewey's notion of "quality," is a contentious one. Paul C. Taylor notes that Dewey seems to be pointing to the immediacy of experience as that which is beyond definition.[19] Taylor argues that aesthetic experience, the paradigm case of experience with a certain immediacy, is definable, although definitions only take one to a certain point. Richard Shusterman, commenting on this same issue, notes a certain useful dialectic between immediacy and nonimmediacy, as well as discursivity and nondiscursivity.[20] For instance, one's somatic experience often influences what one can discursively say about this experience, and verbal guides can help improve somatic action. In another work, Shusterman notes five ways that Dewey uses the qualitative elements of experience to come close to a foundationalist notion of knowledge justification, although such a position is not necessarily in Dewey's thought as a whole (contra Rorty's critique).[21] What I think can be said about this controversy is that Dewey can be taken in a nonfoundationalist sense and can still maintain that there is some aspect of experience that is separate from propositional reports. This traces back to the basic division that Dewey notes in *Experience as Nature* as well as in *Art as Experience*—immediate experience is different in *feel* from reflective activity. To take reflective experience for *all* experience is to commit the fallacy of intellectualism. Knowledge is a reflective endeavor involving conscious thought, justification, and propositional statements. Immediate experience is just that—immediate and prior to detailed reflection. If there are discursive elements to immediate experience, it is because the concepts/words have been rendered as habitually meaningful. This is a point on which both Taylor and Shusterman seem to agree. One sees the flag of one's nation and immediately connotations spring to mind without forced reflection. One hears a simple word like "dog" and the meaning is there, with no need for mediated interpretation, deep thought, or reflection on its context of usage.

I would argue that the experience of something is not *exhaustible* in a specific linguistic formulation, since it lacks that immediate feel that comes with experience that is prereflective. I think here of the opening lines of the *Tao Te Ching,* in which Lao Tzu is recorded as describing the mysterious *Tao* (Way): "As for the Way [*Tao*], the Way that can be spoken of is not the constant Way. As for names, the name that can be named is not the constant name."[22] This verse can be taken either as saying that the *Tao* is simply indefinable and that no definitions or linguistic conceptions come close to it, or that no definition or linguistic characterization *exhausts* its meaning totally.[23] The latter explanation entails that many characterizations are possible, each highlighting an aspect of the *Tao,* but no definition standing so accurate that a person would say "that *is* the Tao." What linguistic characterizations leave out, of course, is what is not linguistic about the Tao, since (at least in part) "The Way is empty."[24] A similar point can be made for Dewey—experience *is* specific experience and not the reflective activity that characterizes mediated thought and stated definition. A definition is different from the experience of something, and while it may be useful, it always exists for a purpose and lacks something of the immediate feel of an experience of some event. No definition *exhausts* the experience of what is being defined. As Dewey points out in *Art as Experience*, there is a difference between the *experience* of something and *reflection* on something—the latter looks for certain relationships and causal factors for some purpose (297).

To return to (1a), if an artist wants to convey what a certain experience *feels* like, and a stated description of it would fail to convey the immediacy of experience, then he or she must resort to the controlled manipulation of energy and rhythm through a medium of art to evoke that experience in the attentive audience member. In terms of (1b), if an artist wants an audience to pass a certain judgment on an experience, then he or she must offer that experience to the audience in such a way that encourages the reflective analysis of that experience in the desired fashion. Like the *Tao*, ordinary experience cannot be exhaustively described in reflective terms because those terms are separate in kind from experience, per premise (2). Characterizations of experience can capture part of that experience, but even this strays from the feeling of the experience itself. Thus, the artist is forced to use the art object to evoke something like or identical to the experience in question (the one he or she felt and wishes to express, or the one he or she wants the audience to feel).

As we saw in the case of the empirical method (e.g., science), words are used to reflectively describe how one is to have such an experience for oneself. After this experience, individuals can render their own judgment concerning the descriptive validity of the empirical claims made by the original speaker/writer. Art fits this general mold, but differs in that it offers, through its close merging of subject matter and material, an immediate experience (aesthetic) of unity and rhythm within the subject matter being conveyed. Science uses statements, which Dewey compares to a signboard. While it directs a person's course of travel to a city, "it does not in any way supply experience of that city even in a vicarious way. What it does do is to set forth some of the conditions that must be fulfilled in order to procure that experience" (90). Such statements serve as reflective means in communication to direct one to experience, but do not immediately create such an experience in the person reading the scientific report.

In art, the experience of the art object is a felt experience in its own right, and is one that exceeds the reading of journal articles in unity, intensity, and emotional coherence. It is *an* experience, one that is the presentation of material *in* and *through* experience. Discussing Van Gogh's use of art to evoke certain experiences, Dewey notes that "he aimed, through pictorial presentation of material that any one on the spot might 'observe,' that thousands had observed, to present a *new* object experienced as having its own unique meaning. Emotional turmoil [a broken heart] and an external episode [a bridge over the Rhone River] fused in an object which was 'expressive' of neither of them separately nor yet of a mechanical junction of the two, but of just the meaning of the 'utterly heart-broken'" (92). Van Gogh wanted to evoke a certain experience in a viewer so he forged a unique union between his subject matter and the artistic medium to accomplish this, a setting much like the correct selection and use of words to accomplish one's ends through communicative activity. The picture serves as the vehicle of communication, since its structure and form are an integral part to evoking a message that could not be exhaustively described in words that either reflect on everyday matters or call on reflective thinking to get at the new connections that Van Gogh is attempting to make. Thus Dewey argues that "he [Van Gogh] did not pour forth the emotion of desolation; that was impossible. He selected and organized an external subject matter with a view to something quite different—an expression. And in the degree in which he succeeded the picture is, of necessity, expressive" (ibid.). What is implied in the "success" criterion of expression, of course, is the same experiential touchstone that the empirical method relies upon—a picture such as this is expressive if it does or could successfully express some experience to an observer. Since that experience cannot be captured exhaustively through reflective means (or a short paragraph full of descriptive statements would have done the job), it must express through the evocation of the specific experience in question in the auditor.

Continuing on this topic, Dewey emphasizes that art is not merely descriptive, or it would be the same as science; instead, "certain relations of lines and colors become important, 'full of meaning,' and everything else is subordinated to the evocation of what is implied in these relations, omitted, distorted, added to, transformed, to convey the relationships" (93). Thus, not only is the artwork an experience for the observer, but it is an experience that draws attention to new relationships that can then serve as material for reflection and analysis. The artist, in doing so, can use the art object to the ends of (1b), encouraging an auditor to reflect and draw conclusions on a certain aspect of the experience as orchestrated by the artist. To illustrate this point, I will now examine three examples drawn from artistic practices such as film, sculpture, and classical Japanese poetry.

The first example of the evocative employment of an art object to elicit certain experiences, as well as certain reflective/deliberative activities associated with these experiences, can be identified in a recent popular film. Steven Spielberg, in an interview concerning his 1998 film *Saving Private Ryan,* provides an excellent instance of the point I am making. Speaking of the intense combat scenes in his war film, he states: "I'm asking the audience—and it's a lot to ask of an audience—to have a physical experience, so that they can somewhat have the experience of what those guys actually went through."[25] One can see how Spielberg is trying to make a point that cannot be given in the dry prose of a history text. By his own admission, he appears to want to evoke a certain reflective experience in an audience in the best way he knows how—by evoking something similar to the World War II soldier's original (embodied) experience through the medium of film. This will expand the audience's experiential repertoire and will most likely lead to the audience engaging the full meaning of what has been depicted (viz., the values and experiences of soldiers in war, national defense policies, etc.). A certain sort of experience is evoked for a certain purpose, and this purpose is fundamentally communicative. It is not a communicative instance of saying something in one way and then saying something equivalent in another fashion. Instead, it seems that Spielberg wants to convey an experience of "being there" to the audience, and the only way he can do so is by coming close to what the represented experience must have looked and sounded like.[26] The film can compel and shape the experience of the attending audience and a large part of that power comes from its making present an experience or situation that was not present before.[27] Spielberg is dealing (largely) with an audience that had not experienced first-hand the horrors of Omaha Beach, so his film makes present certain aural and visual experiences to the viewers. If what is presented to the audience's attention conflicts with values they hold or expands the reasons why they hold certain values or action strategies, then reflective activity will likely be called forth to solve this temporary disruption of the habitual activities of life and value.

Art objects, such as *Saving Private Ryan,* hold the power to create intense experiences that are saturated with meaning and purpose, so much so that their employment as means *is* equivalent to the end they aim at. I will return to this point later in this study, but suffice it to say that this is precisely why

Dewey extolled art's communicative power as unique—the complex meanings that can be made of a particular art object are connected in a very close sense to one's experience of that art object. Even reflection on such an art object still falls within the experience of it in a more expansive sense, a point that Peter Kivy captures in his concept of a work's "reflective afterlife."[28] The experience of an art object may engage our powers of reflection, both during its time of reception and in periods following its conclusion. During both of these times, though, our reflection is closely engaged with the particulars of *that* art object.

A second example of such an evocative employment of an art object comes from the 1980s and involves the site-specific sculpture *Tilted Arc* by Richard Serra. This work was commissioned by the federal government to adorn the courtyard of a federal building in New York City and was installed in 1981. Richard Serra's ultimate design placed a 120-foot-long, 12-foot-high curved piece of self-rusting steel in the middle of the courtyard. Serra's stated intentions, coming after his art object was accused of being an eyesore, indicated that he designed it with a certain evocative purpose in mind. In defending the effects that *Tilted Arc* had on the individuals using the courtyard, he noted: "I make works that deal with the environmental components of given places. . . . My works become part of and are built into the structure of the site, and they often restructure, both conceptually and perceptually, the organization of the site." This restructuring of space is what Serra was hoping to evoke with works such as *Tilted Arc*, as he bluntly points out that he is "interested in creating a behavioral space in which the viewer interacts with the sculpture in its context."[29] Was he successful in restructuring the space with his large slab of steel in the experience of the viewer? Incredibly so, as evidenced by testimony of individuals who had used the courtyard before and after *Tilted Arc* was placed in its center. Many felt the steel mass disoriented their experience of the plaza, made them alter their habits of entering the buildings, and interrupted the walking paths of the employees around and through the courtyard. Eventually, the government removed the sculpture on a March night in 1989. Regardless of the aesthetic merits of such an art object, a simple point was proved. Artists such as Richard Serra can set out to evoke certain experiences (such as that of altered public spaces) to make a point about habits of transit, gathering, and so on. Even though the reflection brought on by the evoked experiences was eventually its literal downfall, it is hard to dispute that *Tilted Arc* was a purposively evocative, and hence communicative, art object.

A third example of such an evocative employment of art can be drawn from classical Japanese poetry. Take, for instance, the Japanese form of poetry called *haiku* (or *haikai* in its first labeled form). The more or less modern form of *haiku* involving a strict seventeen-syllable form evolved from the party game of *renga* largely due to the artistry of the poet Bashō (1644–1694). Bashō was essentially a wandering ascetic for much of his life, and was involved in Zen practice during major periods of his tenure as a *haiku* poet. A few key parts to Zen Buddhism must be enunciated here, as they will be involved in any analysis of what Bashō is trying to do with his *haiku*. Zen doctrine, following Chan Buddhism in China, focused on cultivating the individual to be present to ordinary experience free of its conceptual encumbrances (chief among which would be the classical Buddhist target of the self). As D. T. Suzuki explains, the goal of Zen practice is *satori*, which is "to become conscious of the Unconscious (*mushin*, no-mind)." The difficult aspect to Zen teaching, however, is that its truths are part of a "wordless transmission"—*satori* "cannot be attained by the ordinary means of teaching or learning. It has its own technique in pointing to the presence in us of a mystery that is beyond intellectual analysis."[30] How does one get to such a stage of enlightenment or awareness of what really is present to an individual? This is not attained through reflective experience, but instead (normally) is reached through the help of a teacher who has experienced this state beforehand. Thus, Zen monasteries feature teachers who use devices such as *kōans*, nonsensical stories or questions designed to jar the rational mind away from concepts such as "the self."[31]

Another way of evoking such experiences of enlightenment is through the composition and reception of *haiku*. Bashō's poetry has been described as being the "moment of enlightenment itself"; his poetry, as Thomas Hoover claims, offers many examples of the "perfect Haiku," a piece of art that "is not *about* the moment of Zen enlightenment, it *is* that moment frozen in time and ready to released in the listener's mind."[32] For instance, take Bashō's most famous *haiku*:

Old dark sleepy pool . . .
Quick unexpected
Frog
Goes Plop! Watersplash![33]

This short and direct poem is powerful, according to critics such as Thomas Hoover, precisely because it does not try to do the impossible—to talk about some sort of end state known abstractly as *satori*. Instead, it is praised because it presents an *image* of what the artist wants the audience to be present to—in this case, a seemingly timeless pond and the sound that a frog makes jumping into it. This may not seem like the ultimate experience in life, but according to Bashō, it is the example that he awakened to in that present situation. Thus, he provides a small, vivid presentation of this event to evoke that image, one that avoids an overemphasis on conceptual description and analysis. Indeed, this is vital for the Zen project, as "Zen eschews deliberation and rational analysis; nothing must come between object and perception at the critical moment."[34] If Bashō were to write a reflective treatise on Zen, a different effect would be had; the focus then would be on rational argument, as opposed to the Zen goal of encouraging a direct mindfulness of the situation one is in. Suzuki praises Bashō's use of "little," terse language in his poems to get around the rational mind and to evoke this direct confrontation with "reality" (in this case, an old pond and its resident frog)—"As long as we are moving on the surface of consciousness, we can never get away from ratiocination."[35] That would be the level of *thinking* in writing about the pond; instead, the aim of *haiku* poetry such as that of Bashō's is to evoke a direct confrontation in the observer, a confrontation that the poet himself has had and wishes the audience to have or think about as well.[36]

Process and Product in the Evocative Use of Art

At this point, I hope to have shown the plausibility of (1a) and (1b) in terms of the aspects of experience that stay with experience, as well as (2)'s insistence on the discursive/reflective inexhaustibility of such aspects. The final point in my argument, (3), deals with art being used evocatively. I have touched on that above, noting that art serves as a particularly vivid vehicle to evoke what the artist wants the audience to feel. It can do this because of its close integration of subject matter and media, the particular nature of the artistic enterprise as separate from highly reflective activities such as scientific or philosophical disputation. Like the empirical method, reflective activity (in the case of art, the artist's creative activity) leads the audience to certain experiences for some purpose—such as knowledge (a reflective endeavor), standards for better experience, improved somatic states, and so forth.

More must be said as to what is conveyed through the evocation of aesthetic experience. It cannot be exhaustible in a discursive/reflective characterization, since it has a qualitative feel that cannot be completely rendered in such a way. What else is unique about the aesthetic experience? What I would like to suggest is that the art object has the power to evoke such a powerful experience because in this total interaction process and product, instrument and end are fully integrated. This is something that cannot be done (to the same extent) with scientific or philosophical writing, and this is the point Dewey notes about his own dialectical method. He states in a 1930 essay, "In Reply to Some Criticisms," that in philosophical writings (such as his own), "dialectic is used, of course, but it is used in order to invite the reader to experience the empirical procedure of experimental inquiry and then draw his own conclusions" (213). What seems to differentiate (reflective) dialectic from aesthetic experience is the size of the gap between instrument and end. For Dewey, argumentative discourse aims to move readers and invite them to draw their own conclusions based upon their own experience, with the directions and the experience being quite separated. In art, however, the process of viewing the artwork *is* the product or the experience. The form and substance of art evoke an experience, an ordered discharge of impulse from the engaged audience, which reaches a consummatory phase. This phase *is* in all parts of the work of art, just as the paint is not a medium *for* the painting but is an integral part *of* the painting. The work of art is instrumental in that it is designed for the purpose of causally affecting the aesthetic experience the artist desired (assuming he or she is a good/effective artist) and it is simultaneously final in that the experience *is* what the work of art is. It is not a simple proposition that can be extracted from the art object ("war is hell" from the film *Hamburger Hill*, for instance), since that would deny the experiential aspect of the aesthetic experience. Like the paint, the means of the art object are taken up in the art object and its affected experience. If its import was a simple proposition, and not an experience to be had, this would imply that the work of art was replaceable by other means. In *Art and Experience*, Dewey writes: "Such external or *mere* means . . . are usually of such a sort that others can be substituted for them; the particular ones employed are determined by some extraneous consideration, like cheapness" (201).

Art, however, uses media, which Dewey notes as referring to "means that are incorporated in the outcome." As bricks and mortar become part of the structure they are used to build, so do the parts of the art object become integral parts to the experience as a whole. As Dewey succinctly puts it, "colors *are* the painting; tones *are* the music" (201). One must add that these qualities are the painting *as experienced,* continuing our emphasis on successful expression involving an audience that experiences that expression. This is why artists such as Spielberg, Serra, and Bashō turn to art objects—compared to rational argument, artistic media are a much more direct way to evoke the experience they want their audience to have and to think about.

What is unique about the aesthetic as given in this Deweyan reading is that it is an experience of a process *as* the product, and not merely a means to improve or exercise one's capacities for empathy. This point is recognized by Philip W. Jackson, who highlights the spirituality of art through its unificatory power over experience.[37] I would add that this power would seem to come from what art does uniquely well—the simultaneous unification of process and product, means and end.[38] Unlike the claims of science that direct the reader to an external experience, attending to an artwork *is* the experience in question. Another commentator I would point to in this regard would be Crispin Sartwell, who notes that the means-end relationship is extremely close in the aesthetic experience brought on by an artistic product.[39] As I argued in chapter 4, Sartwell's analysis is important because it emphasizes the value that means can and ought to have if one values them *as* ends, or at least as valuable as the ends that will be present in future situations. What emerges from these commentators is twofold—first, that the nature of aesthetic experience involves the process as the product (all means are integrally tied to/realized in the end), and second, that a subject's orientation can affect how nonartistic means are valued. The latter point, made by Sartwell, serves primarily as an extension of the reflective orientation discussed in the previous section of this chapter and notes the fact that one's attitude in approaching art can also profitably serve as an orientation toward action in general. The first point, however, is what Dewey himself recognizes as a unique characteristic of art, and would seem to be the way that aesthetic experience progresses. He notes that the artist, in the act of expression, goes through inner and outer transformations in ordering the artistic material and the impulse-derived subject matter, and it is only fitting, given Dewey's continuum-based approach, that the experience of the receiver mirrors this transformation. Thus, the experience of the production of the art object, as well as its reception, involves a reordering and transformation not only of external materials (the art objects, physical reactions to them, etc.), but also internal materials such as one's thoughts, attitudes, and emotions. Art is valuable as a communicative strategy because it is the means and end of an important type of communication—the direct communication of experience.

I will conclude this section by considering one source of worry for such an account of art as evocative. As Richard Shusterman has noted, aesthetic experience is mute and often personal, and seems to be something that cannot be communicated.[40] He attached this worry to the legitimation of critical judgments as well as whole fields of artistic practice (popular art, for example). Whereas Dewey seemed to assert that "nothing but aesthetic experience is needed for legitimation, and criticism is merely a means to bring the reader to have the relevant experience," Shusterman argues that legitimation "is social and justificatory, and thus requires means of consensus-formation that are not as immediate and nondiscursive as aesthetic experience."[41] I wholeheartedly agree with Shusterman that there is a productive dialectic between public discourse and individualized experience, and that neither should be said to be foundational or "trumping." I wonder, however, if the competition in which some authors (such as Richard Rorty) place these two levels is not a case of their kicking up dust and complaining about the visibility. This seems to be Rorty's complaint, one which Shusterman goes an admirable distance toward answering by separating experience from a monolithic reading of epistemological justification as the sole use of experience. I think the complete position will be one that acknowledges that some aspect of experience cannot be captured by discursive, reflective strategies, and that critical, reason-based discussion is needed to ensure that the claims of experience do not mutate into trumping claims of knowledge and certainty. This is especially true in the case that Shusterman notes—popular art. If discourse leaves such an area unjustified and unlegitimated, few if any will direct sustained, serious attention toward such art objects to reap the experience they can provide. Reflective discourse, as Shusterman advocates, is needed to bring about and support the conditions that encourage such experience.

I think, however, that the communicative role of primary, aesthetic experience is also important. For instance, arguing about what shade of red looks the best in one's living room only goes so far. At a certain point, it is best to bring the putative shades of red into the room and experience them for oneself. This is the point that Dewey, perhaps too strongly, makes in *Art as Experience*. The point that an artist is trying to make with an artwork can really only be made in that way because of the artwork's exemplary fusion of experience as process and experience as product. The art object leads the observer to an experience, which happens to be the experience of the artwork itself. This is not something that could simply be communicated using propositional utterances and it is the point, I believe, behind Dewey's worry about trying to convey some simple intended meaning in art. Such discursive reductionism would fall prey to the problem of making most of the whole art object superfluous, a mere means and hence replaceable. Instead, Dewey notes that the artwork is public and so are the elements of audience reaction to it (their experience of the work and its perceived meaning); thus, "it is not necessary that communication should be part of the deliberate intent of an artist, although he can never escape the thought of a potential audience. But its function and consequence is to effect communication, and this is not by external accident but from the nature he shares with others" (275). The artist sets out in a public medium to create a work of art that will affect an audience in some fairly foreseeable ways. This setting allows the artwork to communicate, either intentionally on the part of the artist in terms of wanting to use the experience of the artwork to evoke an experience in the audience (and perhaps their reflective judgments on such an experience), or on the part of the audience in orienting themselves toward this public, purposive, and meaningful object *as if* it were an artistic message meant to evoke a specific response.

Where art excels is where the message is an experience that cannot be conveyed in any better way than through art, in which the process and product are unified. What I have tried to highlight in this section has been a *use* that art can be put to, namely, that of the purposive evocation of experience in order to make the audience aware of that experience or in order to elicit reflective judgment on such experiences. Art can be used as communicative, especially in regard to the transmission of the most illusive message of all—one that is simultaneously and wholly both the instrument and the end of the communicative encounter. I will detail the moral uses of such evocative employments of art in the final section, but I will now discuss auditor orientations that can assist one's experience of art.

The Role of Criticism in Aesthetics

As is the case with much of his reconstructive approach to philosophy, when it comes to reflecting on art Dewey wants to highlight a problem with the common *orientation* or *attitude* toward artistic/aesthetic activity and propose a replacement. This new way of approaching art is to be recommended simply because it improves our experience of art. The reformation of our orientations toward art will be a reflective endeavor, much like Dewey's admiration for the Alexander technique and its conscious reshaping of bodily habits.[42] One has aesthetic experience, which then provides material for reflection and judgment. In some cases, this reflective activity is actually intended by an artist qua communicating participant in a society, but in other cases, such actual intention is not necessarily evident. In either case, such reflection (or lack thereof) on the part of the observer affects future experience, with the possibility of making it richer and deeper in terms of linkages to other meaningful experiences or in terms of detail noticed within that experience. The importance of reflection upon experience is noted by Dewey in *Art as Experience* and occupies a central location in his discussion of criticism. Criticism is vitally important to Dewey's enterprise because it is the locus of individual activity and autonomy in creating better and more fulfilling experiences—which is the ultimate goal of his description of aesthetic experience (of art) as *an* experience.

In this section, I wish to examine two views on criticism that Dewey finds unsatisfactory—those he labels "judicial" and "impressionist" criticism. After noting their shortcomings, I will provide Dewey's description of the critical enterprise in *Art as Experience*. This reflective endeavor can be more or less effective at spurring future experiences of depth and value, so Dewey's analysis of what a *good* critical orientation is will receive attention. Some problems will be noted with this analysis and a modified account will be given that posits Dewey's notions of textual unity and authorial intention as *regulative* criteria that guide critical judgment in an open, pluralistic fashion, with the ultimate goal of improving one's experience and the experience of others. This account extends the previous section's analysis of actual communicative uses of art objects to cover situations that center on the immediacy of observer-art object interaction, with the creating artist occupying a distant or unknown role.[43]

Unhelpful Extremes of Critical Orientation

In chapter 13 of *Art as Experience,* Dewey argues forcefully that critical orientations (effectively identical to what I have been calling "reflective orientations") of those examining art should be of a certain type. He begins his account by noting what the right orientation is not. There are two unhelpful habits that make up many approaches to the critical analysis of art. The first type of criticism Dewey distances himself from is labeled "judicial criticism," since it likens the critic to a judge in a "seat of social authority" issuing "an authoritative sentence" on the artwork in question. Such a critical orientation portrays critics as different from the majority of people in society (the critic is trained, educated, or cultured), and their judgments are grounded on the "touchstones" provided by past works of art. Not all works are touchstones, of course, and such a critical orientation picks out certain works to stand as exemplary pieces that can be used to create standards to measure contemporary works of art. Dewey points out that such an orientation entails that "criticism is thought of as if its business were not explication of the content of an object as to substance and form, but a process of acquittal or condemnation on the basis of merits and demerits" (303). Thus, such an orientation reflects on aesthetic experience induced by the art object with an almost total emphasis on the object, such as a painting or sculpture, and seeks to evaluate it with a touchstone-derived rule of exemplary art. Dewey notes that in such criticism, general rules of measurement of artistic greatness are induced from such touchstone works and then are applied to a given contemporary art object to inform the viewing populace of its worth.

Dewey quickly notes the problems with such an approach to reflecting on art and the experience it evokes. First, the judicial orientation fails to offer any justification of *why* these works are touchstones and hence fails to provide the inductive source of rules that can be applied to future works of art. He notes that judicial critics "do not seem to be sure whether the masters are great because they observe certain rules or whether the rules now to be observed are derived from the practice of great men" (305). In other words, are such rules derived from great artworks or are such artworks great because they follow such antecedent artistic rules? Without a firm answer to this "Euthyphro dilemma" of exemplary artworks and their justification, the judicial critic is merely *telling* the public what to believe and is doing nothing that will enhance creativity or value in and through the arts.

A second criticism is that such an approach is inherently limited in dealing with novelty in life and in art's means of appropriating its content. If one of art's purposes is to address and encapsulate the matter of an organism's interaction with the environment in the medium of art, a critical edifice that only looks backwards to former ways of creating art will not be able to deal with changing future circumstances. New modes of artistic rendering are created from tensions in the art world and the world at large, and new forms of art reflect these changing circumstances. Rules based on touchstones from the past will not be responsive to these new circumstances and will erroneously condemn art as useless/nonvaluable even though it may be extremely valuable given the changed circumstances of the present. Dewey notes just this point, stating that "the very meaning of an important new movement in any art is that it expresses something new in human experience, some new mode of interaction of the live creature with his surroundings, and hence the release of powers previously cramped or inert" (307).

I believe that a third problem with such a critical orientation is evident, although Dewey does not discuss it. The judicial approach fails to analyze or do justice to the subject's appropriative activity in the experience of art and in his or her reflections on that experience. Not only is judicial criticism reserved for "experts" of judgment, but it also focuses so much on the object and rules derivable from its qualities that it ignores the subject's role in perceiving and understanding the object. The latter two operations are saturated with purpose and interest for Dewey, and looking solely at objective qualities leaves out any notion of how the experience and analysis of the object can be inflected by the subject's needs, past history, and so forth.

A second orientation to criticism that extends this idea of the subjective element is labeled by Dewey "impressionist criticism." This orientation is one that is diametrically opposed to that of judicial criticism, instead focusing on the subject's experience of the work of art. Such a position denies the possibility of judgment at all, and strives to replace it with a "statement of the responses of feeling and imagery the art object evokes" (308). The critic does little in terms of criticizing a given work of art, and instead tries to describe his subjective experience of the work of art. This description seeks to do justice to the unique and fleeting nature of *that* encounter with the art object. For the impressionist critic, the focus is on the experience evoked by the art object's interaction with the subject. Dewey's aesthetics also prizes the ability and use of art objects to evoke certain experiences, so it will be important for him to distinguish his own view of critical reflection on art from the impressionist approach.

He goes about separating his views on art and its criticism from impressionist criticism by noting three problems with the conception of criticism implied by the latter approach. Presumably, Dewey's critical orientation avoids such faults, a point that will be explored in the final portion of this section. First, the impressionist critic's denial of the need for judgment cannot be sustained. Such a critic wants to focus merely on the experience (the impression), but to give an account of one's impression is already to go beyond that experience. Dewey believes that the impressionist critic wants to delimit a certain experience to the point of *defining* that specific impression, and "to define an impression is to analyze it, and analysis can proceed only by going beyond the impression, by referring it to the grounds on which it rests and the consequences which it entails. And this procedure is judgment" (308–9). Critical judgment, as a second order operation *on* the primary experience of an art object, is necessary even to those who want to recapture the impressions in that experience. One's description uses language and draws attention to elements in the art object-subject interaction that were not overtly present in the experience, thus going beyond the experience. For instance, imagine that one is greatly moved by Terrence Malick's film, *The Thin Red Line*. One's experience of it is just that—the felt and unanalyzed qualities and effects that such an object has on one in such an attentive state. When one begins to reflect on this experience, specific features are overtly noted and singled out as important causal elements of the film's power over one (or any other similar viewer). One does not experience a well-formed and coherent plot, one experiences *that* plot, and can then later analyze it with such categories as coherence and form. To describe it with language entails adding something to the experience, namely, the new experience of reflecting on the earlier experience.

For Dewey, the impressionist critic ignores the crucial role that judgment and reflective criticism must play in examining one's experiences. A second problem he finds with impressionist criticism is that it fails to account for the objective features that influence a subject's response to an art object. This not only includes the object's features as an art object, but also the objective conditions of the subject's own personal history (surroundings, past actions, experiences with the environment, etc.) that influence her reaction to a particular object. The interests and purposes that are inflecting one's perception and judgment directly relate to objective conditions in the environment, and such conditions are left out with the attempt to track a subject's impression by itself. It is such a contextualized understanding of impression that Dewey wants to convey as that which gives the characteristic individuality to an impression, and reflective judgment is then needed to sort out why this experience was the way it was and how such experiences can be improved in future activity. A third problem Dewey notes with this approach to criticism is that it connects the momentary and unique nature of an impression's occurrence with its value—"the suggestion is that because the impression exists at a particular moment, its import is limited to that brief space of time." This is labeled as the "fundamental fallacy of impressionist criticism" (309).

Dewey wants to maintain that all experience has some importance, even if it resides in the minimal amount of contiguity among a subject's experience. Dewey points out that if the impressionist is right in the extremely momentary import of an impression, she would then "reduce all experience to a shifting kaleidoscope of meaningless incidents" (310). The implied argument here is that experience is connected and meaningful, and that to be in such a state each moment of experience must be meaningfully connected to other moments. What Dewey's point treads upon is the claim that the meaning and the value of an experience come in its relations to other experiences (past and potential), and such relations always fall on a scale of usefulness for the organism. Given this account, Dewey's point against the impressionist orientation is not that it renders (or would render, if true) reality a confusion (a transcendental argument), but instead that it is flawed in not recognizing the value of (unique) experiences for a creature's meaningful/effective acting and thinking in its environment. Experience is valuable insofar as it is adjusted to the environment and reflection on this state can be educational for future action by the experiencing agent.

Dewey on Criticism

Dewey faults the judicial critic and the impressionist critic for their overemphasis on either the art object or the experiential subject. Both are integral parts to the experience, and both must be included in any analysis (criticism) of such an event. Both critics fail to note adequately the grounding for such an activity as criticism—the judicial critics fail to properly diagnose the purpose of such a forward-looking criticism, and the impressionist critics fail to see that analysis is a separate activity from the experience itself. Dewey hopes to avoid these faults in critical orientation, emphasizing instead the reflective critic's role in expanding and deepening future experience through the analysis of experience already had.

Dewey begins his account by distinguishing criticism from measurement by noting the former's qualitative nature. Measurement uses standards, or comparative methods of quantitatively analyzing objects. A relatively unskilled and unpracticed individual can use a ruler with the same precision as a trained measuring agent; both are undergoing a well-defined procedure of measurement using the ruler as a standard. A critic, on the other hand, does not formulaically follow such a quantitative procedure, but instead focuses on the experienced qualities of the object and how these relate to its constitution and effect on auditors. This examination focuses on the subject matter of the art object, and provides a reflective analysis of the values *in* the art object. Such values often are not recognized in the immediate experience of them, but are mostly revealed in the secondary criticism of the art object; as Dewey notes concerning our direct valuing of parts of an art object, "criticism is a search for the properties of the object that may justify the direct reaction" (312). This search occurs largely through discourse about art objects and is open to intersubjective criticism, since both it and its object (the piece of art) are public objects. Instances of criticism are good when they are "of use as instrumentalities of personal experience, not as dictates of what the attitude of any one should be" (313). In other words, criticism does more than merely tell one what an important work of art is or what impression was had; instead, it gives one a possible orientation that is helpful in ordering and improving one's past and future experiences.

Dewey provides two functions of criticism, that of *analysis* of constituent parts of an art object and that of *synthesis* of the parts in a unified whole. The former discriminates the parts of a whole, whereas the latter shows how they are unified in the experience. Both of these operations are connected to each other, largely because of Dewey's analysis of parts of an art object being parts of a whole. Analysis of these parts entails and presupposes a recognition of their connection in a unified work of art, and it is this unified work that can be explicitly commented upon in terms of how it is a unified whole, how the parts fit together, etc. The critic, according to Dewey, needs a mix of interest and insight to be effective at offering criticism that is useful. Interest is needed to attend to a work of art with its encapsulated subject matter, and insight is needed to reflect on a rich and deep experience. This insight is also antecedently produced by rich and deep experience, such that a critic's continuing experience furthers his or her ability to function as a critic. It must be noted that Dewey is not confining this activity of criticism to professional critics, a point that is developed in accounts of pragmatist interpretation and criticism.[44] Instead of the narrow professional mold that judicial critics held as their cultivated self-conception, Dewey seems to be advocating an open notion of criticism that is an orientation toward experience that anyone could take. In line with the discussion in chapter 4, everyone has or can have *an* experience (exemplified by the aesthetic experience, and not constrained to art objects), so everyone must be able to reflect upon it in order to improve such experiences in the future. The crucial decision comes in *how* one goes about this critical examination of one's experiences. Dewey's notion of criticism tries for an ideal of openness to the experience, to values in the experience, and to what can be said about these *after* the experience.

Given this commitment to openness in interpretation, a potential problem arises when Dewey enunciates some guidelines for effective criticism. He notes in *Art as Experience* that the point of art is a unity of form and matter, and that the critic attempts to judge the artwork in such a way as to create some unifying strand or pattern through the parts of the work. Although others have critiqued Dewey's emphasis on unified art and experience at the expense of disjointed and fractured experience,[45] I will assume that Dewey's reading of the role of art as unifying an experience is defendable. The question or problem that this creates, however, is how one is to handle divergent interpretations of the same art object. The good critic is noted as one who is open to various traditions, methods, etc., all of which are desirable because they expand one's range of possible experiences. Why aren't divergent readings of an artwork good for this same reason? Dewey discusses this issue in *Art and Experience*, noting that differing interpretations are acceptable in criticism if they meet two conditions: (1) "the theme and design which interest selects must really be present in the work," and (2) "the leading thesis must be shown to be consistently maintained throughout the parts of the work" (318). Prior to these two explicit conditions seems to be another one, namely, (3) that the critic must expand the background from which to analyze the text by knowing the tradition an author is working in and the intent behind the piece (315–16). This mention of authorial intention is immediately constraining, since it seems to be a move toward limiting applicable interpretations of a text to ones in line with an author's known intention in producing the work. Add to this the content requirements that an interpretation be unified and identifiable in all parts of a work, and one seems to have a fairly closed interpretative system for criticism.

I will conclude this section by suggesting some ways out of this quandary for Dewey. It is helpful to start by looking at the larger picture of criticism that Dewey holds—individuals have *an* experience, which they then examine in terms of how and why it was brought about (e.g., how the art object functioned and held meaning). Notice that the reflective stage is separated from the experiential stage (in this analysis). Both of these activities are interpenetrating in terms of mutually reinforcing/affecting each other, but both have characteristics that lead one to see them as different. *Seeing* a painting is different from *thinking* about why it is so powerful. Add to this the ultimate goal of critical reflection, which is the *useful* discrimination and synthesis of a work of art, and one begins to see how Dewey could use the strictures he stated above concerning divergent interpretations.

In terms of the content requirements, one (including Dewey) must not get so caught up in the claim that a theme/thesis is *really in the object*—criticism happens *after* the experience of the object and therefore is additive to the original experience. We do not experience a theme, we experience a story with characters and later identify a theme that seems to make sense given all the parts of experience we identify. What Dewey must mean by (1) and (2) is that it is a useful principle that we try to find interpretations that fit as much of the work as we can. It seems not as useful in making sense of our total experience of *Hamlet* to focus on one sentence in our critical interpretation (say, Hamlet's dying words), so one should try to encompass as much of the total art object experienced as possible in one's interpretation. Why? The ultimate justification comes from the heuristic justice an interpretation does to our experience, and focusing only on minute aspects of this experience would a fortiori leave significant parts of it unanalyzed and undeveloped. Conditions (1) and (2) are not strict in terms of ruling out interpretations. Instead, I think it is more useful to see them as *regulative* principles governing how our reflection ought to proceed (justified by what tends to be most useful), instead of constitutive principles that actually determine something about the art object (similar to the strictures of the judicial critic). Their employment as guides to criticism also avoids the problems with impressionist criticism and its lack of order in analysis and reflection.

This heuristic employment of Dewey's critical principles (1 and 2) is also supported by Richard Shusterman, who notes that "the project is not to describe the work's given and definite sense, but rather to *make sense* of the work."[46] He highlights that this sense-making activity is not a mere identification of a prior meaning *in* the work, but it is also not a capricious exercise in creating arbitrary (nonuseful) meanings for the work to have. I agree with this point and must note that Dewey's strictures on interpretation cannot be taken as they are given without amending the regulative analysis I have discussed. In general, we find it useful to reflect on the whole of a text, since that whole text is what constitutes the objective part of our experiential interaction with the work of art.

Dewey's nod toward authorial intention does seem worrisome given his insistence on criticism opening up new experiences for us. I argue that Dewey cannot be taken to be an actual intentionalist in the strong sense, since it would conflict with his openness and meliorist leanings (by excluding nonintended interpretations and the experiences they may lead to), as well as his analysis that art often communicates important matters of which its author was unaware.⁴⁷ Concerning oneself with an author's tradition and intention must be taken in a regulative sense. It would then be useful for an individual to interact with a work of art *as if* such-and-such was its intended meaning. I would describe Dewey as being closer to a hypothetical intentionalist, as opposed to an actual intentionalist. To truly see artworks as *communicative*, which Dewey does, one must see them as originating from someone and as conveyed to someone. Trees and rocks do not communicate with us and any recognized instance of communication must be assumed as the result of human-to-human interaction. Yet in many cases, the *actual* author of an artwork does not intend to communicate a certain message to a receiver—this is why Dewey notes at the end of his description of art as unhindered communication that "I do not say that communication to others is the intent of an artist. But it is the consequence of his work."⁴⁸ How do we make sense of this?

Communication must be taken as an activity involving human purpose, but with the caveat that in the context of an artwork detached from a human creator, *actual* intentions are not actually existent in the work of art. Contra Robert Stecker and others,⁴⁹ critical reflection is not the search for *the* intended meaning. Instead, it starts with an object that is meaningful from its context and objective features (its use of recognizable words, for instance). What is useful in making sense of the art object is *what could be intended by its creation*—in other words, what type of experience *could* the (possibly unknown) author be trying to convey? This lends a context to one's experience of the object, one's analysis of that experience (including all parties in the interaction), as well as one's future experience of other art objects (which are immune to the actual intentions of artists far removed in time or space).

Dewey's notion of criticism seeks to do justice to the objective and subjective parts of the experience, noting that both are intertwined and only become individuated upon post hoc reflection. The value of criticism for Dewey, including philosophy as criticism of criticism, is in the opening up of possibilities for newer and deeper experience.⁵⁰ Aesthetic criticism broadens one's thinking about the experience of art, which in turn leads to those experiences being even more meaningful. By portraying Dewey's three guides to interpretation as regulative principles that ask one to take an orientation toward the art object, an orientation that attempts to find unified interpretations that treat the art object *as if* someone were trying to communicate a coherent idea to the audience (regardless of the actual intent to do so), one can see how his guidelines can be useful without being exclusionary in his issuing of judgments such as "interpretation *x* is not what was intended by the author." The latter type of criticism is not particularly useful for enhancing one's experience of a particular art object, as evidenced by the multitude of important works by unknown authors.[51] As Dewey notes, "the value of experience is not only in the ideals it reveals, but in its power to disclose many ideals."[52] Experience is valuable because it always offers a source of tension and novelty, something both desired and dreaded by the live creature. Criticism's use is to lead toward better and improved experience, not merely to disclose "the" truth about why a particular author created a particular work. Thus, Dewey's analysis of criticism should be rendered in such a way that certain guidelines regulate our inquiry without harmfully limiting it. As was the case with the previous section in this chapter, art is seen once again as communicative in a powerful sense. The next section will flesh out how this communicative power is tied to reflective activity and how such activity is morally edifying.

Deliberation, Reflection, and Moral Cultivation

In the first two parts to this chapter, I have attempted to show how artists can use the evocation of certain experiences in a communicative fashion, as well as how the critical orientation of assuming such a use can be useful in improving experience. Both of these readings do justice to the communicative function of art and aesthetic experience. I wish to avoid the criticisms of chapter 2 with such an account by tying the experience evoked closely to the message communicated. This seems to be the most powerful way of avoiding the "multiple realizability" arguments against artistic communication theories. For instance, Rekha Jhanji gives one such argument against the overspiritualization of Indian art—such a reading would mean that the artist's "major concern would be to experience and communicate through symbols a supersensible reality. The mode of communicating this experience could be accidental and contingent."[53] The means of communication would be a *mere* means or mode, and not essentially tied to the message that one wishes to transmit.

The account given in the first portion of this chapter has avoided such an objection by emphasizing the closeness of the experience evoked and the message transmitted. Now I will give an account of how this communicative employment, as well as that brought on through the critical orientation of approaching an art object *as if* its creator wished to evoke certain experiences for a certain purpose, can be morally useful in terms of improving or changing a subject's values, habits of reflection, and beliefs. Such interactions with art objects have the hallmark of evoking thought about something, whether it is the experience that the artist actually intended an audience to have or the experience that the audience has through their assumption of a certain critical orientation. The audience thinks and reflects on the art object, its purpose, and its importance to their experience. Thus, art objects can be integrally connected to reflective activity through the experiences that they compel an auditor to undertake. For instance, an ancient Indian text such as the *Avadhoota Gītā* spurs the audience to make sense of it through reflection due to its many blatant contradictory statements on individuation, the efficacy of action in terms of salvation, and the ultimate nature of the supreme deity.[54] Given that art objects and the work they do on a given audience can be closely connected with reflective activity, questions now arise as to what is the specific nature of such activity, and how does it connect to moral improvement?

The key to understanding the moral value of reflective experience in regard to art objects will be Dewey's reading of the process of deliberation. Deliberation is used in this sense to imply practical decision making (as in moral judgment) and is an important factor in the reflective fashioning or instating of values, as was described in chapter 3. It is vital to understand that for Dewey, like Charles S. Peirce before him,[55] deliberation or reflective activity begins with some sort of impasse being reached by the subject in question. Peirce made this point in terms of doubt, and Dewey makes a similar point in regard to a conflict between habits or impulses the agent possesses. Dewey describes deliberation in his *Human Nature and Conduct* (1916): "Deliberation means precisely that activity is disintegrated, and that its various elements hold one another up. While none has force enough to become the centre of a redirected activity, or to dominate a course of action, each has enough power to check others from exercising mastery. Activity does not cease in order to give way to reflection; activity is turned from execution into intra-organic channels, resulting in dramatic rehearsal" (133).

Reflective/deliberative activity occurs in order to decide which impulse or habit ought to be acted upon, as the organism cannot rely on immediate habitual reactions to decide (as these are contradictory and equally immediate). Thus, one dislikes dishonesty, but also likes a coworker. When an opportunity arises in which honesty with one's manager may endanger the coworker's job, the employee is at an impasse. Reflection must take over to decide which value and accompanying action to value more in this case, given its specific and concrete details. This was the theme of chapter 3's analysis of reflective instatement of values, and this idea comes through in Dewey's discussion of deliberation.

The element that is added here to chapter 3's analysis of value setting is the method or mechanism of dramatic rehearsal. It is important to emphasize that dramatic rehearsal is not the *only* way that deliberation can proceed, nor is it all of deliberative activity.[56] It is an important method of deliberation from Dewey's earliest ethical work to his *Human Nature and Conduct* and *Ethics,* though, and thus deserves attention in this reading of the reflective value of art objects. Even in *The Study of Ethics* (1894), the story is the same. Conflicting ends set by various impulses stymie action and the agent is led to reflectively harmonize such impulses—one is "brought to *deliberation,* the more conscious weighing and balancing of values" (251). The way that deliberative reflection proceeds is identical to the description provided in his later work; "it is a process of tentative action; we 'try on' one or other of the ends, imagining ourselves actually doing them, going, indeed, in this make-believe action just as far as we can without actually doing them" (ibid.). A vital part to this activity is imagination. As Dewey later puts it in *Human Nature and Conduct*: "Each conflicting habit and impulse takes its turn in projecting itself upon the screen of imagination. It unrolls a picture of its future history, of the career it would have if it were given head" (133). Choice then occurs when a suitable outcome is envisioned in imagination, including the outcomes and projections based upon a permutation of starting impulse/action strategies.

To continue the previously mentioned example, an employee may avoid his or her manager to prevent being forced to lie or harm a coworker, or may stick to one of the starting options—lie or don't lie. Either way, the outcome is a new resolve and force toward activity due to the subject's reflective deliberation. In Dewey's earlier work, this was described as the "mediation" of impulse in which its immediate meaning was supplemented by reflection on past and future connections (causes and consequences). Such an "improved" meaning now has the added relational element of hierarchical worth—it has now been reflectively recognized as higher than another competing impulse or habit in this type of situation. The more adaptive to future situations this ranking is, the more "reasonable" the reflective activity that produced it

(135). Thus, the deliberative activities of a cocaine addict may involve imaginative projection, but of an extremely one-sided nature—one that is virtually predetermined to focus on the short-term requirements of a physiological craving for chemical stimulants. The ideal, as in chapter 4, is responsiveness to the details of one's immediate situation, along with the emplacement of habits of reflective adjustment that facilitate future adaptation. Reasonable deliberation focuses on the present in such a way as not to predetermine or foreclose future flexibility in reflection or in action.

Deliberation and the Experience of Art Objects

How does such imaginative projection or deliberative rehearsal relate to aesthetic experience? While it seems that imagination would have a ready link to the attending to artistic objects, the immediate problem arises—our experience of many art objects (including deliberative activity) is removed from the activities of our life. This is not an impassable obstacle for the account that gives reflective value to the experience of art objects, as it is in the nature of reflection to be removed from the actual activities of life. The issue still remains that the deliberation spurred on by an art object, say, a narrative film, is removed from decisions the auditor has to make in her life. There are two ways around such an objection. First, one can argue that we exercise and strengthen our deliberative and imaginative habits while attending to a story. Second, one can assert that stories can also compel deliberative activities that relate themes, values, and action strategies in the story to one's own life story. I will explore each of these in turn.

Initially, it seems obvious that one exercises deliberation and dramatic rehearsal while attending to an art object. I will limit the following comments to narrative art objects, but the same sort of analysis can be given in regard to less temporal art objects (statues or paintings), as Dewey argues that even these are temporally perceived and given meaning. When one attends to a story, film, or poem, one's attention is on one given scene or portion of the art object. This present attention, according to Dewey's reading of *an experience*, incorporates what came before it (earlier portions of the narrative, for instance). The portrayal of the elder Private Ryan in Steven Spielberg's film *Saving Private Ryan* has different meanings in the initial scenes with him and his family compared to the last scene. What is added to the later portrayal, of course, is all of the intervening narrative events displaying his World War II experiences. Dewey is making the important point in *Art as Experience* that aesthetic experiences summarize and incorporate what came before, much as he describes (in his earlier ethical works) impulse as being "immediately mediated" in terms of its meaning being carried over from previous experiences. A child does not have to reflect on the meaning of touching a flame a second time; the immediate meaning of flame touching has been mediated by the past (most likely painful) experience of flame touching. Artistic objects possess this integration of parts to an exemplary degree.

Dramatic rehearsal comes in during the second half of the present—that of its anticipation of future events. The present not only immediately incorporates the past, it also looks toward a future. In terms of art objects (especially those of the narrative variety), this is another way of saying they are story structured, with a beginning, middle, and end. As one reads through *Hamlet*, one is lead by one's interaction with the story not only to supply past meanings to what is presently given (say, Hamlet's conversation of the moment), but also to anticipate future actions by certain characters and how they will turn out. Should Hamlet simply go along with the usurpers or actively resist? What ways of resistance are suggested by what is concretely given in the scenes one has been a witness to so far? There is a sort of deliberative activity or imaginative projecting that goes into thinking through one's experience of a story and this seems to be a reflective element of aesthetic experience of art objects. This is what Dewey means when he points out the possibilities "embodied" in art. The art object *is* the sensuous presentation of the meeting of a fairly determined past (as already experienced) and an uncertain future (anticipated in some general way, though). The meaning of the present both takes in what was known of the past and (through the thought process of the auditor) looks toward the future or conclusion of the art object. Of course, certain art objects can perplex or enable such anticipatory activity on the part of the viewer, but the activity occurs nonetheless. An important part to such activity is the dramatic rehearsal of what the characters ought to do and what seems to be coming next from the tensions within the present scene.

Another related way in which art objects can foster deliberation is the extratextual sense of what one thinks of oneself in relation to the substance of the art object. Steven Fesmire notes that there is an important structural affinity between aesthetic/artistic activity and moral activity in Dewey's writings, but maintains that art can be only a useful *metaphor* for understanding moral activity.[57] As is evident from chapter 4, I want to argue the stronger point that aesthetic activity *is* moral activity and not just a metaphor for approaching morality. Fesmire argues that deliberation is importantly connected to aesthetic experience in that they are both story structured with a beginning, middle, and end, but he does not give a detailed account of how readers alter *their* story based upon interaction with a *fictional* story. This is an important arena for deliberation and I believe it can be further examined through the concept of "identification" in regard to narrative art objects. Although relatively simple conceptions of identification have been harshly criticized in the literature,[58] I believe there is room for a heuristic notion of identifying with something or someone in an art object.

For instance, one is tempted to say a reader identifies with an account when he or she sees the character in the story as following a certain way of acting that would fit the reader's life. Often, the noting of this fit comes from the experiences of the character being similar in some key regard to the experiences of the reader. In other cases, it is the values of the character that resonate so strongly with the reader. While the specific lives differ, the reader sees a similar way of orienting him or herself to the world in the fictional character. Often this activity of identification involves thought and choices as to whether there is some meaningful identity between part of the character and part of the reader's life. This is deliberative when there is some tension in what is accounted for in the narrative—for instance, when a character portrays characteristics of which the auditor only partially approves. *Dirty Harry* portrays a rough police detective who often "has to" resort to force to solve pressing crimes. The viewer, we can assume, has a general aversion to the use of torture, but also has sympathies for innocent victims of crime. The viewer is now forced to deliberate and reconcile not only what Dirty Harry ought to do in the given narrative events, but also how the reader ought to instate the two separate values/action strategies that have now come into conflict (stopping the harming of the innocent, never resorting to torture).

Notice that the reader does not have to already hold all of these values for this to be a case of identification with Dirty Harry—what is identical is the value/strategy extrapolated from the character and the value/strategy that the reader judges as desirable (regardless of whether he or she presently holds it or not). This could be the reinforcement of his or her held values and action strategies with the additional meaning of a new hierarchy among them, or it could be a switch to a new value found in the narrative portrayal. Walter Fisher, discussing the process of identification in light of narrative as communication, argues that "we *identify* with an account (and its author) or we treat it as mistaken. We identify with stories or accounts when we find that they offer 'good reasons' for being accepted. . . . Reasons are good when they are perceived as (1) true to and consistent with what we think we know and what we value, (2) appropriate to whatever decision is pending, (3) promising in effects for ourselves and others, and (4) consistent with what we believe is an ideal basis for conduct."[59] This is the sort of imaginative, reflective engagement with narrative that offers benefits for how a reader takes certain ways of acting or believing away from fictional art objects. There is more to be said on this process, of course.[60] It is clear that many narratives provide an imaginative presentation of certain characters and the sort of consequences their actions and values yield, but readers must reconcile this with the specifics of their own situation. Thus, they are led to dramatically rehearse what such values and action strategies would be like if they were to adopt and adapt them to their life. This can be an actually intended outcome of an artist's purposive creation of an art object, or this can be due to a critical orientation that audiences take in relation to being confronted with an art object (removed from its creator). Either way, the art object engages the auditor's imagination in a reflective and useful manner.

Why is such imaginative, deliberative activity spurred on by an art object *morally* valuable? Chapter 4 painted a picture of moral value and cultivation that integrally involved attention to the present situation as the spirit and method to conduct that made it morally worthy. In Dewey's later works, such as *Human Nature and Conduct*, he equates morality with the process of growth.[61] By "morality," he "means that kind of expansion in meaning which is consequent upon observations of the conditions and outcome of conduct. . . . It is learning the meaning of what we are about and employing that meaning in action" (194). The sort of change we ought to aim for is progress, or growth that is sustainable and more likely than not to be adjusted to present and future circumstances. Thus, one sees a continuation of the concept of progressive adjustment from Dewey's early work in ethics to his later writings. Progress is "the present reconstruction adding fullness and distinctions of meaning, and retrogression is a present slipping away of significance, determinations, grasp" (195). This is fundamentally connected to his earlier work in that meaning and reconstruction are functionally equivalent to mediation of the present situation, including what we contribute (impulse, habit) and what the environment contributes (opposing forces, stations, etc.). In *Human Nature and Conduct*, Dewey explicitly calls the result of deliberation "the mediation of impulse" (137). In both of these notions there is an integration of the past and future in the present, with successful attention to the present more fully and richly incorporating past experiential meanings and anticipated connections to future states of affairs. It is no accident that this form of experience is the same as that of aesthetic experience—indeed, Dewey notes this by beginning *Art as Experience* with a description of this general pattern of experience. Thus, it is also no surprise that Dewey's way of approaching art objects would foreshadow an account of identification such as the one I have given. Art objects involve the observer engaging in anticipatory activity concerning the future of the experience of the art object, and morality involves "the future [as] a projection of the subject-matter of the present, a projection which is not arbitrary in the extent in which it divines the movement of the moving present."[62] In moral matters, attention to the present is adjustment to the present and simultaneously some measure of adjustment to future situations (as these are meaningful and anticipated insofar as their significance is seen in present concrete circumstances).

When an artist evokes an experience from an observer with a created art object, or when an observer interprets an art object *as if* this were the case, what is occurring is the focusing of attention on objects made present through reflective activity. As recounted in chapter 3, reflective experience is different in content than immediate experience, as the former brings in connections to other states of affairs (viz., causes and consequents) that are not immediately present. They are made present, however, in reflective activity. Deliberation is attention to conflicting impulses or habits (accepted pathways of action) and the possible consequences of these if they are followed. Dramatic rehearsal is merely an imaginative way to reflect on what one ought to do without first doing it, and it entails attention to something that one may have overlooked—certain consequences that are connected to values or action strategies that are now somehow in conflict. Such an imaginative means of deliberation is not the mere "calculation of indeterminate future results. The present, not the future, is ours. No shrewdness, no store of information will make it ours. But by constant watchfulness concerning the tendency of acts, by noting disparities between former judgments and actual outcomes, and tracing that part of the disparity that was due to deficient and excess in disposition, we come to know the meaning of present acts, and to guide them in the light of that meaning."[63]

Thus, as was the recommendation in Dewey's early ethical works, one's focus should be on what is concretely given to us. Of course, there are ways to make such attention more or less useful for future presents. Our attention ought to be focused on the present, and in situations where the present stymies our impulses and established habits, reflection (via dramatic rehearsal in this case) makes present certain factors that should be attended to now. In the here and now, we ought to foster "those impulses and habits which experience has shown to make us sensitive, generous, imaginative, impartial in perceiving the tendency of our inchoate dawning activities."[64] This is what dramatic rehearsal through the imaginative engagement with art objects results in—cultivation through instantiation of the tendencies of intelligent attention to the meaning of the present.

I return at the end of this chapter to the power of the evocative and communicative use of art objects. Why are they so effective in getting individuals to look at held values, to change them, or to strengthen them? I would trace this to the power of art objects to make certain values present, or to evoke reflection on certain values by foregrounding a conflict of values and/or action strategies in a sensuous form in the art object. This is the power of communication that Lenore Langsdorf contrasts against a purely representational theory of language; she points out that language not only *represents*, but in a real sense also *presents* a world to us.[65]

Our communicative practices highlight what we talk about, know, value, and despise. Richard Shusterman, in his analysis of art as drama, also notes this power of art to focus attention. Drama, like most of art, is characterized by its framing of a certain vivid portion of natural activity and life. This framing of some of the energies of life, be it on stage, in a museum, or in a wood carving, functions as all frames do: "A frame not only concentrates but demarcates; it is thus simultaneously not just a focus but a barrier that separates what is framed from the rest of life."[66] Art makes apparent something that is particularly vivid and powerful, partially because of the framing of such a subject matter "outside" of life and in some artistic object or event (such as a play or song). This framing is still a framing of *life,* something in which we are engaged; this is why our interest is so readily drawn to powerful art objects, and in turn, why our attention is rewarded with some sort of change or added meaning in our selves and our experiences of the world. This sort of reading of aesthetic engagement with art objects, a reading that is found in part in Dewey's aesthetic work, answers a fundamental tension that Steve Odin notes in theories of artistic distance across the East and the West—that of the tension between auditor detachment and engagement or sympathy with the art object.[67] The framing of one part of life in a narrative is detached from life in one regard, largely because of cultural institutions surrounding the production, delivery, and reception of such an art object. In another sense, however, it is still vividly engaging in a practical sense as it is a framed presentation *of life*. It frames and focuses the audience's attention on some part of life, be it a value, action strategy, etc., and forces the audience to reflect and deliberate on the value of what is presented *for their projects and activities*. One notices this functioning of framing and, more important, attention in Dewey's reading of the value of aesthetic experience of art—it is revelatory, and "'revelation' in art is the quickened expansion of experience."[68] Notice that what art reveals *is* internal to the experience of the art object; life is revealed insofar as it is experienced in the particular fashion that an art object, either intentionally or through the critical orientation of an audience, frames it.

Art objects, such as *Saving Private Ryan*, *Tilted Arc*, and *haiku* poems hold the power to create intense experiences that are saturated with meaning and purpose, so much so that their employment as means *is* equivalent to the end they aim at. This is precisely why Dewey extolled art's communicative power as unique—the complex meanings that can be made of a particular painting are connected in a very close sense to one's experience of that painting. Even reflection on such a painting still falls within the experience of it in a more expansive sense. This chapter has attempted to explicate and clarify Dewey's claims concerning the communicative power of art, the role of critical orientation in one's experience of art objects, as well as the connection of art objects to moral cultivation and reflective activity. The experience of art objects, like the reading of aesthetic experience in general given in chapter 4, can be morally cultivating in a unique fashion due to its integration of means and ends in a sensuous object. What this present discussion adds to the account in chapter 4 is the reflective dimension of deliberation and its associated process of dramatic rehearsal. The intentional nature of art objects gives them this power to frame and focus attention, and in doing so, to hone our ability to be a progressively adjusted and growing agent. Thus, Shusterman points out that "art's apparent diversion from real life may be a needed path of indirection that leads us back to experience life more fully though the infectious intensity of aesthetic experience and its release from affective inhibitions."[69] The point of this chapter has been to show how such a path of indirection can be directed in a communicative fashion, either by an artist or by the audience itself.

6

Orientational Meliorism and the Quest for the Artful Life

Art and morality can and should be connected. Yet not all aesthetic experience should be conceptually tied to fine art as it is traditionally designated. The previous chapters have advanced a sustained argument concerning how experiences can be aesthetic or nonaesthetic depending on a subjective variable. I have alluded to this element as orientation, or a deep-seated way an individual has of approaching and thinking through the objects of experience. Such objects include conventional art objects, but they can also be expanded to *any* activity that one is doing and undergoing. Activity can be aesthetic or artful as a creation insofar as we attend to it in its immediacy, and not as something merely of value as an instrumental means to something additional (be it monetary gain through owning a painting, the paycheck after the ferry ride, etc.). The vital core to Dewey's aesthetic theory, I argue, is not an analysis of the objective properties of those varied things we dub as "art objects," but instead concerns the spirit and method of one's habits of attending. When one sees an art object, is one captivated and absorbed in what is there in front of one, or is one drawn away to nonpresent issues? When one thinks about and criticizes an art object, is one's reflective activity closely tied to the experience of that art object, or is it removed from the present experience in its details and import? When one undergoes activity, is attention paid to how it structures, shapes, and instantiates one's relations with others, one's desires, and so forth, or does one merely want to get through it to the desired end or goal?

All of these possible alternatives involve similar or identical objective conditions, but all entail different *experiential* qualities to the individual undergoing them. What differs is the subject's *orientation* toward the activity or object in question. In this chapter, I will characterize what I mean by orientation, and how it fits into a Deweyan program of meliorism, or the improvement of one's lived experience. In order to do this, I will discuss orientation and the notion of *orientational meliorism* in general terms. Following this, I will explicate a point that has been hinted at in various ways in the previous chapters—how one's general orientation can shape reflective attention and immediate attention in ways that render human experience more enjoyable and more conducive to growth. Thus, I will return to the topics of aesthetic experience and moral progress in a different fashion; in this case, I approach them from the point of how to make our activities more unified, alive, and absorptive.

In earlier chapters I built such a case from foils in the philosophy of art literature, but here I will do so from the perspective of Dewey's moral theory. What sort of individuals ought we to be? I engage the important issue of how ought we to act from an angle that is particularly Deweyan—with what spirit or method ought we to engage the struggles and demands of life? In the terms I will develop, the question becomes—what sort of orientation ought we to cultivate? This necessitates the qualitative insights of Dewey's reading of aesthetic experience, as well as his notion of growth or progressive adjustment as a moral endpoint of sorts. The latter parts of this chapter therefore deal with what sort of orientation toward activity, desire, and goals we ought to take, guided largely by the demand to make more of our experience unified and adaptively engaged with the present situation in all its obstacles and resources. In other words, we return in a slightly more general fashion to the question driving this entire study—how can we render more of life's experiences aesthetic or artful?

Meliorism and Orientation

What is meant by the term "meliorism?" This is an important term in pragmatism, but its true meaning is sadly missed in many contemporary pragmatist projects. Let's start with a more general question, one that will lead us directly to the melioristic point. What is the purpose of writing or discussing philosophical problems? This question could apply to any instance of theorizing. Richard Shusterman provides a useful distinction between what he notes as the two major approaches of contemporary pragmatists—what he calls *descriptive pragmatism* and *reconstructive-narrative/genealogical-poetic pragmatism*.[1] These also can be seen as approaches to philosophy in general, and not just in regard to pragmatist writers. I will truncate these and call them *descriptive* or *reconstructive* approaches to philosophy. The central point to the former, according to Shusterman, is the production of some correct or accurate account of the world or some set of practices. Thus, one approaching the definition of art may look for a concept of art that accurately and completely describes those practices and objects we call art. Alternatively, a more reconstructive approach eschews mere description of the world and aims to change or reconstruct some aspect of it. Dewey's take on art is consequently different from the descriptive approach—he aims to redefine art in such a way as to get us out of old ways of sequestering art in museums and to establish new habits of thinking that let art into our everyday activity. The purpose of such a reconstructive definition is future orientated insofar as it attempts to affect some sort of change or reorientation toward the world. More descriptive approaches to philosophy will attempt to capture or accurately describe some phenomena; more reconstructive approaches will attempt to change some phenomena.

This is very compatible with the general pragmatist approach to meaning and truth, and flows readily into the pragmatic emphasis on *meliorism*. What exactly is meliorism? It is this reconstructive approach to doing philosophy, and often features some sort of program of moral or ethical cultivation. Dewey describes meliorism in general terms in *Reconstruction in Philosophy* (1920): "Meliorism is the belief that the specific conditions which exist at one moment, be they comparatively bad or comparatively good, in any event may be bettered. It encourages intelligence to study the positive means of good and the obstructions to their realization, and to put forth endeavor for the improvement of conditions."[2] Opposed to the paralyzing doctrines of optimism and pessimism, meliorism entails a focus on the present situation and attempts to work within those constraints to improve the quality of present and future experience. Much is packed into this description of meliorism, but we can extract three main features:

1. Meliorism must include an analysis of some sort of end state or goal.
2. Meliorism must involve attention to the means needed to reach this end state.
3. Meliorism involves (a) some unit of analysis and (b) some vector of change.

Before I delve into the specifics of my program of orientational meliorism that I draw from Dewey's work, it is important to briefly discuss these general parts to the reconstructive or meliorative way of doing philosophy.[3]

First, meliorism must include an analysis of some sort of end state or goal. This is essential to what makes such an approach future oriented—this is the state toward which one wants to move the present. As detailed previously, Dewey is against any strong separation of the ideal from the real. The goal will be implied in the present insofar as the present has good aspects that we wish to maximize and bad aspects that we wish to minimize or remove. In previous chapters, I have discussed the moral endpoint of progressive adjustment. In the latter parts of this chapter I will return to this topic, albeit in the form of growth, as this is emphasized in Dewey's later work in ethics. A scheme of meliorism on such an account would be one that provides an analysis of growth such that one is better able to reach and instantiate that desired state. This is what makes a melioristic account of growth different from a merely descriptive account of what growth is—the former is actionable insofar as it can guide one's actions after the philosophical activity is done.

Second, meliorism must involve an analysis of means. Part of the way such melioristic accounts guide action is through attending to ends *and* the means required to reach them. This is essential, as it clearly separates meliorism from wishful thinking. The latter notion would be mere daydreaming about how one wants the world to be. Of course, there is no guarantee that such wishing would result in any changes. One must act to improve oneself and others, and such action is the means to attain such an end. Thus, pragmatists such as Dewey give attention to the positive means needed to maximize the good of our experience and to minimize the harmful aspects. This also renders pragmatist approaches to meliorism and ethics compatible with social science, specifically those projects that seek controlled ways to intervene and measurably improve the quality of human life.[4] The basic point is that means must be attended to in some fashion. For my current project, this involves paying attention to how one changes orientations toward activity as much as one attends to what orientation ought to be fostered. I will discuss the idea of means later in this chapter.

Third, an important part to considering means is attending to *what* one wants to change, and *how* one plans to affect that change. These are what I refer to as one's "unit of analysis" and "vector of change." The former is one's target—what exactly is one trying to improve? Is it the community or each individual? Is it one's own self? What part specifically? I have been arguing for the importance of the subjective, individually located unit of analysis of one's orientation, and I will more explicitly examine this unit of analysis in the next section. Melioristic projects, however, must pay attention to where their change will be located. Related to this will be the method of affecting such change. Is the vector of change individualized, or something at the group level (viz., a particular way of organizing people)? Choices here will impact your version of meliorism in important ways, so attention must be paid to what you want to change and how you want to change it. In the remainder of this chapter, I will highlight the fact that orientation, while formed and influenced by group membership and culture, is in an important sense individually located (as a habit), and that individualized methods of rethinking activity can change such an orientation.

If meliorism is reconstructive and entails a focus on ends, means, and the specifics of such change, I must give a general account of the sort of melioristic project I see as stemming from Dewey's account of aesthetic and moral activity. A central feature to such an account is experience and how it is shaped by habits that guide the individual's engagement with the world. Habit, character, consequences, and values are all linked to experience at either the individual or collective level. Humans face their environment with certain ways of acting and responding (viz., habits), and this adds up to what is called their character. This in turn is shaped and changed by the environment (both social and natural). What Dewey adds to such a reading, however, is the dialectical point that character can be changed by altering the environmental conditions. An important example of this is education—in *Democracy and Education*, Dewey clearly states that "we never educate directly, but indirectly by means of the environment. Whether we permit chance environments to do the work, or whether we design environments for the purpose makes a great difference" (23). Thus, educators create an environment that in turn creates certain sorts of people with certain habits. As we have seen, this is also a point that holds for the purposive creation of art objects.

What is interesting about Dewey is that he describes ways of thinking about and responding to the world as habitual. Humans not only have habitual ways of reacting to oncoming buses, say, they also possess engrained patterns of how to approach solving problems, how to evaluate paintings, and so on. In *Human Nature and Conduct,* Dewey goes as far as to equate mind with habits, and notes that it is habit that determines the boundaries, flexibility, and ways of thinking and perceiving (70). By reconstructing these habits in an intelligent fashion, one reconstructs one's character and the very way that one approaches and sees the world of people, needs, and action possibilities. This is the basis of what I call "orientational meliorism," which takes its lead from Dewey's pragmatism.

The particular habits I am concerned with are those that are of and related to what we can usefully call the mental—namely, those related to the *ways we think* about the world (including objects and individuals, environments and roles, etc.) and the *ways of action* that are opened up as a result. Dewey discusses such habits in a variety of places, but he is particularly clear in *The Public and Its Problems* (1927): "Faculties of effectual observation, reflection and desire are habits acquired under the influence of the culture and institutions of society, not ready made inherent powers" (334). Notice that habit applies not only to specific actions or reactions (one commonly accepted analysis of habit), but is also related to general ways of discharging emotion, desire, problem solving, and so on. These are general, wide ways of engaging the world, or of turning away from parts of it that are deemphasized. While these habits are still embodied insofar as they are located in a physical organism, they do differ in important ways from habits such as those of posture and of one's golf swing. Thus, I heuristically label these as "mental habits" to distinguish them from those other sorts of habits, all the while acknowledging that the former do involve embodiment in an important sense. In that same chapter of *The Public and Its Problems,* Dewey notes that habits per se are not opposed to the mental, but instead that mental operations are habitually directed: "Habit does not preclude the use of thought, but it determines the channels within which it operates. Thinking is secreted in the interstices of habits. The sailor, miner, fisherman and farmer think, but their thoughts fall within the framework of accustomed occupations and relationships. . . . Thinking itself becomes habitual along certain lines" (335).

Notice that such individuals as the sailor and the farmer have physical habits established to accomplish certain skilled tasks on the deck or in the field. Dewey's claim here is subtly but importantly different than this point, however—both individuals have different habitual ways of approaching tasks, goals, problem solving, and so forth. This is the sort of general habit that affects a human's engagement with the world and with others, and this is what I capture in my concept of orientation.

In broad terms, orientation can be said to be a general mental habit that addresses (1) what is in the world (call this the ontological aspect of orientation) and (2) what is of value in the world (call this the axiological aspect). These two aspects of orientation join together to produce another part to orientation—(3) recommended paths of action, including physical and mental ways of interacting with the environment (call this the actional aspect). Thus, one's orientation tells one what is in the world, what value it has, and, consequently, how one is to act in this world. One's orientation concerns what constitutes the world and the self, as well as the value of the parts of the world or the self. Thus, one who approaches the world as a hostile, unfriendly place has a certain orientation toward the world, and thereby has certain action and belief strategies foregrounded (perhaps a protective egoism). Such orientations are not necessarily consciously held and noticed at all times; as habitual ways of thinking (like habits of the body) they often operate without conscious acknowledgement.

As a habit, one's orientation is formed by past activity and shapes future activity. It is deep seated, but like all habits, orientation is not immune to reconstruction and rehabituation. At some point, however, habits can conflict or cause problems, and it is here that a person (or others) may wish to change these general habits of thought that comprise one's orientation. The following Deweyan connection is twofold—first, certain orientations that a subject can take may be better than others in terms of their adaptive value to the environment (including social environments) and their value in terms of the quality of a subject's experience, and second, individuals can work to improve their experience by changing their orientations toward the world, self, and others. Thus, orientational meliorism addresses the use of one's mental orientation toward self and world (both of which imply and foreground certain action strategies) to improve the quality of one's lived experience.[5] The altering of one's orientation (viz., the vector of change) can have its locus in the activity of others (as in education), or can occur through one's own initiative. While social means are possible, I will focus the later sections of this chapter on the second path (via one's own initiative), as this highlights an important strategy of self-cultivation that lies undeveloped in Dewey—that of individuals using mental and somatic means to transform their orientation toward the world in order to improve their experience. It can also occur through cognitive means, or through somatic means that affect one's way of seeing and experiencing the world. The former is what I call "mental/cognitive" means of orientational meliorism, and the later can be dubbed "mental/somatic" means of changing one's orientation. The former is exemplified by cognitive therapies for depression, say, whereas the latter would be exemplified by traditions of meditation or bodywork. Regardless of the means of change, one must engage the fundamental question of the general program of orientational meliorism—what sort of orientation ought we to take, and how can we cultivate such an orientation? To start this investigation, we return to the contested but important topic of progressive adjustment to one's present situation, or as we will now call it, growth.

Growth Revisited

The sort of orientation that answers our question of the artful life will be the sort of orientation that is conducive to growth. This was the argument in chapter 4 of this book, albeit couched in the terminology of Dewey's "progressive adjustment." Here I will approach the topic of growth from a different angle—that of addressing the criticisms of one of Dewey's recent critics. What I hope to establish is the sort of specific program of orientational meliorism that a Deweyan take on moral cultivation and aesthetic experience would advocate. Like the previous chapters, the main point will be some way of going about activity, a specific orientation to activity. The melioristic project will then focus on ways to bring about this sort of orientation such that more of our activities and experiences can have the unity and absorption characteristic of the aesthetic. This is what would render our purposive and meaningful activities as artful or aesthetic. To motivate my discussion of growth and its connection to the mental orientations or habits that one brings to activity, I start with a critique given by John Lachs in "Stoic Pragmatism" of the Deweyan account of growth. What I will argue, after detailing Lachs's arguments, is that he is close to diagnosing the really problematic point in regard to growth—that growth typically does not occur in cases where experience is fractured, mechanical, and generally nonaesthetic. What causes this sort of state? Is it something inherent in Dewey's notion of growth? I will argue it is inherent only in one way orienting one's self toward activity and its ends. Given another orientation, activity can be experienced as aesthetic and artfully done.

John Lachs criticizes Dewey's notion of growth in a thorough, but sympathetic fashion. His argument proceeds in three steps, and the first step addresses the incorporation of limitation within pragmatism. In Lachs's words, "intelligent pragmatists have to be stoics from time to time" (96). What it means to be a stoic in this usage of the term is to be ready to replace the drive toward growth with acceptance. Lachs's point is that growth is always in relation to some situation, and often the objective features of that situation confound further growth. In such cases, "seeking growth is unintelligent; we are better advised to accept what cannot be changed and thereby reduce frustration and pain" (96). He gives the example of quadriplegics who "undergo a period of growth after their accidents. . . . But soon, they master their meager repertoire of actions possible for them and, at least in that important respect, acceptance of limits must take the place of trying to do more" (97). This is a case, according to Lachs, where "continued attempts at amelioration [are] futile and thus irrational" (97). The same sort of recognition applies when we consider human abilities—unaided flight is not a possibility, but we get around this acknowledged barrier through technology. Lachs seems to think that many of these limits push us toward some larger sense of acceptance, though—an acceptance of limits that can't be overcome with technology. This is especially true in regard to human mortality, the uniqueness of youth, and the physical forces of objects (103). We must learn to see when meliorative action is possible, and when acceptance is the better course of affairs. In certain circumstances, growth is impossible or limited by the effects of certain givens, be it facts about the situation, human nature, and so on. Lachs notes Dewey's failure to address this sort of situation, noting that he "says relatively little about circumstances in which growth is impossible and must therefore be supplanted by a less activist value" (98).

This initial point of Lachs's argument leads him to conclude that an intelligent pragmatism will incorporate stoic surrender to some extent. The harm in the traditional pragmatist urge to ameliorate is that it "fails to guard against crushing disappointment. The probability of frustration and consequent disenchantment is directly proportional to the immensity of our expectations; the more we want to accomplish, the greater the chance that we will fail." By incorporating the stoic emphasis on acceptance, "stoic pragmatists" live a more efficacious and enjoyable life as they "tend to scale down their hopes even as they increase their efforts to make life better." Thus, we have acceptance on two levels—first, in the notion of growth itself (the acceptance of limits), and second, at a larger level of orientation toward action in general ("knowing how far to push and when to hang it up") (105). It seems that an orientation that fails to appropriately acknowledge limitation leads us to live less happy or effective lives. This is the (appropriately pragmatist) bottom line to Lachs's stoic pragmatism—it avoids the orientation that focuses too much on what we think we can do and that causes us to become "fixated on an activity" or life itself.

I want to offer another diagnosis of what is wrong with the orientation that Lachs identifies as so harmful. I also want to do this by using resources within Deweyan pragmatism, as this will highlight a side or aspect to Deweyan lines of thinking that take him farther from readings that focus on improving life through solely focusing on objective features of the situation. I'll explain such a version by first considering if growth really is faced with the limits and problems that Lachs identifies. I think Lachs's notion of growth and of inherent limits to growth only works when one builds into it some sort of efficiency in changing objective conditions.

For instance, the example of the quadriplegic seems to presuppose physical challenges that must be met solely by the bodily activity of the paralyzed agent. Why must we assume this, especially in light of the emphasis on subjective factors defended in previous chapters? If we take Dewey's notion of growth, in its best sense, to imply some sort of meaningful engagement with the present (funded by past meanings, habits, and expectations of future states) that sets up future states of similar equilibrium between the organism and environment, then I don't see how growth will be limited in such a fashion. The paralyzed individual can meet the challenges of the environment through enabling the agency of others, through technology that his or her society invested in, and so forth. I do not think growth is limited—just that agent's physical range of activity. It does seem as if such individuals are able to orient themselves toward their injury and their lives (assisted by others) in a way that is useful (in terms of the quality of their lived experience) or in a way that is less than useful (viz., more conducive to frustration and suffering). How they view the assistance of others, how they go about sustaining care relationships, and how they reorient the goals of their new activities are a matter of growing to meet the challenges of environments, especially the ones they will now be faced with. Physical activity is limited, but I would argue that growth isn't.[6]

At this point, I would like to offer a characterization of growth that addresses some of these issues that I have broached in relation to Lachs's analysis. Growth, on my Deweyan account, involves subjective and objective (viz., environmental) factors. Like my earlier analysis of progressive adjustment, growth can be seen as denoting a state of equilibrium reached between the needs of the organism (the subject) and the resources/obstacles resident in the environment. In *Art as Experience,* Dewey describes this sort of equilibrium as change that sets up future reaching of equilibriums. Growth is said to be organization to change, specifically that sort of ordering that completes a previous organism-environment interaction and thereby sets up future successful interactions. Such an account may tempt one to lean toward the sort of reading Lachs gives of Dewey on growth—an analysis that fixates on the successful achievement of ends or goals related to a creature's needs (desires) in light of a resistant environment. The focus here, in other words, is on the objective results produced (say, actually procuring and eating the food needed to survive).

This is not incorrect, but it is misleading in its emphasis. If one looks at the sort of account Dewey gives of growth in *Art as Experience,* one sees something peculiar. In a passage in which Dewey discusses growth as organization in change, he states that "time as organization in change is growth, and growth signifies that a varied series of change enters upon intervals of pause and rest; of completions that become the initial points of new processes of development. Like the soil, mind is fertilized while it lies fallow, until a new burst of bloom ensues" (29). What is curious about this way of putting things is the absence of emphasis on the *physical* interactions with the world. Dewey draws one's attention here not so much to the (albeit important) part of the organism-environment interaction that involves the achieving of goals in relation to needs of the organism, but instead to the mind or mental disposition that occurs during and after periods of growth. Thus, an important part to growth is the mental direction and meaning that is given to certain parts of the environment, as well as certain ways of interacting with that environment. An account of growth that starts from some notion of successful ways of such interaction (physical activity such as procuring food or throwing a baseball) has it wrong on Deweyan grounds. When one is discussing human growth, the proper place to start is not at the physical interaction between the organism and the environment, but instead at the sort of mental habits that are a response to the needs of the subject and the forces of the environment. Of course, such mental habits or dispositions are also a way of changing or dealing with those needs and that environment. Growth involves possessing and creating the right sort of mental dispositions or habits.[7] What makes these the right ones to possess?

To answer this question concerning growth, we turn to what may seem an unusual resource—Dewey's writings on religion. What I would like to emphasize is that the right mental dispositions—dispositions that include how we act and react, value and think about our environment—can be conceived of as dealing with the way we *orient* ourselves toward some challenge or part of the objective situation at hand. As Dewey puts it in *A Common Faith*, our adjustment or orientation to the world can be a combination of accommodation of the self to environmental realities *and* an adaptation of the environment to the desires of the self (12).[8] Dewey discusses accommodation, pointing out that "the two main traits of this attitude, which I should like to call accommodation, are that it affects particular modes of conduct, not the entire self, and that the process is mainly passive" (12). Thus, if a group of humans live in a harsh environment, certain things may not be possible or practical (such as building structures out of a certain material). What occurs in this process is a changing or subduing of an individual's hopes in light of the environmental realities, and they thereby accommodate themselves to this check on external action in that environment. The other side to growth, adaptation, occurs when "we modify conditions so that they will be accommodated to our wants and purposes" (ibid.). Here the individual or group changes the environment so that it more fully meets their needs or wants.

This latter element (adaptation) is the notion of growth that Lachs and others seem to attribute to Dewey. What must be pointed out, of course, is that it is only *half* of what Dewey means by adjustment to an environment. What seems to be more accurate is to say that adjustment to the environment (or growth in some environment) entails a rich and general combination of these two strategies. In some cases, more of one or the other strategy would work best; in other cases, a more or less equal combination of both would be the most effective way an individual (or a group) could react to a given situation. Dewey is far from relying solely on one side of this split, and both factors highlight the point I want to make about growth—that it deals with the individual or group effectively orienting themselves toward the environment at some general level more than it deals with certain ranges of action/reaction (physical responses or challenging the givens of nature, say). An individual in a harsh desert environment may not be able to do certain things short of extraordinary effort (produce certain vegetables), but growth is not thereby limited. Instead, growth occurs when the individual takes an orientation toward her situation and possible actions that holds the correct measure of adapting the environment to the self and accommodating the self to the environment such that her experience is enriched now and in future situations. In the desert environment, there may be more accommodating than in resource rich environments, but the point is still the same—holding the right orientation towards one's environment and what can be done is crucial to states of experience being those of growth.

The correctness or rightness of the orientation in question is simple—what best conduces to a richness of experience in that present situation as well as in future presents. Physical activity is included, but it does not exhaust all of growth—indeed one can think of a variety of ways of accommodating to and adapting environments that would meet basic and advanced needs of individuals and groups. What I am interested in analyzing is what Dewey believes is the general orientation toward activity that *best* results in growth of a certain quality. This quality that I refer to has to do with the subjective experience of the live creature (viz., the human), and connects to the problem that Lachs describes as "crushing disappointment" and "frustration and consequent disenchantment" related to our expectations not being fulfilled in our interactions with the physical world.[9] What exactly is wrong with such experiences? In other words, why are such crushing disappointments not instances of growth? Instead of arguing that this is due merely to a failure of action, I want to argue that the negative quality of such human-environment interactions is due to a certain orientation that the agents in question donned.

Orientation and Activity in the Face of Desire

In this section, I want to explore what exactly is wrong with the orientation noted above—the orientation that individuals take to experience that leads to the bruising defeats and painful quality of failed activities that Lachs draws upon in his critique of the notion of growth. This orientation is problematic insofar as it represents and encourages a fragmenting of the agent's attention, as well as opposing his or her full engagement and attention to the environment and demands of the present situation. The problem with incorrect readings of growth are the same as misleading accounts of aesthetic experience—both notions really involve a subjective orientation that shapes an agent's attention and engages him or her to the activity of the present in an enlivened fashion.

If growth doesn't have inherent limits, why can there be varying levels of disappointment at failed projects? In other words, why can agents set themselves up for bigger disappointments and suffering by the way they orient themselves to the situation and their role in it? Although Lachs is right that certain obstacles may pose challenges to certain activities, I think a different answer can be given from one rooted in certain natural limits in nature and in ourselves. I want to argue that another answer can be drawn from one's orientation toward desire. More specifically, the orientation that harms the pleasure and effectiveness of present action is that of *attachment* to and *fixation* on the (remote) objects of one's desire. Of course, Dewey does not judge desire to be a bad thing in general. I need to explain how it becomes harmful in such a Deweyan account. It is fairly noncontroversial, however, how Dewey analyzes desire in such works as *Human Nature and Conduct*. Desire is said to start with an obstacle to impulse, at which point a desire for some object or state becomes foregrounded to the agent. This then focuses the agent's attention on that object, which "is (or taken to be) the key to the situation. If we can attain it, lay hold of it, the trick is turned" (172–73). The role of intelligence, according to Dewey, is then to make sure impulse is checked appropriately such that the greatest possible mix of desires can be satisfied.

What I want to argue is that this inherent focusing of attention that desire entails is what can get out of control (thus resulting in attachment to the objects of desire), and thereby cause the harms that Lachs discusses as connected to a pragmatist view of activity. Desire pushes us to actualize something that is not present and it focuses our attention on that which is not present. In some cases, this is useful. Dewey holds a high regard for ends-in-view, or guideposts for directing present action in the here and now of the concrete situation. What is harmful to growth and to the qualitative, aesthetic feel of experience, however, is when certain orientations toward the objects of desire become instantiated. For instance, the example of building a house is given as a perfect case in which the object of desire (a completed house) can be used to guide activity effectively in the present. In this case, the object desired guides activity in the present (following the plans to build the house one wants). What is important to note, however, is that the focus of attention is on the present situation (the materials and lot in front of the builders), and only secondarily on the object of desire. The end-in-view informs *present* activity, the "only one really under control" (184). A harmful way to experience the building of the house would be to focus too much on the end—the finished house as investment, status symbol, much needed necessity, etc.—and not give enough attention to what one is actually living through in the present (the activity of building). That would be a case of the general orientation toward objects of desire that Dewey deplores—he notes that "as things are, men so habitually scamp present action in behalf of future 'ends'. . . . But everywhere the good, the fulfillment, the meaning of activity, resides in a present made possible by judging existing conditions in their connections" (184–85). The orientation that attaches attention and exclusive value to the object of desire in its remoteness is what ought to be resisted.

Instead of fostering the sort of consummatory, fulfilling, and aesthetic experiences that Dewey describes in *Art as Experience,* such habits of action in the face of an environment and a subject's desires separate the activity from the product, and places the value in the latter. Dewey notes this point in *Human Nature and Conduct* shortly after the house example, claiming that "the moment production is separated from immediate satisfaction, it becomes 'labor,' drudgery, a task reluctantly performed" (186). This occurs when one fixates so on the *object* of desire that one fails to attend and adapt to the present situation. Not only is the present situation mishandled because of this diversion of attention, but it also becomes a painful mere means through which the individual must trudge to achieve that remote goal that will bring satisfaction. Needless to say, when that future goal (or state) is reached, the individual will probably postulate, through the influence of this orientation of attachment to the object of desire, another remote goal that now must be obtained. So the struggle goes on.

What is important to note is that in this discussion, Dewey connects the notion of a general orientation toward how one views activity to the idea of growth. Describing the harms of modern economic life, he claims that "most workers find no replenishment, no renewal and *growth of mind,* no fulfillment in work. They labor to get mere means of later satisfaction" (186, italics added). Growth in the case of work has less to do with the physical limits and activities undergone, and more with the mental orientation the worker takes (or is encouraged to take by social forces). This is the harmful orientation of attachment to the objects of desire, and attachment that practically results in the harming of present experience by constantly fixating an agent's attention on that which is not present. This will consequently hinder growth and adaptation in future instances as well.

The same situations and same activities can have a different connection to growth, depending on the mindset that the agent takes to them. For instance, in *Art as Experience*, Dewey notes mechanization in habitual orientation toward activity with another case that I've previously mentioned: "One student studies to pass an examination, to get promotion. To another, the means, the activity of learning, is completely one with what results from it. The consequence, instruction, illumination, is one with the process" (201). Both students do the same activity, but the second *experiences* the goal or object of desire as part of the process of education, not as a mere means to be suffered through.

The harm in pragmatism's view of progress, I would submit, is not so much in the ignoring of inherent limits to growth, but is instead resident in how attached and fixated we are to the nonpresent goals of our activity. Too much attachment and the present literally gets glossed over. Of course, the rub is this—happiness always occupies a present, and taking the habit of focusing on what is not present will forever put that which we think will satisfy us one step beyond our reach. Dewey notes just this point in *Human Nature and Conduct*, as well as its connection to mental orientation: "We have insisted that happiness, reasonableness, virtue, perfecting, are on the contrary parts of the present significance of present action. Memory of the past, observation of the present, foresight of the future are indispensable. But they are indispensable *to* a present liberation, an enriching growth of action. Happiness is fundamental in morals only because happiness is not something to be sought for, but is something now attained, even in the midst of pain and trouble, whenever recognition of our ties with nature and with fellowmen releases and informs our action" (182). Thus, our capabilities for growth and apt adjustment to the situation primarily come down to the mental habits toward action that we possess. These make the difference between pleasurable activity and drudgery, mechanized mere means and consummatory experience, growth and stagnation. In other words, these mental habits are central to determining if one's life is to be artful or not.

Before I turn to what orientation Deweyan pragmatism would offer as the alternative to this problematic attachment to the objects of desire, it would be helpful to look again at the larger goal Dewey is pursuing. In *A Common Faith,* Dewey discusses the sense of adjustment that he finds as captured by religious faith—that sense in which it deals with changes that are general and deep seated in the ways we think of and act on the world. In an important passage, he notes that such adjustments, or orientations as I have been calling them, affect "a composing and harmonizing of the various elements of our being such that, in spite of changes in the special conditions that surround us, these conditions are also arranged, settled, in relation to us. This attitude includes a note of submission. But it is voluntary, not externally imposed; and as voluntary it is something more than a mere Stoical resolution to endure unperturbed throughout the buffetings of fortune. It is more outgoing, more ready and glad, than the latter attitude, and it is more active than the former" (12–13). Although Dewey is talking about the religious and its effects on some types of individuals, I believe that his point is the same one that he made in *Art as Experience* when he describes growth and equilibrium as an "inner harmony" that is "attained only when, by some means, terms are made with the environment" (23). What he is getting at is the rich, deep-seated ways of seeing and approaching the environment *and* our subjective desires that are enshrined in our orientation.

Certain sorts of orientations see or conceive of the environment and our desires in ways that reduce the quality, meaning, and vitality of experience; these are not instances of growth, and a ready example of such an orientation has been given in this section concerning the attachment of a subject to the objects of desire. In his religious writings, Dewey argues for an orientation that involves an imaginative re-visioning of the human-nature relationship.[10] I'd like to extract a similar solution to the riddles of growth and artful living through a reorientation of the subject, but in regard to the particular problem of valuing ends and the objects of desires in a harmful manner. The orientation that I would offer as a Deweyan solution to the problem would involve imagination as it entails a creative refashioning of the materials of experience and activity, as well as a revision of how one values certain parts to this equation (viz., the objects of one's desires). Instead of taking the path of the religious here, however, I will seek this deep-seated and harmonizing orientation that combines Dewey's notions of accommodation and adaptation in his discussions concerning work and play.

The power of the notion of orientation that I have been developing is that it, like Dewey's discussion of adjustment, includes accommodation (or acceptance) and adaptation. It also involves an imaginative aspect insofar as it deals with *how* the world is portrayed, valued, and acted upon differently by different agents. How can one address the orientation that reduces activity to nonaesthetic drudgery by its overemphasis on the objects of desire? While one may offer a remedy that involves changing the physical conditions (say, removing the objects of any particular desire), this would not seem to be a deep-seated change as it would not apply to many of the situations in which one has (different) particular desires. One may also advocate giving up desire in general; this, however, would be problematic on a Deweyan account, as desires are a large element to what motivates thought and action in the first place. Indeed, it is hard to conceive of activity at all without some reference to states of affairs that are desired or undesired, valued or devalued. The solution I want to offer is a mental/cognitive means of changing one's orientation. It will involve the imaginative refocusing of one's attention from the objects of desire and remote ends to the activity itself. In contrast to solutions such as Lachs's "stoic pragmatism" and its scaling down of hopes to make life "better,"[11] the solution I will describe will address the problem through the imaginative reorientation of the focus of an agent's attention.

Orientation and the Re-visioning of Activity

The orientation that I believe is available and promoted in Dewey's work on growth and moral activity is one that prizes an individual's attention to the present, concrete situation in all of its richness. This is diametrically opposed to the focus on the remote objects of desire noted above that characterizes so much of current ways of thinking of activity, be it vocational or moral. Dewey believed that such habits of thought, whether it involves a focus on a remote moral law or on a remote end to the work activity (viz., a paycheck), harm experience. The orientation one ought to adopt, in terms of being more conducive to that quality of experience that I have previously noted as growth and as aesthetic, is one of rapt attentiveness and absorption in the present situation. In this section, I will do the following. First, I will flesh out this sort of orientation from Dewey's discussion of work and play. This will serve as a complement to the analysis of the same sort of orientation involved in the experience of art noted in earlier chapters, one that does not separate means and ends, situation and value, and so on. Second, I will discuss how such an orientation meets Dewey's concerns regarding the distracting of attention and effort from one's present situation, while not failing to capture the richness of moral activity. Finally, I will offer some mental/cognitive strategies as to how one can instantiate such an orientation in one's everyday life.

How is one to imaginatively refocus and re-vision one's experience and its relationship to the objects of desire? One important discussion of this topic that is so crucial to Dewey's thought (including his ethics and aesthetics) occurs in an unlikely place—his reading of how one conceptualizes work and play in education. Dewey's discussion of play and work touches on a vital point—namely, that it matters how we orient ourselves to activity and its ends or goals. Of course, as in many things Dewey analyzes, there are two sorts of distinctions that can be made—one that Dewey advocates based upon its meliorative value, and one that society tends to indoctrinate into its members (at the expense of the quality of their experience). The latter sort of distinction between play and work puts the stress on work as distinguished by its focus on some remote object—namely, that which is the product of some process. Play is seen as the opposite sort of activity, one that is spontaneous and merely momentary. Play may be valued as an activity, but it is literally worthless if the criterion of worth is seen as external to the activity itself (its products and their value to life). Work, on the other hand, is said to be undertaken for the sake of its products, while play is for its own sake.[12]

Such a way of orienting one's self toward activities called "work" is to render them as drudgery. This is how Dewey describes such activity and its quality in *How We Think* (1933), and, I would argue, such a manner of description mirrors his worries over the harmful way to orient one's self to the objects of desire in general. The key to an activity being drudgery (and nonaesthetic) is that it focuses attention on the object of desire qua remote end to activity, and thereby alters the value (and attention) given to the means: "*exclusive* interest in a result alters work to drudgery. For by drudgery is meant those activities in which the interest in the outcome does not suffuse the process of getting the result. Whenever a piece of work becomes drudgery, the process of doing loses all value for the doer; he cares solely for what is to be had at the end of it. The work itself, the putting forth of energy, is hateful; it is just a necessary evil, since without it some important end would be missed" (346–47). Thus, conceiving of work and play as separate kinds of activity with different values placed on ends and means is not good for work, as it reduces it to drudgery, or for play, since it reduces it to what Dewey calls aimless "fooling" (346). Dewey makes a similar point in other places as well—the standard, externalist reading of work activity places its value outside of the activity and thus tends to make individuals dread the lived experience that this activity represents.[13] Drudgery is simply characterized by this external locus of value, which consequently focuses one's attention outside of the current activity and toward the remote object of desire.

If one looks to Dewey's corrective reading of this harmful conceptualization of work and play, one can find the resources to build the sort of orientation that one ought to take to activity. Throughout this book, I have been arguing that the key to growth and aesthetic experience lies more in the mental habits we take toward activity than in any given set of physical actions we may undertake; this sort of approach also lies at the base of Dewey's take on play. What one is to fix is how one sees play and work, which consequently will lead to a way to reimagine the relationships among agents, their activities, and their desires.

We start this account with Dewey's preferred take on play. While many think of play as a sort of activity, Dewey notes that the important part to what we call play is its attitude—what he describes in *How We Think* as an "attitude of mind." This attitude is one that orients the individual toward the activity at hand, and one that uses objects merely as "vehicles of suggestion" or as bearers of meaning merely at the behest of the individual (285). Thus, children "play house" and assign meanings to rocks, bushes, and other objects that are not literally connected to household activities. Here, the interest is not so much on the objects in their particular relationships to one another and to the goals of activity, but instead is focused on continuing the activity itself. Where work differs from this attitude of playfulness is not in terms of its focus of interest on something that is not related to that activity, but instead lies in how it conceives of the present activity and its materials.

Dewey describes this difference in a passage from *How We Think*: "For work (as a mental attitude, not as mere external performance) *means interest in the adequate embodiment of a meaning* (a suggestion, purpose, aim) *in objective form through the use of appropriate materials and appliances*. Such an attitude takes advantage of the meanings aroused and built up in free play, *but controls their development by seeing to it that they are applied to things in ways consistent with the observable structure of the things themselves*" (286). Thus, the attitude or orientation enshrined in those activities that truly deserve the name of work involves the embodiment of meaning in some object or expression. This is the focus of activity, and the end-in-view of the present activity is what gives each part of its means value and a role in building toward some sort of consummation. In instances of skilled work, this would be the production of a product in and through a process of skilled making. In the case of argument, this would be the focus on argument and counterargument with attention to their relationships and their weaknesses (particularly important in lines of work such as that of a trial lawyer).[14] In all such cases, the attitude of work does not focus attention away from the resources of the present; like play, it involves meanings, but it tethers these meanings to aspects of the objective situation in ways that can lead toward some sort of consummation or new state of affairs.

Is this the final sort of orientation that one ought to take toward activity to curb the extreme focus on desire that our ordinary orientation toward work brings with it? Dewey's answer is "no" for a very interesting reason. Dewey thinks that play and those that typically engage in it—children—have something important to teach us about work. In the notes taken during Dewey's lectures in China from around 1920, Dewey is observed to make this sort of point—"from a child's point of view, there is no sharp line of demarcation between play and work. We are all familiar with situations in which children get fun out of such tasks as cooking and cleaning which adults tend to regard as drudgery. This is worth remembering."[15] Like the points he makes in *Art as Experience,* the orientation that the subject takes toward work activity makes a difference. What he is pointing out here, however, is that children can provide a clear example of the possibility of combining the attitudes of work and play in a useful synthesis in their own activity.

What Dewey identifies as the ideal sort of orientation combines the attitude of playfulness and its focus on the continuation of activity and its meaning with the object-focusing feature of the work attitude. He argues in an important passage from *How We Think* that

> to be playful and serious at the same time is possible, and it defines the ideal mental condition. Absence of dogmatism and prejudice, presence of intellectual curiosity and flexibility, are manifest in the free play of the mind upon a topic. To give the mind this free play is not to encourage toying with a subject, but is to be interested in the unfolding of the subject on its own account, apart from its subservience to a preconceived belief or habitual aim. Mental play is open-mindedness, faith in the power of thought to preserve its own integrity without external supports and arbitrary restrictions. Hence free mental play involves seriousness, the earnest following of the development of subject-matter. It is incompatible with carelessness or flippancy, for it exacts accurate noting of every result reached in order that every conclusion may be put to further use. (347)

Thus, the ideal orientation is one that focuses on the present—both in terms of the immediate responsiveness noted in chapter 4 and the open-minded critical attitude noted in chapter 5. One is absorbed in and open to the present. The use of the word "present" here indicates the *rich* present—it covers what is and what could be (based upon the resources of the actual), what is resident in the mind and what relates to the objects of manipulation and expression in the situation, and what is here present and to what it inclines in a consummatory sense. What this enshrines is a recognition that the work attitude too often falls prey to the sort of one-sided and remote interest in the objects of desire, and that this must be tempered by the open-mindedness and imaginative re-visioning made possible by a playful engagement with the materials of activity.

This ideal mental condition is therefore one that is focused on the material of the present situation, while maintaining a flexibility to new ways of reacting to such material and to the myriad meanings resident in such a situation. It is the striking of a fine balance between routinized habitual response to objective stimuli and the aimless and nonconsummatory flailing in regard to the material offered by some present situation. In terms of Dewey's *Art as Experience,* it is the aesthetic middle ground between aimless and mechanical ways of experiencing activity. Instead of randomness or routine, the individual focuses on the present, and aptly attends to its demands and resources in the richest sense of that term. It is this sort of re-visioning of the goals of activity and the value of present activity that can address the overemphasis on goal achievement that characterizes the "crushing defeat" spoken of by Lachs. Of course, this sort of orientation of attentiveness to the present that I am extracting from Deweyan pragmatism is not a mere focus on the disconnected present (viz., without connection to past and future activities)—although this may avoid some defeats, it certainly would not lead to a long and rich life. Attention to the present means attention to one's desires, one's station, the expectations and projects of others, and the resources and realities of the environment.

Moral activity in the widest sense of that term is activity that attends to all these matters in the right amount and without distortion that would prove harmful for further growth (such as that harmful alignment of attention and focus that characterizes a criminal).[16] This sort of reading of the meaning of present experience (viz., its possession of projected ends and expectations from one's station and from others) is readily evident in Dewey's moral work. This theme also appears in his reading of play and work: "To live in the present is compatible with condensation of far-reaching meanings in the present. Such enrichment of the present for its own sake is the just heritage of childhood and the best insurer of future growth."[17] This is the sort of orientation that we ought to adopt to be best ready for growth in our lived experience—one that, like the child, is raptly absorbed in the details of the present, but that, like the driven adult, attends to objects with foresight and connection to the projects and desires we wish to consummate in and through experience. This avoids the one-sided focus on desire and its objects that makes the present a continual nonaesthetic drudgery that all too often is then seen as worthless or as a crushing defeat when some part of it (viz., the projected desire) is not achieved in part or in whole. One has projects and goals, duties and outcomes wanted, but most important, one is oriented toward and focused on all of these things *in* and *through* the present—the goals connected to desire as instantiated *in* the present, the expectations as resident *in* the individuals and groups in the present situation, and the object of desire as closely connected to the present activity.

This is the sort of imaginative reconstruction of present activity that I believe grasps what Dewey wanted in his religious and aesthetic works—the rendering of life as "the supreme art." In his early work, Dewey described this artistic approach to life requiring "fineness of touch; skill and thoroughness of workmanship; susceptible response and delicate adjustment to a situation apart from reflective analysis; instinctive perception of the proper harmonies of act and act, of man and man."[18] Life, when done right and with the sort of approach that would best result in that quality of experience called "growth," would be done with this artistry of touch and attention to the very materials that make up our desire and our interactions with others. When done less than desirably, there will be a mishandling of the materials of the present such as that which occurs in action guided by an overattachment to the remote objects of desire.

This connection of artistry and attention to the present is not unique to Dewey's early work or his aesthetics. Indeed, he concludes *How We Think* with his connection of the attitudes of play and work in activity: "When the thought of the end becomes so adequate that it compels translation into the means that embody it, or when attention to means is inspired by recognition of the end they serve, we have the attitude typical of the artist, an attitude that may be displayed in all activities, even though they are not conventionally designated 'arts.'" (348). Activity can be artistic if done with a certain mindset. More important, what is meant by the term "art" is a re-visioning and consequent revaluing of the relation of the present and the future, the process of activity and the products of activity, the means and the ends of activity. Dewey makes much of this in his aesthetics concerning the experience of means and media, and the sort of orientation that I've extracted from his discussion on the attitudes of play and work extends this point.

I will provide some thoughts on how one is to fully instantiate an orientation that strikes at the heart of a harmful attachment to and focus on the objects of desire separated from the means of present activity. In order to cultivate an orientation of attention to the present, one must practice being attentive to the present activity and its materials. One could complain, however, that this is easier said than done. I would like to enunciate three types of practices that can be consciously engaged in to cultivate this sort of orientation. This will by no means be an exhaustive discussion of the mental/cognitive method of orientational meliorism aiming at this attitude of attentiveness, but it will represent a beginning to such an account. Further work is called for to fully test such melioristic means of change. I will take as a typical yet important test of such a specific account of orientational meliorism the case of work or occupational activity. In many cases, work activity is done by individuals to get through the workweek to the blessed weekend or to earn a paycheck that enables them to enjoy what they want to enjoy. Dewey noted the case of work (taken here in terms of an occupational activity) as a truly important one—he claims that the "greatest evil of the present regime is not found in poverty and in the suffering in which it entails, but in the fact that so many persons have callings which make no appeal to them, which are pursued simply for the money reward that accrues."[19] As was the case with his complaints about the lack of aesthetic experience in everyday life, part of the problem (and solution) lies in the objective makeup of society and its economic realities. The important part to the solution, however, seems to be the orientation of the individual—be it in the more perfect society or in the one that we currently possess. For even great occupations and careers can become drudgery with the wrong orientation. Dewey notices this in his discussion of vocation and how to realize the ideal situation in which everyone holds an occupation that enriches themselves as well as society: "For the change [that is needed] is essentially a change in the quality of mental disposition—an educative change."[20]

Dewey thought that by altering the ways of education one can better equip individuals to enjoy their work activities. I believe that such a change can be

(1) self-initiated and (2) directed by one's own conscious effort. This is a point that is not lost on non-Western ways of thinking, and although Dewey often denies the efficacy of direct activity, one must admit that there are grounds to sense the need for intelligent reconstruction of one's habits or dispositions.[21] What I want to sketch here is the sort of self-initiated and directed program that can cultivate the orientation toward work activity that an individual may possess. Of course, such a program does not exclude the assistance or help of others. What I want to illustrate is the sort of mental/ cognitive melioration one could adopt should one sense that one's orientation toward activity and desire is the cause of a degraded quality of experience in one's work activities. How can such an individual go about addressing and improving how they experience and approach work activity? In the terms of my larger project, how could their work activity be made more artful and less nonaesthetic?

First, such an individual could begin to imaginatively re-vision her work activities not as drudgery, but as something that is suffused with the value of a larger goal. One could consciously tie one's activity to the goal of the organization in which one is located. For instance, a religious person could connect the way he or she treats individuals on the job (say, as a telemarketer) with the larger goal of treating all individuals with love and respect as his or her religion commands. Thus, the value of the present would be suffused with the value of the end of this person's reading of the goals of life, as directed by some substantive religious commitment. The focus would not be merely on some remote religious state of bliss or holiness, nor would it be on the drudgery of work keeping one from one's religious practice. Instead, the means of work would be integrally connected to the end-in-view provided by religious belief.

A more secular example is provided by the research of Amy Wrzesniewski and her colleagues. In their study of workers and the happiness they have or lack in light of their jobs, they arrived at the conclusion that meaning and happiness is due more to what I have been calling the orientation of workers toward their work activities than to the objective makeup of those activities themselves.[22] For instance, hospital cleaners who see their job as an integral part to a hospital's mission of healing lives and bodies report greater levels of happiness and job satisfaction than those who merely see their job as cleaning up undesirable messes. Martin Seligman takes this as proof that individuals can recraft or rethink their work activities to make them more meaningful.[23] This is an empirical take on what I have been describing as the Deweyan project of orientational meliorism—the project of making one more attentive and focused on the meaning in the present situation, and less focused on the pullings of remote objects indicated by an attachment to desire. Seligman and others are approaching this same goal through empirical study, but the point is the same—there are methods that one can take to change the orientation one brings to work activity to make it less drudgery and more meaningful, valuable activity. The way that has been suggested by these psychologists is simply what Dewey described as letting the value of the end suffuse the means (activity). In the rubric I have been using, this would entail attending to the activities of the present as integrally connected to some greater project or idea—be it a moral code, religious beliefs, thoughts on how one ought to treat others in one's relationships, and so on.

Another method of meliorating the problematic sort of approach to work that renders it drudgery would be to focus on the personal relationships involved. Deweyan pragmatism recognizes the importance of human relationships to the quality of one's individual experience and progress, and such a factor is not absent from the place of work. Whether one has a socially desirable job (say, as a neurosurgeon) or one that may tend to be seen as drudgery (say, the hospital cleaner), one is enmeshed in relationships with other people. Part of these relationships is the interaction that they entail. Thus, one could go about consciously focusing on creating certain climates or qualities to their interactions with others. The work done by Wrzesniewski and colleagues finds that such a method was at work with some of the individuals they studied; for instance, some hospital cleaners foregrounded this aspect of their jobs and deliberately pursued certain relational behaviors such as talking to patients and kindly showing visitors around the hospital.[24] Thus, they tied the value of their work to the value and quality of the relationships in which they participated, and this consequently affected (for the better) the relational interactions that actually occurred. In the Deweyan reading of orientational meliorism that I have provided, this would be a mental/cognitive method of rethinking and imaginatively altering the meaning of the relationships one is involved in at work, with the overt goal of giving a certain meaning to what otherwise may be seen as an eight-hour shift that one would skip over if one could. This would be a case of one giving a certain sort of attention to the present situation—a focus not on the remote object of *one's* desire, but instead on the needs and interests of those involved in the present interaction (oneself and others). Such activity would possess the quality not of the mechanical or aimless, but of the aesthetic and artful.

A final suggestion for how one is to cultivate and instantiate such an orientation of attentiveness to the rich materials of the present would be to focus on overlooked aspects to the activity. In the case of one's job activities, this would entail an increased and creative attention to the activities that one has previously taken for granted. Dewey notes that humans have an inherent interest in multiplying their acquaintances with things and people, a fact of childhood that often gets repressed in working adults.[25] One could use this aspect of human engagement with the world and further one's engagement with the situations evident in the workplace. Instead of focusing on what one wants *from* the job (say, monetary resources, prestige, etc.), one would consciously direct one's attention to the aspects of experience *in* the job. As previously discussed, this could be attention to and enjoyment in the very details of relational interactions in the line of work. Alternatively, the point here could be deeper. One's job could put one in interesting positions and environments that go unnoticed because one's attention is directed by an attachment to the objects of desire. By consciously focusing on what is present, one may see what one has missed—the managerially overlooked insights of other workers in some lost memo, the beauty of one's field of corn, the feel of the water from the water cooler, or even the comforting buzz of the busy workplace.

Experience and its value does not stop at this sensory level, of course. For instance, Martin Seligman and his colleagues have designed and tested empirical interventions aiming to make one attentive to certain key aspects to one's work experience, such as important events that have gone unnoticed in the past work day. They have also successfully tested and validated ways to actively recraft and revise one's daily work activities in light of attentiveness to personal strengths.[26] The point to take away is that there are ways to cultivate attentiveness to one's embodied presence in the various activities and levels of work. What one is effectively instantiating is a sort of Deweyan mindfulness—an absorbed engagement with the materials of the present, ranging from one's projects as an engineer all the way to the smoothness of an office desk that has seen the palms of untold numbers of employees with their myriad dreams, projects, complaints, and expectations. This can then be seen as yet another way of mental/cognitively directing one's activity with the goal of reorienting one toward the experience that one previously denigrated and overlooked at the behest of desire's direction.

Suffering, Growth, and Meaningful Activity

These suggestions about how one can meliorate work experience may seem too simple to be of use. What if one's job experience is inherently demeaning or unbearable? Could that person create the conditions needed for growth—both in the sense of accommodation and adaptation? If the artful life is one that has a sort of meaningful unity to it, this is a fair challenge. I will meet it with the brief consideration of one powerful example from the twentieth century—that of Viktor Frankl's experience in Europe in the 1940s. This example, while not illustrating all of the aspects of orientational meliorism discussed previously, does illuminate the general project of using mindsets and mental habits to reshape experience into a more meaningful and valuable form.

Viktor Frankl was born in rather inauspicious circumstances in Vienna, Austria in 1905, the second of three children. Vienna, however, was well known as the hometown of two famous psychologists—Sigmund Freud and Alfred Adler. Frankl evinced an interest in psychology and mental health and took it on as his professional calling. He studied at the University of Vienna and earned his medical degree in 1930. He even corresponded with Freud about his work. As the Nazis came to power in the region, his professional position began to slip because he was Jewish. He was eventually put in charge of the only medical facility in the city that served Jews, the Rothschild Hospital. Just before the Americans entered the war against Nazi Germany, Frankl received an invitation to the American Embassy in Vienna. He was eligible for a visa to the United States, which would certainly ensure his safety and the survival of his work on existential psychotherapy he so valued, called "logotherapy." It was clear what the German occupiers wanted to do with local Jews, so no one would have judged his attempt to escape to America. Yet Frankl made a fateful choice—he and his wife chose to remain in Vienna. He knew that his parents could not emigrate and would be in grave danger. He also knew that the important psychiatric and neurological work with which he was charged would be abandoned. Thus, he remained in his hometown and cared for his family and let his American visa lapse.[27]

In 1942, Frankl's luck ran out. He and his family were ordered to transports. Separated, they went their own way on crowded trains, carrying luggage that contained their prized possessions. Frankl did not know of his destination until he and other Jewish prisoners saw the sign "Auschwitz" from a small window in their crowded train compartment. Even at that time, Auschwitz was well known and feared for its crematoriums and gas chambers. Upon arrival, Frankl's every possession was taken away from him—even a completed manuscript on logotherapy that he hoped to publish was confiscated. He would never see any of these possessions again.

After this initial processing, Frankl and his fellow captives were stripped of every last bit of humanity. Their clothes and possessions were taken, their bodies shaved, their names replaced with administrative numbers. The physical surroundings Frankl found himself in while at Auschwitz and three other concentration camps were equally atrocious. The sleeping accommodations were crowded, unheated, almost a special kind of torture. Multiple prisoners had to find a way to sleep on a bench that wasn't big enough for even one person. Often, sanitation and water were cut off by freezing pipes. Yet life indoors was not the extent of camp existence. Frankl recounts how he and his fellow prisoners were made to assemble at dawn in the freezing winter, dressed insufficiently in tattered clothes. Food was scarce and individuals survived on small portions of bread and watery soup. They had to work long, brutal days at pointless tasks (such as digging trenches in the frozen ground) in the Nazi effort to work prisoners to death. Once people were unable or unwilling to report for their day's work, the battle was over for them. They were then sent to so-called special camps, but everyone knew that meant the gas chamber or crematorium. Either way, the message inculcated into the prisoners was that their time was limited. They were the walking dead, a fact that was reinforced by their own skeletal frames.

The concentration camps of 1945 were clearly a place without hope. The objective conditions were horrible. Escaping such conditions seemed impossible, and the most one could do to improve one's lot was to "run into the wires," or commit suicide by touching the electrified fence surrounding the camp. Yet Frankl began to notice that humanity in such extreme circumstances both floundered *and* flourished. Of particular interest was the fact that certain individuals did quite well, whereas others sought refuge in the electrified wire or in a slow death by starvation. The prisoners who used their cigarette coupons (given as payment by the Nazis) instead of trading them for soup portions had given up on the most basic need, namely, nutrition. In the language of this chapter, the prisoners that *grew* or successfully *adjusted* to their environment were those that adjusted their orientation toward camp life. In Frankl's words, "the intensification of inner life helped the prisoner find a refuge from the emptiness, desolation, and spiritual poverty of his existence" (39). In some instances, imaginative recollections of the past and of potential futures gave Frankl the meaning and power to survive in *this* awful present situation. The thought of seeing his wife again, opening his apartment door, and so on gave him a strong motivation to see his present ordeal through. The present situation, as full of suffering as it was, had to be met by Frankl's attention and effort. For instance, he recounts how he and other prisoners began to witness the beauty of sunsets and nature, even if it was from the grounds of their imprisonment.

In some cases, individuals "escaped" using their imagination into memories of the past. But this was not the only or the best way to cope with the horrors of camp life. Frankl notes:

> We have already spoken of the tendency there was to look into the past, to help make the present, with all its horrors, less real. But in robbing the present of its reality there lay a certain danger. It became easy to overlook the opportunities to make something positive of camp life, opportunities which really did exist. . . . Instead of taking the camp's difficulties as a test of their inner strength, they did not take their life seriously and despised it as something of no consequence. They preferred to close their eyes and to live in the past. Life for such people became meaningless. (71–72)

Frankl saw the camp and its suffering as a chance to *make* meaning out of the present. When he was confined to his hut, he imagined giving psychology lectures to a captivated audience dealing with the details of his confinement. He even gave a shadow of such a talk to his depressed hutmates in complete darkness one night, imploring them to continue to find meaning in how they confronted their suffering. Ringing through his head was the quotation from Dostoevsky, namely, that the only thing he feared was "not to be worthy of my sufferings" (67). The present situation demanded that he meet suffering with noble action. The easy way out was to focus on a remote past or give up—and then wishfully think of a better future as one was led away to a "special camp" for those who were unwilling to continue working.

In various official and nonofficial roles in the camps, Frankl began to give psychiatric advice to despairing prisoners. The lesson he always tried to convey to them was that "*it did not really matter what we expected from life, but rather what life expected from us.*" We must not think of there being *an* answer to the meaning of life, we must instead think of life questioning us without end. How does one answer such questioning? Frankl argues that the response to life's questions occurs in "right action and in right conduct." Like the account I have been giving in this book, he asserts that "these tasks, and therefore the meaning of life, differ from man to man, and from moment to moment. . . . 'Life' does not mean something vague, but something very real and concrete." For a prisoner, whose lot was to suffer, Frankl argues that he must "accept his suffering as his task; his single and unique task" (77). It has meaning when one realizes it cannot be changed by other means, and when one sees that it is a unique and particular individual who must bear it.

For Frankl and his fellow prisoners, the future held little of certainty beyond their highly probable demise in the camps. What could be controlled, of course, was how they faced that fate. In the discussion of these issues he had with his hutmates, Frankl puts it quite clearly:

> I spoke of our sacrifice, which had meaning in every case. It was in the nature of this sacrifice that it should appear to be pointless in the normal world, the world of material success. But in reality our sacrifice did have a meaning. . . . I told them of a comrade who on his arrival in camp had tried to make a pact with heaven that his suffering and death should save the human being he loved from a painful end. For this man, suffering and death were meaningful; his was a sacrifice of the deepest significance. He did not want to die for nothing. (83)

Such cognitive overlays could give meaning to one's struggles and suffering while in camp. Whether one lived or died, one still experienced potentially meaningful present situations. And as Frankl notes early in his recollections of the camp, it was the individuals who lacked meaning in their everyday activities that simply gave up at some point. In the context of this study, Frankl serves as an exemplar of the power of orientation. Certain orientations give strength, meaning, and efficacy to one's actions in the present. Other orientations lose their grasp on the present, and with it, any pleasure, meaning, or effect one may have in the here and now. If Frankl could live meaningfully in the harsh objective environment of the four concentration camps in which he was held, should not a contemporary individual be able to manage even more of a successful balance between accommodation and adaptation that will render the present activity valuable and worthy of his or her attention?

Although this chapter—and its culminating example—has been a rather brief overview of the sort of practical project that the Deweyan form of orientational meliorism calls for, I hope my general point stands sufficiently developed—growth and artful activity, in such an account, are tied closely to the orientation that one takes toward one's activities in light of personal impulses/desires and an environment. If, as Frankl puts it, "it is possible to practice the art of living even in a concentration camp, although suffering is omnipresent" (44), shouldn't the art of living, the art of attending to and growing in the present situation, be even more manageable in instances of lesser suffering? In any and all environments, certain orientations that direct and shape interactions that play out in personal experience and activity can be helpful in creating the meaningful experience of growth in the present and in future presents, or can incline the individual to focus on an unreal, non-present goal—the removed object of desire that one's orientation attends to and that it places one step beyond the present that one now (and in the future will) occupy. It is this latter sort of orientation, I argue, that Dewey attacks in his religious, moral, aesthetic, and educational work as unduly separating the present from the future, the means from ends, and the values that these relational connections hold. Part of the challenge of growing is to realize the sort of relationship one holds to desire and its directing power over attention. The Deweyan reading I have explicated in this chapter has demonstrated that there are resources in Dewey's variety of pragmatism to deal with this challenge in a constructive and imaginative way at its very root—the orientation that one takes to the self, the world, and activity.

7

Practicing the Art of Living

The Case of Artful Communication

I have argued that a Deweyan take on aesthetic experience is an expansive, wide-ranging reading of what is connected to the aesthetic and the artful. I have also claimed that aesthetic experience connects to moral value in immediately being an instance of the absorbed, engaged endpoint of moral cultivation. The previous chapter has introduced the more general project of orientational meliorism, the attempt to improve the quality of our experiences through the adjustment of our orientation toward the world, self, others, and action. While I emphasized the notion of growth in that chapter, the linkages with the aesthetic should be clear—both represent a unified, consummatory, and absorptive engagement of a live creature with its present situation. The vitally important part of my account is the sort of mental habits that guide, shape, and tone this transaction between a creature and its environment. These mental habits are what I have labeled "orientations," and they are what can be meliorated to increase one's chances of growth.

From the aspect of subjective quality of experience, orientations are what make the difference between conduct being artful or being fragmented drudgery.

I concluded the previous chapter with some ways that one can imaginatively rethink one's activities in order to render them more aesthetic in quality. I will continue this practical side to my Deweyan account of how life can be artful by examining another common part of our lives—the case of everyday communicative activity. While many writers focus their analysis of Dewey's theory of communication on the rather mundane point of taking the position of one's interlocutor, I want to explore a tantalizing and unexplored question—can ordinary instances of everyday communication be made more artful and consummatory? In other words, can one's meliorative project extend to the rectification and enlivening of everyday communication?

Why should one even subject communication to this test? First, we have good reason to from Dewey's own writings. At various places Dewey includes tantalizing sections of praise of the power of communication. He notes in *Experience and Nature*, for example, that "of all affairs, communication is the most wonderful" (132), and in *The Public and Its Problems* that communication plays an important part in the individual's attempt "to learn to be human" (332). Some scholars who study communication have sensed the important but undeveloped role that communication plays in Dewey's thought and have attempted to use his work in analyzing rhetorical practice, cultural studies, and the role of journalism in society.[1] Although such studies strive to clarify the value and process of communication in Dewey's thought, they fall short of explaining one seemingly simple point that is also implied by Dewey—that communication can be experienced as aesthetic or artful. Nathan Crick identifies such a lacuna in the literature and notes that "beyond its utility as an argument against elite forms of academic criticism, the value of Dewey's aesthetic theory for communication studies remained underdeveloped."[2] While he does an admirable job of tracing the relation of aesthetics to communication in Dewey's evolving thought, Crick comes no closer than others in answering the fundamental question of how communication can be artful or aesthetic—he simply argues for the general point that "communication, whether it occurs in an oration, a conversation, or a television, is best understood as a form of art that has the potential to bring about aesthetic experience in its participants and open their eyes to the world of possibility embodied within each of us."[3] How exactly does this aesthetization of communication occur? Crick concludes with the interesting claim that "in its aesthetic form communication becomes rhetorical. It turns communication into an art whose goal is a presentation that unites form and rhythm in a manner that can reach down into the experiences of the audience and literally transform them into something new."[4] How *exactly* does communication meet such standards? Does such a high art of communication fit everyday communication, the vast majority of human communicative practice?

Second, everyday communication provides a useful test of one of the main points of this book—that any activity can be made more artful. If everyday communication can be rendered artful, then one has successfully shown the applicability of Dewey's notion of aesthetic experience to a major swath of human experience. I focus on everyday communication because there is a tendency in many commentators on Dewey and communication to read the word "communication" as implying finely wrought, thought-out speeches. Crick's sustained analysis of rhetorical eloquence, timing (*kairos*), and decorum, while insightful, does not seem to completely capture the informal nature of everyday interaction.[5] While one may be able to analyze Martin Luther King, Jr.'s "I Have a Dream" speech according to traditional artistic, rhetorical, and aesthetic standards, I think the heart of the Deweyan challenge strikes deeper. How can we render everyday communication, such as that experienced in mundane conversations with friends, cashiers, and so on, as aesthetic? This, I believe, is a real challenge, and one that fits the Deweyan project of expanding the notion of the aesthetic to cover as much of life as possible.

Third, Dewey himself makes communication central to one of his major projects—the melioration of human society. Thus he places the potentially artistic and aesthetic aspects of communicative practice at the very heart of his social and political philosophy. In describing the "Great Community," he announces that it will take place when two conditions hold: "The highest and most difficult kind of inquiry and a subtle, delicate, vivid and responsive art of communication must take possession of the physical machinery of transmission and circulation and breathe life into it. . . . Democracy will come into its own, for democracy is a name for a life of free and enriching communion. . . . It will have its consummation when free social inquiry is indissolubly wedded to the art of full and moving communication."[6] This is a vital passage for understanding Dewey's aims, as it clearly links a scientific habit of thinking (his preferred method of inquiry) with a form of communication that can be taken as an art. Yet scholars of communication systematically miss this part of the Deweyan equation. For instance, Lary Belman concludes his early study of Dewey's view of communication by analyzing this passage on the two conditions of the Great Community, and states: "The basic conditions for the creation of a Great Community . . . were, Dewey postulated, the presence of (a) vigorous, systematic, and continuous social inquiry to reveal the influential agencies at work in society and their mode of operation, and (b) widespread and rapid distribution of the findings of this inquiry in a form readily understood by those for whom these findings have significance."[7] It is remarkable that Dewey's "art of full and moving communication" is reduced by Belman to effective forms of rapid distribution. Again, the question of how communication can be artful fails to receive a clear answer.

I will argue that what can make everyday, mundane instances of communication aesthetic or artful is the *orientation* of the individual communicator. My analysis will serve as an application of the view of aesthetic experience and orientation developed in previous chapters. In particular, I will argue that a specific sort of orientation that focuses one's attention on the present communicative situation is what will make that instance of communication possess the quality denoted by Dewey's term "aesthetic," or will be what makes it an instance of what Dewey calls "expression." Not all of what is usually taken to be art is expressive, but at its highest point art is connected to aesthetic experience and is expressive; in the same way, not all communicative activity is inherently aesthetic and expressive in Dewey's terms, but it can reach this height if certain conditions are met. This is when the purposive activity of communication truly becomes artful. This chapter builds such a case by first examining what Dewey means by the aesthetic or, in terms of art objects, what he means by something being expressive and therefore connected to the production of a unified, aesthetic experience. My analysis will demonstrate the hurdles that one needs to overcome to argue that everyday communication can reach the qualitative heights of the aesthetic or artful. I will then argue, however, for the overcoming of these obstacles by examining the role of orientation in aesthetic experience, as well as in what Dewey calls "artistic media." Ultimately, it is the attitude the subject brings into the communicative experience that will render it aesthetic. I will then speculate on practical strategies that can be drawn from this conception that contribute to the goal of making communication more aesthetic.

Dewey on the Aesthetic and the Expressive

In *Art as Experience*, Dewey provides a wide account of aesthetic experience. Aesthetic experience is called by Dewey "*an* experience," the interaction of a subject and its environment such that "the material experienced runs its course to fulfillment" (42). Notice that Dewey doesn't start such an account by closely tethering it to art; instead, his first three chapters focus on the live creature and the qualitative ways it can interact with its environment. Certain ways of interaction can reach this highpoint "with its own individuating quality and self-sufficiency" (42). Such vivid, live, and qualitatively enhanced experience *is* aesthetic experience.

Dewey believed that this qualitative unity and integration inherent in aesthetic experience could be realized in any type of experience in life. He did believe that art objects, when done well, had an increased chance of fostering the subjective absorption and attention to present detail that made such an experience unified in meaning and value. Dewey's use of the term "art" is notoriously imprecise and prone to lead one to confusion. Many commentators take the word in a descriptive, classificatory fashion—in other words, as covering the extension of a certain concept (viz., identifying all those objects called art). Dewey sometimes refers to art in this typical fashion, and at other points in a more evaluative fashion—as indicative of human processes and activities *at a certain pitch of experiential quality.* Dewey did not care much if this failed to account for bad art; instead of a "wrapper definition" of the class of "art," he was pursuing a conception of art that would help us maximize those sorts of (aesthetic) experience in our production and reception of art objects.[8]

Specifically, Dewey shifts the focus of his definition from *objects* to certain *processes*: "Art denotes a process of doing or making. . . . Every art does something with some physical material, the body or something outside the body, with or without the use of intervening tools, and with a view to production of something visible, audible, or tangible" (53). Notice that the *product* is derivative from what Dewey really emphasizes—the *process*. At a later point in *Art as Experience,* he gives this expansive reading of art: "Art is a quality of doing and of what is done. . . . When we say that tennis-playing, singing, acting, and a multitude of other activates are arts, we engage in an elliptical way of saying that there is art *in* the conduct of these activities and that this art so qualifies what is done and made as to induce activities in those who perceive them in which there is also art" (218). The vital point here is not so much the objective features of some object (what Dewey calls the "art object" or "product of art"), but instead in the sort of experience it required in its production and the sort of experience it engenders in its reception by some audience. Like the chapter 4 discussion of the certain spirit and method that characterizes moral conduct, the term "art" is said to denote a certain quality surrounding those processes of creation (or execution) and reception.

One can see a potential confusion arising due to Dewey's various uses of the word "art." He often uses it to refer to the practices we naively would refer to as art, and he also uses it in a normative, reconstructive sense of how we *ought* to think about art. Take the example of painting—a child rubbing paint on a canvas requires some minimal amount of skill and somatic habituation, but this process (and its product) differs in the artistry of production and reception from the case of Monet rubbing paint on canvas. The second case is art in Dewey's favored sense, since it involves a unity of experience in the production and reception that is at a particular height of absorption, integration, and unity. In the case of the true artist, the process of production is one of ordering materials, thoughts, and emotions through and in a material; this will be further identified by Dewey as the process of expression. The case of the child painter does not reach this height of unity (hence expressivity) and most likely would not evoke such a response in the audience as well.

In terms of communication, one can see the same confusion arising when I refer to the art of communication. Is all communication aesthetic, or is this an achievement of skill and artistry? The answer that I will give is the latter—the process of communication, like rubbing paint on canvas, can be routine, mechanical, or disjointed, or can be characterized by the qualities of aesthetic, integral experience that are the hallmark of absorbing works of art. For instance, Dewey uses the example of an interview to illustrate the aesthetic—the discourse between two individuals can be "mechanical, consisting of set questions, the replies to which perfunctorily settle the matter." Or the interaction could truly be alive and charged, moving toward "its own consummation through a connected series of varied incidents" (49). Dewey did not follow this example with an extended discussion of communicative activity, but one can see the point he glosses on his way to a general discussion of the aesthetic—everyday communication (as in this example) can be *either* aesthetic or nonaesthetic. The question now becomes, how can one make the activity of communication possess more of the former quality?

Art works, taken in the evaluative sense of *true* works of art or human activity, are integrally connected to aesthetic experience—"art, in its form, unites the very same relation of doing and undergoing, outgoing and incoming energy, that makes an experience to be an experience [viz., aesthetic experience]" (54). Aesthetic experience can be evoked by nonart objects (say, a sunset), but good art (art that does *work* in Dewey's sense) will be good insofar as it is connected aesthetic experience.⁹ In *Art as Experience,* Dewey argues that art has a twofold connection to aesthetic experience. The artist purposively works through her ideas, emotions, and the material she is dealing with, all the while imaginatively anticipating what sort of reactions will take place to certain manipulations of the artistic media. These connections to aesthetic experience are also captured by Dewey's talk of an art object's *expressiveness*—its embodying of meaning and emotion in a unified sense through the experience of its creation, as well as its reception by an audience. This experience of creative expression or *production* on the part of the artist can reach levels of unity and integration that would make it an aesthetic experience; alternatively, the attentive audience in perceiving or *receiving* the art object and its qualities can go through a similarly progressive and unified experience that renders their experience aesthetic. As Dewey notes, "in both [the experience of the artist and the audience], there is a comprehension in its literal signification—that is, a gathering together of details and particulars physically scattered into an experienced whole" (60). Aesthetic experience is a parallel phenomenon, occurring in the interaction in the artist-art object relationship, as well as in the audience–art object relationship.

The interesting point for my project of providing an analysis of the "full and moving art of communication" in Dewey comes in his discussion of the process of artistic creation. This is what he labels as "expression," a term that can be used to label both the process of creation and the art object created and received by an audience. This is important insofar as expressive objects (an expression as a created object) are implicated by Dewey in the evoking of aesthetic experience in an audience. Thus, if the process of communication and its utterances are to be aesthetically experienced in any significant degree by their conversational producers or receivers, they must be an expression. These are the public, objective actions or objects of art (for instance, a novel, play, or sculpture) that are causally connected to aesthetic experience. Can an instance of everyday, mundane communication (say, a conversation at the supermarket) be expressive in this sense?

Initially, one would think not. Dewey's account of expression in *Art as Experience* distinguishes the sorts of meanings in actions that can or cannot render them aesthetic in the way that art objects are expressive. The key to art's creation and reception imbuing experience with the quality of the aesthetic is that it is closely connected to experience in its unified sense; commenting on how art is so absorbing for an audience, Dewey notes that "it [art] presents the world in a new experience which they [the audience] undergo" (89). Thus, art does not mirror reality or experience as much as it *re*-presents some sort of experience the artist underwent and wishes to convey to the audience in a certain fashion.

There is a close connection between the experience of attending to the art object and the meaning of the art object. Dewey speaks of words, such as those used in instances of everyday communication, as having a "purely external reference" much like a signboard along a highway does—"it stands for something by pointing to it. Meaning does not belong to the word and signboard by its own intrinsic right" (89). These are what Dewey calls "statements," which, like the signboard, "directs one's course to a place, say a city. It does not in any way supply experience of that city even in a vicarious way. What it does do is to set forth some of the conditions that must be fulfilled in order to procure that experience" (90). Scientific statements and claims are examples of such signboards in linguistic practice; they point toward the experience of certain things (say, through experiments) and provide the "recipes" for confirmation of such claims in replicative actions. Discussing the general nature of such statements, Dewey states: "Statement sets forth the conditions under which an experience of an object or situation may be had. It is a good, that is, effective, statement in the degree in which these conditions are stated in such a way that they can be used as directions by which one may arrive at the experience. It is a bad statement, confused and false, if it sets forth these conditions in such a way that when they are used as directions, they mislead or take one to the object in a wasteful way" (90). This seems to adequately capture everyday linguistic utterances as nonexpressive, and therefore as not integrally connected to the production of aesthetic experiences in either the producer of the communicative message or its receiver. They appear to serve as instrumental, routinized shortcuts to coordinating activity.

Furthermore, Dewey characterizes the term "expression" in such a way as to connect it to experience and traditional art and remove it from everyday instances of linguistic performance—an art object qua expression "does something different from leading to an experience. It constitutes one. . . . Art is an immediate realization of intent" (91). Opposed to statements that have an external connection between object and meaning, expressions feature an internal relationship between an object and its meaning. Thus, one can be told how to get to a city, or how a city is laid out, but this is different in the meaning featured when a subject *experiences* that city firsthand. Similarly, art objects are expressive insofar as they put the audience through an experience, versus linguistic statements (such as in science) that are removed from any actual, concrete experience. The former are constituted by and connected to experience at that height of unity called "aesthetic" by Dewey.

This reading of expression is closely connected to Dewey's analysis of means and media in his aesthetic theory. For Dewey, media are contrasted to mere means, as media unify and collate preceding particulars of experience and *compose* the effect that is desired. This is the sort of internal connection between object/material and meaning that one sees in expression. Paint *is* the painting in a real way, as opposed to being a mere means of painting. In terms of Dewey's notion of statement, the analogue here is mere means, which feature an external relation to what they implicate and thus can be identified by their replaceability and their externality to the effect desired. One can alter car engines such that gasoline can be replaced by ethanol, motivated perhaps by external concerns—pollution, efficiency, availably, and so forth. The nature and meaning (use) of the vehicle is unchanged by the substitution of alternate means (viz., fuel). If one changes the composition, phrasing, and so on of Wordsworth's "Goody Blake," however, one has changed the art object. The experience of those words by a subject *is* the aesthetic experience produced by that art object; thus, in a real way, the material of the art object both causes the aesthetic experience and constitutes it. The medium (or expression) is the end desired, and not a mere means to an external, unconnected end. Expressions are objects produced such that they are instances of a medium manipulated. Expressions produce aesthetic experience primarily because their creation and reception can be said to involve this internality of means and ends, the diametrical opposite of the nonaesthetic—"all the cases in which means and ends are external to one another are non-esthetic. This externality may even be regarded as a definition of the non-esthetic" (202).

Even though Dewey exclaims in *Experience and Nature* that "of all affairs, communication is the most wonderful" (132), it is hard to see it as artful or as connected to the aesthetic in its everyday form. Dewey ends his discussion of expression in *Art as Experience* by concluding that "in the end, works of art are the only media of complete and unhindered communication between man and man that can occur in a world full of gulfs and walls that limit community of experience" (110). Communication, especially in its mundane and everyday discursive form, seems firmly aligned with statement and not with expression. One can discern at least three general reasons why everyday communication would be classed as statement, and therefore not as expressive or aesthetic.

First, there seems to be an experienced split between means and ends in communication that violates the idea of an integrated medium of expression. In communication, words or concepts are employed to stand for past objects of experience, emotions experienced, actions to undertake, and so on. Thus, Dewey notes that even when word meanings have been internalized (habitually made immediate), they still involve an action-coordinating function among individuals.[10] A police officer yelling "stop!" begins with an understanding of how the other individual will perceive and react to such a command, and the situation usually ends with the other individual's reaction that is based upon the sort of past habituation to the imperative use of language that the officer assumes. Communication here operates at a remove from experience, but with a reference to possible and anticipated experience (viz., the action of stopping). This is substantively different from artistic expression, where the "utterance" of the painting and its experience is that which the artist hopes to evoke through the manipulation of paint, reflected light, and so forth. Everyday linguistic communication would seem to point to experiences undergone in the past or anticipated/desired for the future, but would not seem to hold the same experienced unity between means and ends that constitutes aesthetic, expressive activity.

Second, there appears to be an evaluative split between means and ends in communicative activity that is absent in artistic expression. For example, perhaps one needs a particular form from a certain government office to apply for a job. One constructs a certain utterance with the explicit goal of getting that form. The value of the utterance, say, "can I have form 7.132?," is conditioned upon actually receiving that form, as well as on holding the end of wanting to get the job that form 7.132 lets one apply for. If that way of asking for a form was known to be utterly ineffective, it seems that it would be devalued as an action not in line with one's desired goal of gaining that sort of employment. Crispin Sartwell, writing on Dewey's aesthetic theory, notes that most individuals so value the ends of activity that the value of the means gets subordinated to achievements represented by the desired end. Indeed, he notes the disparity in value between the means and ends in such a way by stating that "if we could achieve the end by sheer force of will, if we could realize it without performing the means, we would."[11] If the utterance doesn't get us what we want, the desire seems to be to scrap the utterance as an action; conversely, the utterance is valued insofar as it can achieve that result—be it anticipated action, lack of action, transmission of one's feelings to another, and so on. Unlike artistic expressions, everyday communication seems to hold to a strong separation of means and ends, along with a subordination of the former to the latter in terms of what is of value. This is ontologically and axiologically the opposite of what occurs in instances of media in Dewey's integrated sense.

Third, everyday communication seems too intentional to be what Dewey cherishes as artful activity. Discussing the communicative power of art, Dewey seems to discount the artistic value of communication due to the notion of explicit intentionality in the latter: "Because the objects of art are expressive, they communicate. I do not say that communication to others is the intent of an artist. But it is the consequence of his work. . . . If the artist desires to communicate a *special* message, he thereby tends to limit the expressiveness of his work to others—whether he wishes to communicate a moral lesson or a sense of his own cleverness."[12] An artist that sets out to communicate something about social policy in eighteenth-century France will be thereby limited in what his or her audience finds moving about that expression in today's society. A didactic fable will seem heavy handed and limited in its artistry, and the audience may consciously try to resist the manipulation on the part of the writer. I addressed related concerns circling around art as communicative in chapter 5 of this book, but for now it is enough to note the tendency of communication to be explicitly tied to problem solving and action coordination, as Jürgen Habermas puts it in his attempt to distinguish art from everyday communication.[13] Such a characteristic of everyday communication would, for Dewey, render it different in kind and value from expressive, artistic objects.

Everyday communication, with its mundane subject matter and orientation toward valued outcomes would seem to violate the implied unity of artistic expression and render it just another mere means toward the achieving of those desired outcomes. Like any given conversational utterance, expression that was related to an external goal could be replaced with another utterance of equivalent use. It is hard to see, given this objection as well as the proceeding two dealing with the separation of means and ends in communicative activity, how communication can reach the level of "the art of full and moving communication" prophesied in Dewey's work on political philosophy.

Rebuilding a Notion of Communication as Aesthetic

How can one move everyday communicative activity from the realm of statements to the realm connected with aesthetic experience or expression? How can communication, an inherently practical endeavor, be experienced as an integrated whole, as opposed to merely one means toward some desired end or outcome? In other words, how can communication be made artful or aesthetic? The answer to this question lies not in changing the objective features of the world (what words are said, how one uses ink to write), but instead resides in what Dewey saw as the essential element to aesthetic experience—a subject's *orientation* toward experience, be it of a painted canvas, of painting a canvas, or of the commute to work. This sounds like a wide definition of the aesthetic, but I hope the previous chapters of this work have shown that it is the project that Dewey advocates. In other words, part of his rebelling against the museum concept of art is to expand the reach of art, along with the highly unified experiences we often correlate with art objects, to more of life. These are truly the high points in subjective experience, and it requires no great leap in inference to say that Dewey's project follows from this valuing of aesthetic experience, and consequently aims at making more of life's activities and objects aesthetic.

In terms of the activity of communication, what could make it and its products (viz., verbal and nonverbal messages) expressive in the way that art objects produced by skilled artists are expressive? I suggest that communication can become artful or aesthetic *if* a subject dons the sort of orientation toward that activity that (1) *attends* to means and ends as integrally connected, and (2) *values* means and ends in a connected fashion. This reading, incidentally, has been the template for how one can render the various other domains covered in this book as aesthetic; here it will be expounded in relation to communicative activities.

I have been building an account of the aesthetic in Dewey that places a particular importance on the orientation of the subject. As evidenced in the ferryboat commuter example and the test takers example discussed in chapter 4, the same objective circumstances can be experienced differently because of a difference in the subjective orientation toward the activity in those circumstances. In each case the difference in orientation concerns seeing the process as part of the product, or in seeing the activity as a *medium*, and not as a mere means to some externalized goal. Some commentators have picked up on the connection here between process and product, but none have emphasized the role that subjective orientation can play in making basically any activity a product or something valued in and of itself.[14]

These two examples from Dewey's aesthetic theory show that the attitude of a subject can render an activity aesthetic (with a connection of means/ends) or can render it nonaesthetic. The former chapter and its focus on growth featured a similar analysis—one ought to foster engaged, enlivened, and meaningful activity that one does not want to skip over if one could. Compare Dewey's definition of the nonaesthetic—"all the cases in which means and ends are external to one another are non-esthetic"[15]—to his description of drudgery and its manipulation of means/ends in terms of value: "*exclusive* interest in a result alters work to drudgery. For by drudgery is meant those activities in which the interest in the outcome does not suffuse the process of getting the result. Whenever a piece of work becomes drudgery, the process of doing loses all value for the doer; he cares solely for what is to be had at the end of it. The work itself, the putting forth of energy, is hateful; it is just a necessary evil, since without it some important end would be missed."[16] The first commuter and the first test taker share one important subjective trait in common—an overpowering focus on an end or goal that is (1) separate in an important sense from the process that is seen as achieving it, and (2) separate and superior in value to the means undertaken to reach it. Just like the agent who makes her present activities into drudgery by overly fixating on nonpresent objects of desire, the commuter and test taker also render their experience disjointed, devalued, and nonaesthetic. The end is what counts. These two factors deal with how the subjects focus their attention and thought in the present, how they act, and how they value such activity; consequently, the fragmented and hierarchical way of orienting oneself toward commutes and tests renders those activities nonunified, replaceable, and nonaesthetic insofar as one sees them as subordinated to some end that is truly of value.

An additional factor in communicative activity is that it is a purposive, interactive practice that involves the production and reception of material messages. This, on Dewey's account, renders it an art. The way that this art can be expressive is through the quality of the process involved in the production of the messages, as well as the quality of the process of message reception. The quality of producing and exchanging messages in communication (say, at the supermarket register) can be habitual and mechanical, or it can be more akin to an integrated, consummatory situation in which each part has value. Dewey was quite adamant that the qualities so lauded in art depend on the individual: "For quality is concrete and existential, and hence varies with individuals since it is impregnated with their uniqueness."[17] The meaning and impact of the color in a painting depends on an audience's receptivity to it and related meanings and reactions that they have developed over time; to the wrong audience, a great painting can be meaningless and unmoving. The central point in the equation is the subjective factor. This is what allows the art object to evoke the sort of unified experience that is called aesthetic experience. If one's way of attending to the communicative utterances of others is at a mechanical, goal-driven (and hence external) level, one's experience will not reach the level of the aesthetic. If one cultivates a way of attending to and valuing the present communicative activities, then that process can be rendered aesthetic, and the produced utterances of self and others will possess a true expressiveness (and not merely an externalized value as pointers to future coordination of action and ends).

Thus, the key to making everyday communication reach the qualitative heights of aesthetic activity—namely, activity that unifies means and ends in the eyes of the subject—lies in changing how one sees and values those activities. If one conceives of an interaction at the register in a market as merely a way to procure goods and then leave, then that is the sort of replaceable and valueless (in terms of experienced quality) interaction that one will have. If one instead focuses on the act of communication itself as part of the goal desired, then one can experience the exchange of money and goods with the cashier as a unified, qualitative whole. How does one go about uniting activity and outcome in one's activity? The answer is deceptively simple—one ought to focus one's attention on the materials of the immediate situation, and not on some remote goal or outcome that desire inclines one toward. This is the natural enemy of the sort of Deweyan mindfulness to the present activity that I argue is the key to making communication aesthetic or artful—as I detailed in the previous chapter, desire focuses one's attention on a particular remote object (or state), which seems to be the key to all of one's plans, *if* one could attain that which one lacks (viz., the object of the desire).[18]

The problem, of course, is not in the mere existence of orientations toward the objects of desire, but instead lies in the *overemphasized* value and separateness placed on the goal of activity. Dewey notes the harmfulness of such an orientation to activity in general, let alone in communication, pointing out that "as things are, men so habitually scamp present action in behalf of future 'ends'. . . . But everywhere the good, the fulfillment, the meaning of activity, resides in a present made possible by judging existing conditions in their connections."[19] This also applies to the large part of our waking life that is spent talking in interpersonal or organization contexts. Such communicative interactions can be affected either by an orientation toward present communicative activity as *instrumentally* good for reaching some end separate in location and value, or by an orientation toward present communication as enjoyed with its own meaning. This is the sort of reading Dewey gives in a long, important passage about communication and its dual status as means and end:

> Discourse itself is both instrumental and consummatory. Communication is an exchange which procures something wanted; it involves a claim, appeal, order, direction or request, which realizes want at less cost than personal labor exacts, since it procures the cooperative assistance of others. Communication is also an immediate enhancement of life, enjoyed for its own sake. . . . Language is always a form of action and in its instrumental use is always a means of concerted action for an end, while at the same time it finds in itself all the goods of its possible consequences. For there is no mode of action as fulfilling and as rewarding as is concerted consensus of action. It brings with it the sense of sharing and merging in a whole.[20]

Communication is *both* a means to future states of affairs and an immediately valuable, felt instantiation of harmony and coordination with others. One's orientation toward communicative activity can focus one's attention in such a way as to foreground its value as a mere means; it is at this point that communicative interaction loses any felt, immediate value and instead gains the promised value only of the end yet to be achieved. In other words, the activity of communication becomes nonexpressive insofar as it is seen and experienced as a mere means of attaining remote goals.

The more enjoyable and rewarding quality of communicative experience can come when one conceives of the discursive activity as connected to the desired end in terms of value and ongoing process. As in the previous analysis of communication as both instrumental and immediately valuable, community now and in the future exists because of communication in the present and the quality of communication now will tone the quality of communal interaction in the future. Dewey captures this point succinctly by stating that "society not only continues to exist *by* transmission, *by* communication, but it may fairly be said to exist *in* transmission, *in* communication."[21] Instantiating aesthetic or artful forms of communication now is not only a way to help create desired forms of enlivened community in the future, it is also the creation of the desired goal *now*. Aesthetic or artful communication is seeing, using, and experiencing utterance as not merely statement, not merely as a means toward coordinated action; it sees the activity of discourse as the sort of coordinated, valuable action we want to maintain in future states of affairs. In other words, the process of communication *is* the end of communicating—individuals attentively responding to each other and the situation in such a way as to truly instantiate a community of interacting beings.

With such an account I believe that I have built upon past readings of Dewey that recognize the important connection of art and communication, but that fail to fully explicate *how* communication can be artful or aesthetic in the way that artistic expression is aesthetic. The difference lies in the subjective orientation toward that activity just as much as it hinges upon the audience of a painting attending to *that* object and its presented qualities instead of to how much it would help one's financial standing *if* one possessed it. What one ought to focus on is the present situation. As I have shown in previous chapters, this is a common theme from Dewey's early work on ethics in the 1890s and it is a vital part of the characterization of aesthetic experience as absorptive in his work of the 1930s.

The artful life is one that is finely adapted to the particular demands of the situation, which includes the inner needs and drives of the subject as well as the outer demands imposed by one's station, other individuals, and the social and natural environment itself. Finely attending to the properties of an art object is what makes it expressive and artful, and the fine-tuned and attentive focus on meeting the demands of the present situation is what makes our present activity most adapted and immediately valuable, as well as most instrumentally valuable for reaching consequent states of affairs that hinge on how we handle the here and now. The sort of absorption Dewey describes in *Art as Experience* is not far from this line of thinking. When he discusses the live animal as "fully present, all there, in all of its actions," a state that humans can reach when they achieve the "aesthetic ideal," he notes that it is instantiated only "when the past ceases to trouble and anticipations of the future are not perturbing [only then] is a being wholly united with his environment and therefore fully alive" (24).

Of course, one may demur and question why all communication *already* isn't experienced as expressive. The reply to this is simple—too many individuals have the wrong orientation toward interaction. In other words, too many possess bad habits regarding how they communicate with others. For instance, scholars have noted the tendency to think of argumentative communication as "war" or as the persuasive changing of others in accord with one's will.[22] In a Deweyan diagnosis these would be identified as habits that degrade the value and effectiveness of communicating with other members of a community. Dewey provides a similar answer to a similar question—why aren't more objects expressive? The answer he gives is simple; habitualized ways of thinking and perceiving render these objects dull and easily glossed over. He remarks: "Yet apathy and torpor conceal this expressiveness by building a shell about objects. Familiarity induces indifference, prejudice blinds us; conceit looks through the wrong end of a telescope and minimizes the significance possessed by objects in favor of the alleged importance of the self."[23] All of these indictments point toward habits of how we *attend* to objects. In many cases, familiarity and the slackness of routine blind us to the properties and qualities of objects (and, I would add, experiences such as discourse). We can ruin the expressiveness of an object by focusing on what it could mean to us if we *could* own it, how knowledge of it *could* impress our friends after the museum visit, and so forth. The focus and value is not in the present in such cases. Our own conceit often focuses us on what interactions and objects mean *to us* in future states of affairs, and minimizes the attention we give to the particular details of the concrete situation or object confronting us in the present. This is not the fineness of touch evinced by the art of living. Instead, it is the following of an ossified orientation that renders the present subservient to a future state of affairs that is conceived as more valuable and worthy of attention than the here and now. Of course, such a focus is ironic insofar as the present is more real than either the past or the future.

Orientational Meliorism and Artful Communication: Three Proposed Maxims

The answer I have given to the question broached at the beginning of this chapter—how can we make more of our communicative activities aesthetic or artful?—lends itself to the pragmatic project of meliorism. In the case of making more communication have the quality of being aesthetic, the challenge is clear—what are some ways that we can instantiate this orientation in subjects such that their experience of the processes of communication is meliorated?

As opposed to the aesthetic attitude theorists who prized a subject's disinterested attention to an art object, Dewey very much prized an engaged, absorptive, and interested attention to art objects. The key is the *focus* of attention and *how* things are valued. One can be practically engaged with a situation *and* be absorbed in it. Dewey makes this point in saying that he opposes readings of aesthetic attitudes that feature detachment or psychical distance. In his version of the aesthetic experience, there is a merging or absorbing of self and object in attention such that "there is no severance of self, no holding of it aloof, but fullness of participation."[24]

I will return to the theme of absorption of self and object momentarily, but for now it is enough to emphasize that my reading of Dewey on aesthetic communication would not render the process as passive. Instead, a thoroughgoing engagement with the present situation is due to one's orientation and its attention-focusing power, and results in the transformation of the materials of the present. This transformative aspect has been part of Dewey's account all along, of course; the live creature, the artist, and, I would add, the communicator, are all engaged in confronting some material environment with certain mental habits of action in place. How they shape and transform that material, and how that material and its reaction shape them, is all part of this transformative story. The communicator, through his or her careful attention and valuing of the means of communication, transforms a material just as much as the sculptor does, and both do it with thoughts of the reaction of an audience (formal or informal) in mind. The central determinant of whether such an interaction with stone or sound is aesthetic in quality is how individuals focus their attention, and whether their way of valuing means and intermediary steps renders them as *mere* means, *mere* routines that must be navigated in order to reach what is truly valuable. Thus, the orientation toward communication that I have been detailing holds its meliorative promise in that it offers a way of transforming how we communicate and how it will be experienced.

How can such an orientation be instantiated or cultivated? This is equivalent to our starting question, how exactly can we render everyday communicative activity as artful or aesthetic? Like all arts, fine or technical, artful communication will be a learned and cultivated skill. Also, like all acquired skills, it is only perfected by and in present instantiations (viz., use). Recognizing communication as instrumentally valuable for future states of affairs as well as immediately valuable as an instantiation of community activity with others, I propose the following three guidelines or maxims as means for how to make one's communicative activities more aesthetic, more expressive, more unified in terms of how they are valued and how they related to remote states of affairs and values. In the terminology advanced in the previous chapter, these are mental/cognitive ways to imaginatively recraft one's communicative activities.

First, a communicator is well served to avoid focusing on a remote goal. Instead, one ought to develop the orientation of attending to the present by consciously attending to the communicative interaction itself. One way of doing this is by reimagining the present activity as intrinsically valuable. This is the tactic Crispin Sartwell pursues in his reading of the *Bhagavad Gītā* and its general relation to action—one should see activity as more than a mere means, as instead sanctified.[25] Thus, using religious motifs, an emphasis on one's present duty, and so on, one could begin to experience the situation in a different fashion. One could start to see the means of interacting with another person as intrinsically valuable, regardless of the ultimate outcome of such a purposeful endeavor. Seeing another person as intrinsically valuable due to a conceptual overlay, whether it is from Kant or the New Testament, could also be an imaginative way to re-vision what is occurring and what the immediate value of the other participants is. As noted in chapter 6, psychologists have studied the power of imagination and how it can be used to forge new ways that individuals can relate to their vocations; thus it is not unwarranted to believe there are more or less effective ways to rethink the values of others and the communicative situation itself.

Additionally, one ought to consciously cultivate habits of attending to the demands of the present communication situation. In any given situation, there will be the desires, projects, needs, and capabilities of the individual agent, as well as the external factors of other participants and the environment. The former elements determine and direct our activities, and the latter are always some sort of consideration in how and why we act in certain ways. If an individual desires a higher financial position and finds that she can take a job in a neighboring city, she is drawn to such a course of action. Yet the present situation holds more resources for and obstacles to action than that. For instance, the demands and needs of her relational partner are a relevant factor, as well as any duties she may have toward her present employer. When she communicates with these other individuals, the outcome and the quality of that communicative experience itself will be radically affected by how she attends or fails to attend to the situation with its myriad of particular details.

If individuals attend only to *their* needs, the situation will most likely be mishandled, and the resulting quality of the interaction with others in that situation will not be at the most effective or enjoyable level that could be attained. If one sees the situation offered by the present as a valuable opportunity that demands certain responses, then one may respond to it in an integrated, holistic, and, most likely, effective manner. To varying extents, individuals will be artfully and finely responding to the needs and desires of self and other, the forces in the social environment, and so forth, in the manner in which they ought to be addressed. The important aspect emphasized here, of course, is that to be empathetic and intelligent at the same time is to intently focus one's attention on the means and process of communication. This is also the key to experiencing communicative activity as aesthetic and expressive in the unified, qualitatively alive way that great art is experienced as expressive and absorbing.

Finally, one should avoid the pitfall, noticed by Buddhist philosophers for millennia, of focusing too much attention on the idea of a reified, separate self. Dewey also noted the harm in focusing too much on what is not present, an observation connected with his attacks on remote ideals and abstract notions of a transcendent self that have no connection to our concrete activities of the present.[26] One is bound to mishandle the particulars of the present and render one's experience of it fragmented and nonaesthetic if one is focusing on a remote ideal of ego, self, or the kingdom of God. Such a remote focus of attention draws attention away from the here and now—the self that one *is* in the situation, who (exactly) others are, and how the community is actually formed (both for good and bad). No transcendent self breaks through, according to this view of communication, in one's interactions with another individual. To use an everyday example—that of a teacher and a student—the self of the speaker is the self qua teacher and the self of the other participant is that person qua struggling student. Their desires and expectations stem from their social placement in those roles and in that culture, and each person's reaction is determined by their expectations. Focusing on a transcendent self doesn't help one communicate with that concrete person. Instead, attending to *why* they are struggling and *why they think* they are struggling provides the better way to craft a unified, valuable response. This in turn will help one experience that interaction not merely as valuable insofar as it leads to some remote end that really possesses value, but instead will help one experience the situation as suffused by the value of the ends that stem from the contextualized expectations and needs of the agents in that situation.

Artful Communication and Artful Activity

How does the previous chapter's project of orientational meliorism fit into this account of making more of our communicative activity artful or aesthetic? The previous three maxims, like the three guidelines proposed in chapter 6, may seem too abstract and general to be of use. Indeed, one could even claim that such artful communication and activity does not exist. Yet I would argue that most of us have experienced intense absorption in conversation at one point or another. Why were we so enthralled? Perhaps it is because a certain interest animated us, such as in a conversation over a shared hobby. I want to conclude this chapter with a case in which activity and communication are infused with that sort of value and meaning because of a consciously held orientation. In other words, I will examine a case in which an orientation serves as a meaningful overlay to the activity—communicative or otherwise—that consequently gains in quality. Whereas the previous chapter culminated with the example of Viktor Frankl, this chapter will take the more mundane example of Brother Lawrence and his activities as a lay cleric in the 1600s. What this example will show is that even in everyday affairs such as cooking and conversing with others, there is the opportunity for meaning, unity, and absorption. In the case of Brother Lawrence, the orientation that enables such engagement with the present is religious in content.

"Brother Lawrence of the Resurrection" is the assumed religious name of Nicholas Herman (1614–1691), a man born into a modest family in what is now eastern France. He had a simple childhood, and his parents' financial position eventually forced him into military service. It was around age eighteen that Nicholas first saw military action in the Thirty Years' War. During his years of service, one must assume he saw or possibly took part in the looting and violence that characterized this charged conflict.[27] He was captured, released, and eventually injured in the course of his military service. Approximately six years after starting this career, he left to become a lay brother of the Order of Discalced Carmelites in Paris. He sought out the religious life as a way to atone for his past transgressions and as a way to make up for his admittedly awkward and unrefined demeanor. What is of interest is not the story of the soldier turning to religion, but rather the sort of ideals that animated Brother Lawrence during the very religious portion of his life.

A variety of letters survive from Lawrence's time as a lay brother, as well as a short text on "The Practice of the Presence of God." What is fascinating is the extent to which Brother Lawrence's religious ideas infused his daily activities. As a lay disciple in the monastery, he was put to work helping the order with its business demands. He first assumed the job of cook and later was forced by recurrent gout to take the position of shoemaker for the other brothers in the order. Throughout both of these mundane occupations, Brother Lawrence still found a way to make them have the quality and meaning of religious activity. For instance, he implored others to adore God in their work: "In the midst of your work find consolation in him as often as possible. During your meals and conversations, occasionally lift up your heart to him; the least little remembrance of him will always be most agreeable. You need not shout out: he is closer to us than we may think" (69). We can find religious meaning that gives our everyday work value and importance. The secret to this, for Brother Lawrence, was to practice the "presence of God." This practice is driven by the belief that "we do not always have to be in church to be with God. We can make of our hearts an oratory where we can withdraw from time to time to converse with him there, gently, humbly, lovingly" (ibid.). Brother Lawrence's orientation toward the world entailed an omnipotent, omnipresent God—one that was directly available to everyone's communicative endeavors. In the terms of communication literature, he was having an "imagined interaction," or an intrapersonal conversation that no other human could observe.[28]

Wouldn't such an intrapersonal discussion distract Brother Lawrence from the immediate present? What his letters and conversations reveal, however, is that this discussion with God actually imbued the activities in which he was participating with more value and unity. There is not much evidence that his discussions with God were as long and detailed as normal human conversations are. Instead, they served as a focus of love, a way for Brother Lawrence to feel that God was present and that he was doing his work activity for God's sake. He is recorded as saying that "our sanctification depends not on changing our works, but on doing for God what we would normally do for ourselves." Instead of a focus on his self and his goals, he conversed with

God by doing his actions out of love for God. Brother Lawrence was said to find "no better way to approach God than by the ordinary works required in his case by obedience, purifying them as much as he could from all human respect, and doing them for the pure love of God" (97–98). Brother Lawrence *sees* his task in a different way: he imagines it as part of a conversation with God. Instead of being driven by human regards (such as the desires of the self), he gives all of this worrying over to God and does his task out of pure devotion.

Put another way, Brother Lawrence was using his willpower to change his habits of acting and thinking. To get rid of his ordinary human sins, he saw it was necessary to give all of his activities to the service of God, a God that was an observant communication partner to him. Indeed, in his occupations as cook and sandalmaker, he reports that he felt closer to God than he did during his institutionalized prayer activities (93). He was cultivating an inner adoration of God, and he did this through the imaginative presence of God. He even notes how his goal was to make this way of experiencing the world habitual (63). One sees here a path of mental/cognitive orientational meliorism insofar as he was using certain ideas (viz., of God) as a way to give meaning and value to a range of activities.

Even more important, one sees how his *communicative* activities were given a new value. Outside of his communicative encounters with God during his occupational activities, Brother Lawrence's correspondence with other followers was similarly imbued with meaning. He wrote to them (in many cases, in response to their letters) not to achieve any given end, but to comfort them (in some cases) or to teach them how to experience God as he did. He always kept "constant guard . . . not to do, say, or think anything that might displease him [God]," and this oversight extended to his interactions with others (81). If the interaction concerned a woman's worry over her soldier husband's well being, he answered the demands of this communicative situation by explaining his practice of the presence of God when done with "sword in hand" (63). One gets the distinct impression that Brother Lawrence gave meaning to all of his actions—including communicative ones—with the orientational overlay of God's presence. Instead of distracting him from these activities, the religious orientation gave even more meaning and value to the concerns of others and the demands of his ordinary tasks. Instead of merely cooking, he was honoring God in his cooking. What was diminished by his orientation was desires of the self—a concept that could easily change his actions and interactions with others. His brothers remembered his charitable and giving nature, and so we must continue to see his words and actions as an example of the inner orientation toward experiencing the world in a religious sense. Communication and everyday work for Brother Lawrence gained the sort of unity and meaning in itself that this book has described as the hallmark of the aesthetic. In other words, Brother Lawrence was living, teaching, and communicating in an artful fashion.

Although the religious orientation practiced by Brother Lawrence is not essential to the general project of orientational meliorism, it does serve as an example of one way it can be undertaken. It also shows how orientations can alter and shape our communicative activities as well as our occupational tasks. Thus, we reach an answer to the question that perplexed us from the start of this chapter—how can communication be rendered aesthetic or artful? The answer, as I have argued, stems from the orientation toward communication that one holds. As evident in the example of Brother Lawrence, certain orientations tend to connect means/ends and process/product in the activity of communication, and tend to suffuse each part with the value of the other. Orientations that render communication incomplete, fragmented, and less effective at building community are those that tend to separate means/ends and process/product, and that tend to make the value of the means (in this case, interacting with others) depend solely on the value of the end that one desires.

One may question, though, if the best way to address the problem of fractured communication is a refocusing of attention to the present activity itself; is this not too vague an account of the relation between orientation and communicative activity and how one *exactly* should behave? Even though such an objection grants that my account answers the starting question of how communication can be aesthetic, it does challenge its practicality. Brother Lawrence's example shows us that a life of absorbed and valuable activity can be actualized, but such an example is extreme in its employment of a specific religious tradition. Whether or not it is a typical example need not concern us, though. For the pragmatists, as well as for Aristotle, one must expect only the sort of precision that one's subject of inquiry allows. Just as one cannot codify in specific rules how *exactly* to paint a creative masterpiece, one cannot specify what this attentive, fine-touched, and balanced response to a particular situation will be in all of its detail. For the only thing certain is that the details of one's communicative response to a situation, if artfully done, will be closely connected to the details and demands of that communicative situation.

How we use specific orientations—including religious ones—to do this remains a topic of exploration. What can be said is that the present, concrete situation holds the resources for mindful, attentive communication. As was noted in my previous discussions of growth and progressive adjustment, desires, ends, duties, lines of response, expectations, and so on are all *there* in the interaction between, say, a teacher and a student in a specific class. The agents merely have to figure out how to use such resources and in what measure. It comes down to the choices that will render communication as either aesthetic or nonaesthetic and routine. This is why the orientation that is most artful, most aesthetic, most unifying of life and its experiences will be that orientation that directs purposeful activity by attending to the actual location of such activity—the present situation confronting one with all its demands and opportunities, risks and promises.

8

Beginning to Live the Artful Life

We have effectively reached the end of this investigation of a Deweyan take on the aesthetic and its connection to life, activity, and moral improvement. Dewey's reading of aesthetic experience is controversial and fresh, if it is anything. I have attempted to figure out how such a reading could answer the debates concerning art and its connection to moral cultivation, and how Dewey's analysis could be conceptually grounded in an account different from traditional accounts of intrinsic and instrumental value. Whether my account is ultimately satisfactory to those wishing to pursue these questions in the fashion current in Western intellectual circles is an open question. I rest content with having at least opened the possibility of such a reading of means/ends and the experiential value to the absorptive and engaged reading of aesthetic experience discussed in this work.

Why do I continue here? As Walter Lippmann once wrote, "the last chapter is merely a place where the writer imagines that the polite reader has begun to look furtively at his watch,"[1] and by all means, the previous chapter did seem to culminate a long and detailed look at the complex topic of the artful life. I do want to examine a variety of objections to my account, however, and provide what I believe to be decent answers to such criticisms. This final section is aimed not at those looking at their watch, but instead at those who continue to cast a skeptical eye toward the pages of this book.

Objection 1: This Account of Aesthetic Experience Is Too Subjective or Subject-Focused

This objection can be phrased in a variety of ways, but it essentially boils down to an objection to my emphasis on the *subjective* aspects of nonaesthetic experience and its melioration. One may claim that I am making Dewey an "aesthetic attitude" theorist by means of an inaccurate focus on the power of an individual's disposition to magically change the quality of his or her lived experience. It could be claimed that I ought to instead do justice to the interactive, transactive foci of Dewey's aesthetic work. Alternatively, one could claim that no amount of subjective change will overcome the obstacles posed by objective conditions, either in regard to economic structures or the actual properties of the art object itself. Such criticisms also accuse me of not taking seriously the object or the external conditions in my putative withdrawal into subjective passivity.[2]

In responding to such criticisms, I in no way want to leave out or exclude the material aspects to life, activity, or art—indeed, these aspects give our particular experiences their unique qualities and joys. I also do not want to imply that Dewey has a reified division between self and object, the subjective and objective. Indeed, Dewey notes that habits integrally incorporate parts of the environment, such as the habit of breathing and its intimate contact with the air. There is a sense, though, in which habits or ways of approaching activity can be said to be of the subject. For instance, in describing habits and how habits function as will in *Human Nature and Conduct,* Dewey notes that "the essence of habit is an acquired predisposition to *ways* or modes of response, not to particular acts except as, under special conditions, these express a way of behaving" (32). One can see that the conception of orientation that I have been elucidating in this study fits this wide notion of habit as "a predisposition to *ways* or modes of response"—particularly toward how we *attend* to and *value* parts of present activity. These are habits that address how we respond to the present situation and its materials, and these responses in turn affect how our habits and dispositions are formed and reformed. There is a way, then, that we can talk of subjective habits without hermetically sealing the subject off from the outside world—these are the predispositions to action that are formed in light of past interaction, and, most important, the ones we bring qua subject into future situations of action.

This analysis merely establishes a working notion of self, however, and does not address the objection that material aspects to melioration are left out of my account. What I want to maintain is that the *key* to making more activities aesthetic lies in the subjective orientation of the individuals involved—artists and audiences, speakers and hearers, agents and actors. With any locking mechanism, there is more to the story than just the key (viz., the rest of the lock). Material conditions do matter. Nevertheless, I give a particular level of importance to the subjective habits I call orientations, and this choice must be defended. I focus on orientation as the key to meliorism for the following three reasons.

First, one cannot explain the two examples of aesthetic experience I gave from *Art as Experience* without the central variable being the subject. The ferryboat riders and the test takers both do the same physical activities, but the *process* and *experience* is radically different. Why? The only explanation I can see as defendable is that the individuals differ in how they attend to and value the activities at hand. Of course, this difference may lead to different physical manifestations—increased physiological arousal, boredom, a gaping mouth, and so on—but the primary and initial difference that puts all of the other differences in motion is how these individuals approach the activities in the first place. This conclusion also is born out by empirical work in psychology on work satisfaction. Studies about happiness at work find that for nearly any type of job, roughly a third will rate that occupation as a calling, a third will rate it as a career, and a third will rate it as a mere job.[3] The latter seems more akin to Dewey's notion of drudgery, and the descriptions Wrzesniewski and her colleagues give of the first category strike one as having the integration, meaning, build, and purpose that Dewey packs into his notion of *an* experience. The important point here is that *regardless* of the objective activities of the job (CEO, administrative assistant, hospital custodian), one will find individuals who *experience* those same activities differently. One can find individuals who see *any* of these jobs as callings, and one can find individuals who see *any* of these jobs (including high status and power jobs) as *mere* jobs to trudge through. Notice that I am not claiming that objective conditions (say, of working conditions or of internet chat rooms) are meaningless. They may, given certain established habits in individuals, be more or less conducive to the realization of certain qualities of experience (say, aesthetic experience). The point is that one *always* will find the subjective factor at play, but one will not find a certain class of objective features *always* at play.

Second, one would be hard pressed to identify objective features of a situation that are vital in any generalizable sense. In the case of aesthetic experience and artistic expressivity, one would be at a loss to identify (in a principled fashion) which properties of physical art objects correlate with a certain quality of experience. Is it a certain way of creating a line? Does a certain color make a painting sad? Which properties render a three-hour war film moving (or tedious)? Certain aestheticians in the pragmatist tradition have given up attempting to argue that there are determinate aesthetic properties of objects that everyone could identify; instead, they fall back to the claim that such properties are *determinable* by subjects, but that the specifics of this process rely heavily on enculturation and habit.[4] This line of thought is not foreign to Dewey; he bluntly claims that "the fundamental mistake is the confusion of the physical product with the esthetic object, which is that which is perceived. Physically, a statue is a block of marble, nothing more. . . . But to identify the physical lump with the statue that is a work of art and to identify pigments on a canvas with a picture is absurd. . . . For an object is perceived by a cumulative series of interactions."[5] This series of interactions, of course, is the interplay between the subject and whatever objective material there is in the object at hand—be it a statue or a spoken utterance. As detailed earlier, the expressiveness of each sort of lump depends on *how* we attend to and value it. If we see the statue as a doorstop, or the conversational greeting as a cue to hand money to the cashier, that will tone the experience and speed it along to the next disjointed activity. If we attend to the statue or utterance *now* and value it in itself, we will better handle the situational demands and not deprive it of the aesthetic unity Dewey finds available in each activity or process. Material or objective features are important in a subject's interaction with an environment, but one cannot specify the vital ones in the same way as one can the orientational features of attention and valuing. This, of course, has the meliorative implication of telling us where to start our efforts.

Third, an emphasis on orientation is useful insofar as it can effectively guide individual and social projects of melioration. In the terminology of meliorism, an emphasis on orientation is useful insofar as it provides both a unit of melioration (the individual and his or her mental habits toward activity) and a vector of change (viz., ways of instilling a new orientation toward activity). One still could maintain that this is not the most important factor in melioration. This alternative emphasis on systemic objective conditions would seem to lack the ease and effectiveness of implementation that the individual level of orientation provides, however. If one maintains that the factor preventing us from enjoying a life of reveling in present activity is the economic, material setup of society and its occupations, one may be hard pressed to change all of this. Such a change would require massive reorganization of people and energies, a change that is not only difficult (indeed, a Deweyan naturalism would be much better predisposed for gradual reform or change), but may be warranted only by a high level of certainty that a major societal reorganization (which would most likely need to occur coercively) is *the* way society ought to be.

Alternatively, orientational meliorism as a program is compatible with the further organizing of communities to change objective conditions, but insists that attention be given to the factor that will continue to affect the happiness and quality of experience no matter what the objective conditions are—the factor of orientation. The Buddhists (and many schools of Hindu philosophical thought) saw this point clearly in their analysis of desire; no matter what you achieve or fail to achieve in the way of your projects and goals, you will continue to suffer if you do not address how you orient yourself toward desire and its objects. This conclusion is born out in the modern empirical research on work—no matter what the material accouterments of a position, one's approach to it and its value can render it painful drudgery. Thus, an eminently helpful project is the improvement and optimization of one's orientation, both for the philosophers of India as well as for pragmatists such as Dewey. The subjective focus of orientational meliorism provides a workable starting point for such improvement, as individuals can immediately begin examining how they approach activity. Furthermore, interventions can be designed and tested in regard to improving orientations such as those toward communicative activity, in much the same way that interventions have been conducted in positive psychology and occupational satisfaction research.[6] Such an approach also echoes and reinforces Dewey's point that aesthetic experience is interactive or transformative in nature.

Objection 2: This Account Encourages Passivity in Victims of Immoral Treatment

This objection is related to the previous one, but specifically concerns the putative passivity that is encouraged by my account of aesthetic experience. Thus, one may say that one should not be focused on the present in situations of painful existence; instead, one should remain fixated on something in the future and strive to make it a reality. One could even take my advice about transforming drudgery into satisfying work as a placating inducement of false consciousness—the making of an oppressed individual into a happy and content oppressed individual. Like the previous complaint, such an objection is based on an oversimplification of my position. I would offer the following two responses to such a criticism.

First, the conception of aesthetic experience and artful activity I have developed from Dewey's work does not encourage passivity or the ignoring of the demands of the present. Instead, as indicated in my reading of aesthetic experience, progressive adjustment, and growth, the ideal is an agent who is integrally connected to the needs, demands, and resources of the present. Why is this the ideal? It not only provides unity among an agent's successes and failures, it also serves as the most effective way to negotiate the situation. Remote ends and goals disconnected from the rich present would be the method to placate individuals *now*, since they avert the agent's focus from what is right, what is wrong, and what can be done about it now. The Deweyan point is merely that it is the living *subject* and her *experiences* that should guide this meliorative project. No passivity is necessarily entailed by this account. Activity is always there—the only variable is how one goes about that activity.

The best way of handling a situation and setting up future successes is to attend to the situation in the rich sense of the word "attend." This means that one does not merely *notice* what is happening, but instead one actively and attentively *engages* the specifics of the situation in the most intelligent way possible. Thus, if one is in the atrocious position of being a captive or a slave, one's attention is best directed about how to improve that situation and possibly escape it. One's lived experience is not helped by saying that one will get one's just dessert in some remote afterlife. Religious belief can assist with melioration, but the Deweyan point is that this occurs only when it encourages an imaginative engagement with the materials of the present—

not when it encourages a wholesale slighting of what one is currently experiencing. The point I am stressing is not that passivity is good, but simply that artful living concerns how one engages one's situation, whether this is in regard to work, captivity, familial interactions, and so on.

Second, this objection seems empirically falsified by significant cases in which individuals could not change their objective situation. As was exemplified in the Frankl example, one can take the well-documented case of Jewish occupants of Nazi concentration camps. Here is a case in which individuals did not have much hope of changing their situation in the short term—they were forcibly detained and had little chance of escape. Yet many of the prisoners who survived significant lengths of time in the camps found ways to adjust themselves to the situation such that they could give it the sort of meaning that was conducive to their survival. Again, the question is not whether the concentration camps as objective situations should be changed; obviously they are reprehensible and no one should be in such circumstances. But what happens when people were forced to be in such circumstances? How does one give meaning and significance to that experience such that one has the resilience needed to adjust, grow, and survive?

This is a point that extends beyond Frankl's experience. In her qualitative research involving Holocaust survivors, Roberta R. Greene found that those individuals that survived the mental and physical challenges of the concentration camps tended to be those that could alter their subjective approach to the situation to give the present (deplorable) circumstances a greater meaning. Many of the survivors stated that they found ways to undercut the Nazi efforts by sabotaging military parts they were working on. While this had a negligible impact on the Nazi war machine, it had a great impact on those individuals' beliefs in their ability to make choices and to control their inner life.[7] The choice many of them had was simple—to give up and wait for death, or to try to give meaning to their choices and themselves in such awful circumstances. The latter approach not only contributed to a more satisfying experience in circumstances that were deplorable and inescapable, but also proved to be more favorable to survival and growth. My account does not wish such circumstances on anyone, but it does maintain the adaptive and experiential value of engaging with one's present situation, good or bad. For it is in this fashion that the greatest hopes for meaning and melioration are to be found.

Objection 3: This Account Does Not Exhaust All That Can Be Said About the Objective Features of Art or Artistic Practices

Such an objection may emphasize the time Dewey spent analyzing certain objective artistic practices, such those involved in certain schools of painting or sculpture. Or the objection can come from those individuals who are unsatisfied with my wide account of aesthetic experience, and who desire an airtight description of the artistic and the aesthetic such that speed boats and Porsches can be excluded from the realm of art. I would agree with the objection as originally stated, since my account does not preclude individuals from investigating such issues. The freeing solvent of pragmatism merely asks that all those involved in such labors keep a close watch on what they accomplish. I believe I have constructed a wide account that is of use precisely because it gives us an answer as to how aesthetic experience can be morally cultivating and how we can render more of our life artful or aesthetic. Mere correctness does not entail usefulness. Others may not feel the draw of these issues emphasized by a Deweyan take on art and the aesthetic, but that does not count as an objection to such an account's value. Pragmatists never shy away from a healthy and heuristic pluralism—in theory or in application.

Objection 4: This Account of Moral Cultivation Is Too Broad

Such an objection is simply saying that attention to the situation is not useful, which is a viable pragmatic objection to my pragmatist account. First of all, my account of aesthetic and moral experience does not preclude further moral theorizing and analysis. Indeed, more specific investigation must be undertaken, say, in the case of internet privacy, to even ascertain all the demands, desires, and interests involved in such a complex ethical issue. Second, as a general theory of moral *cultivation,* my account is satisfactory. Such an account cannot give specific steps that make and instantiate an ideal moral agent; on Deweyan grounds, it simply does not make sense to reify and freeze character at one determinate state. What situation would your list of moral traits or actions assume? It would have to assume some concrete situation if a specific account were to truly be concrete, and the rub of life is that nothing is concrete for long.

The account I have given argues for a fluid, adaptable, and unified way of approaching activity. This is what Dewey was getting at when he characterized moral conduct by its spirit or method, not by what specific act was called for in that specific situation. Education, like moral cultivation, aims to produce agents that are sensitive to the demands and opportunities of a given situation, be it inquiry over truth claims or deliberation over what one should do in relational contexts. Short of limiting one's domain of investigation to one specific area of conduct, the most one can say is what I have been arguing for here—that the sort of character we ought to develop is one that is attentively and absorptively engaged in the situation at hand. In some cases, this attentive engagement is a reflective engagement, as in engrossing problem solving or in difficult art. In other cases, this engagement is a second-natured connection with an absorbing situation, be it in the theatre or on the ball field. Moral cultivation, like aesthetic experience, involves a certain live and absorbing interpenetration of the organism with the situation at hand. Such a quality of experience is not only higher in terms of subjective satisfaction, but also in terms of the likelihood of growing, adjusting, or thriving in light of that situation's demands and opportunities.

Objection 5: Your Account of Aesthetic Experience as an Instance of Moral Cultivation Is Easily Falsifiable

This objection is related to the previous one, but could be couched in terms of a counterexample—for instance, the Nazi doctor who truly understands and appreciates classical music, but ignores the moral status of the Jewish prisoners on whom he experiments. Is this not a case of aesthetic sophistication and attentiveness being disjoined from what we would class as virtue or morally cultivated behavior? One may think such cases show an obvious flaw with my argument, namely, that aesthetic experience and attentiveness is not an instance of the endpoint of moral cultivation. An individual who is focused on aesthetic matters and aesthetically cultivated is shown to be lacking in simple moral matters.

This is a powerful, but ultimately flawed, objection. The way such examples get their traction is by featuring an agent who attends to aesthetic matter (viz., an art object) at the expense of other morally relevant features of the present situation. Thus, the caricature is drawn of a person staring at a painting while a fellow human drowns nearby. Such a situation indicts the habits of attentiveness of the individual in the example, not the general claim that aesthetic experience and moral experience involve ways of attending to a present situation. People can be more or less attentive to a situation in a holistic sense; in the case of aesthetic matters, one can attend to the art object in a rich fashion or in a constricted fashion. In terms of art objects, this is the point I explicated in chapter 5 with the example of the doctor who examines the statue with too much emphasis on his practice as a doctor; the experience is affected in a negative fashion by the art object becoming just another part of that doctor's practice instead of an object in which to be immediately engrossed.

The point I have been getting at in this book is that the key to the aesthetic is that it is connected to a shaping of attention through one's orientation. Incomplete ways of shaping attention in a present situation are cases calling for melioration, not evidence that shaping and focusing attention is incorrect or not helpful for the quality of one's lived experience. The Nazi doctor is not a case of a truly cultivated person, since he is not attending to vital parts of the situation in front of him—namely, the interests and desires of the other humans involved. One could hope such selective attention could be meliorated and further cultivated. The deficiency in attention of the Nazi doctor does not impugn a Deweyan take on aesthetic and moral experience involving attentiveness to one's situation. It merely impugns the doctor's habits of attending in that situation.

A related concern would be that such an instance of aesthetic experience would render one excused from further cultivation. One attends to an opera in an absorbed fashion. According to my logic, the objection goes, this is an instantiation of the endpoint of moral cultivation—attentiveness to one's situation. That individual is then excused from all other moral striving or cultivation. The objection would press that the individual is now perfect. Of course, this is a *reductio ad absurdum* argument, since no one believes that the individual in question is done with morality simply because he or she was enthralled in one opera. This sort of objection can be answered in a simple fashion by clarifying the nature of morality. For the sort of pragmatist take on moral cultivation that I have been explicating, the name of the game is to be attuned to one's situation in the present. What is life but an interconnected series of presents?

Thus, the overall goal of a life well lived would be one that is attentively engaged in as many lived presents as possible. Being absorbed in an opera is great; that moment was well played, so to speak, as long as one was not giving selective attention to the opera and ignoring one's starving child at home. All things being equal, that sort of experience was alive and the individual was engaged with the present. Could one ever just enjoy the opera? Yes, in those situations in which the opera was the central concern of one's rich present. But there is often more to life than that opera, and there are many more instances and opportunities to be engaged and absorbed in the present. One's habits of attentiveness helped one attend to the art object in the form of the opera and such habits will more often than not prepare one for the next situation in life that calls for a fineness of touch.

Objection 6: Your Account Is Non-Deweyan Because It Uses Non-Deweyan Distinctions

Such an objection balks at my talk of mental and physical habits, the present and the past/future, subject and object, and so on, and perhaps would gesture toward the rich concept of experience as being truly Deweyan. While I have addressed some of these worries earlier in this book, here I would present two lines of response to such a general objection. First, a methodological response. While I agree that Dewey's sort of pragmatism rejects *hard* dualisms, distinctions that purport to grasp onto the nature of reality in a strict way, I do not see him opposed to *using* distinctions in reflectively analyzing the whole of lived experience. Indeed, it seems that reflective analysis and problem solving is forced to make such distinctions. Where the distinctions must not lead us is the judgment that these concepts exhaust reality. I make no pretense to the latter judgment in the previous chapters. Instead, I merely want to entertain one way of differentiating habits *with a certain purpose*—to meliorate certain general ways of approaching activity that renders it nonartful and mere drudgery. If the proceeding way of talking about certain habits that are more mental than they are of specific bodily motions, say, is useful, then so be it—how can a pragmatist object to such a useful and meliorative exercise? If they turn out to be nonuseful, then their fault lies in that feature, and not in their violating of some veridical notion of what is Deweyan.

The same goes for the topic of experience and subjects/objects. If one can usefully (and reflectively) analyze the lived immediacy of experience with the concepts of subject and object, shouldn't this be allowed on pragmatist grounds? Indeed, Dewey does this in *Art as Experience* when he discusses habits of attention *of subjects* in museums, in classrooms, and on ferryboats, a point I have discussed in previous chapters. He does not retreat into the dark amorphous night of experience in order to leave all reflective and heuristically valuable distinctions behind. Immediate experience is more than any given set of conceptual distinctions, but the latter can justifiably be employed to discuss the former. Such distinctions can be used to meliorate or improve lived, holistic, and immediate experience. In the terms of my project, such working distinctions as subject/object are used as an entry point to the question of how *one* can make more of *his or her* experience aesthetic or artful in quality.

My second response concerns the more specific issue of dividing temporal processes into seemingly distinct parts (viz., past, present, and future). One could object that Dewey interlinks these *processes*, the past funding the present and the present anticipating the future. This indeed is the picture Dewey paints in the first two chapters of *Art as Experience*. What I think such an objection misses is the *use* of such distinctions in reflectively diagnosing and meliorating harmful ways of orienting one's self toward such processes. As I have explored in earlier chapters, Dewey was concerned in the realms of work, aesthetic matters, and education with certain orientations that force a subject to attend less to the rich present and more on remote, detached goals. This renders work drudgery, experience nonaesthetic, and education boring and less effective. Simply saying the present *is* connected to the past and future misses Dewey's point—certain ways of orienting oneself toward this present *distorts* or *overlooks* this connection for a subject, rendering his or her experience not as enlivened or qualitatively pleasing as it could be. Again, distinctions are employed because they seem to be of a certain use. In this case, separating future from present, say, gives us the meliorative leverage to distinguish helpful orientations toward activity from harmful ones. The former orientations, of course, are what I have been arguing are the vital part to making more of life aesthetic or artful.

Living the Artful Life

The artful life is the life that is lived in the present, the life that instantiates engaged, absorptive attention to the demands of life *now*. Of course, this instantiation helps one develop and solidify those habits that will help one attend to the next present situation. Like Dewey's general reading of moral development in *Human Nature and Conduct*, the vital move is the development of habit. The type of habit that I have identified as being particularly important is one's orientation to the world, self, and activity. With a bit of conscious attention to one's orientation, one can improve the quality of experience one has in front of art objects, desks, customers, and conversational partners. Like all things involving habit, conscious effort and intelligent direction will be necessitated. People can make more of their life artful, more of their life like the unified production and playing out of a great work of art, primarily through realizing the key to the aesthetic.

I conclude this study with a point that Dewey found important enough to employ in ending one of his works. This is the idea, held through much of this study, that moral cultivation implicates a close relation between self and community. This interrelation extends to descriptive claims about the ontology of individuals, but more important, it holds an important position in rectifying and improving the quality of lived experience. Dewey notes this perspective on self and community in ending his collection of essays on the "lost individual": "To gain an integrated individuality, each of us needs to cultivate his own garden. But there is no fence about this garden: it is no sharply marked-off enclosure. Our garden is the world, in the angle at which it touches our own manner of being. By accepting the corporate and industrial world in which we live, and by thus fulfilling the precondition for interaction with it, we, who are also parts of the moving present, create ourselves as we create an unknown future."[8] Like Dewey's early ethical pronouncements in the 1890s, cultivating the self is the improvement of the community, and vice versa. This is also a theme that is resident in his works on education; in his contribution to an encyclopedia on education in 1921, he notes the reciprocal (but often unnoticed) relationship between improving the harmony of individual faculties and the production of a better society.[9]

The trick is to realize that the means are the ends in this situation—the world of the individual is the world of the community and the improvement of one is not sequestered from the experience of all. In a very real sense, we create the world in which we find ourselves and in which we will find ourselves in future presents. The challenge is to intelligently form conditions and selves such that we can grow and adapt to conditions, and so that our lived experience is as we truly want it. The lived experience denoted by aesthetic experience in the Deweyan scheme is important because it is a lived instance that can tell us about the quality of a certain way of being, as well as the imaginative connections that such states share with other possible states of affairs. We see the end of our efforts and struggles to be alive, and we simply want more of it.

Like most of life, the key to the artful life lies in attending to what one is faced with *now*—attending in the rich sense of noting and reacting in the correct measure. As with great works of art, no specific recipe or set of rules can be given for exactly how one is to live such an artful life. The hope of pragmatism is that it gives us the sort of general direction and guidance that one can reasonably expect in such matters. In the case of the artful life, one can succeed if and when one wakes up to the demands and opportunities of the rich present in which they are situated. Artful living is a way of living as if the present was your goal, as if that self and world you are creating through your actions were a work of art worth attending to with all your energy, care, and devotion.

Notes

Chapter 1

1. Weingarten, "Pearls Before Breakfast," W10.
2. Some may object to my usage of the terms "art," "artful," and "aesthetic." Indeed, they carry much conceptual baggage. Part of the argument of this book will be that the experiences connected to the creation and reception of art—skilled making, imagination, foresight, exhilaration, and absorption—are part of what we denote as "aesthetic experience."
3. For an account of the relationship between Western artistic practices and the concept of aesthetic experience, consult Carroll, "Aesthetic Experience, Art, and Artists," 145–65.
4. Gaut, *Art, Emotion, and Ethics*, 35.
5. Shusterman, *Pragmatist Aesthetics*, 34–61.

Chapter 2

1. Lee, "Subway Books Give Mexico a Novel Way to Fight Crime," A8.
2. Shusterman, *Performing Live*, 15–34, and "Aesthetic Experience," 80.
3. When I use terms such as "wrong" or "incorrect," I imply their pragmatist meaning of "not as useful as other conceptions." The later chapters of this book will illustrate the new directions for meliorative activity that are opened up by taking the term "aesthetic experience" in my different, more useful way. It is in this sense that I believe the path Dewey leads us down is the correct one.
4. Stolnitz, *Aesthetics and Philosophy of Art Criticism*; Bullough, "'Psychical Distance,'" 233–54.
5. Budd, *Values of Art*.
6. Bell, *Art*, 25.
7. Bahm, "Aesthetic Experience and Moral Experience," 837–46.
8. Bullough, "'Psychical Distance,'" 234.
9. Ibid., 239.
10. Dickie, "The Myth of the Aesthetic Attitude," 56–65.
11. Carroll, *Beyond Aesthetics*, 41–62.
12. Dickie, "The Myth of the Aesthetic Attitude," 64.
13. Carroll, *Philosophy of Art*, 200. Carroll also continues this focus on internal aesthetic properties in "Aesthetic Experience, Art, and Artists," 159.
14. For the latter point, see Mothersill, "Beauty and the Critic's Judgment," 152–66.
15. Aldrich, "Back to Aesthetic Experience."
16. I would submit that a better question would be whether texts can argue for or against certain action strategies or normative judgments. See Stroud, "Narrative as Argument in Indian Philosophy,"

42–71; "Multivalent Narratives," 369–93; and "Simulation, Subjective Knowledge, and the Cognitive Value of Literary Narrative," 19–41.

17. See Lamarque and Olsen, *Truth, Fiction, and Literature*, 1.
18. Carroll, "The Wheel of Virtue," 3–26.
19. Stolnitz, "On the Cognitive Triviality of Art," 191–200.
20. Lamarque and Olsen, *Truth, Fiction, and Literature*.
21. Lamarque, "Tragedy and Moral Value," 62.
22. Lamarque, "The Uselessness of Art," 209.
23. Lamarque and Olsen, *Truth, Fiction, and Literature*, 396.
24. Diffey, "What Can We Learn from Art?," 30.
25. Ibid., 31.
26. Novitz, "Messages 'In' and Messages 'Through' Art," 85.
27. Ibid., 5. Budd continues to connect the intrinsic value of art solely to an appreciation of its aesthetic properties in his essay "Aesthetic Essence," 28–29.
28. Carroll, *Beyond Aesthetics*, 41–62.
29. Gaut, *Art, Emotion, and Ethics*, 11.
30. James, "The Will to Believe," 717–35.
31. Gary Iseminger joins in as one of the many partisans in this debate over aesthetic experience and value that emphasizes the role of states of mind. While he focuses his account on fine art objects and the concept of appreciation, one can still see the sort of value that others place on the role of individual attitude in aesthetic experience. See "Experiential Theories of Aesthetic Value," 45–58.
32. Aldrich, "Back to Aesthetic Experience," 368–69.
33. Danto, *The Philosophical Disenfranchisement of Art*, 117–33.
34. Shusterman, *Performing Live*, 15–34.
35. Ibid., 31.
36. Margolis, "The Deviant Ontology of Artworks," 109–29.
37. Bahm, "Aesthetic Experience and Moral Experience," 842; Stolnitz, *Aesthetics and Philosophy*, 45.
38. Other scholars continue to explicitly or implicitly align the value of art to intrinsic value, cashed out as value that is self-contained and persistent, or independent of ulterior interests. See Levinson, "Intrinsic Value and the Notion of a Life," 319–29, and Iseminger, "Experiential Theories of Aesthetic Value," 45–58.
39. For such arguments against the application of intrinsic value to art objects, see Levinson, "Intrinsic Value," and Beardsley, "Intrinsic Value," 1–17.
40. Budd, *Values of Art*, 5 (emphasis added).
41. Beardsley, *Aesthetics*, 574.

Chapter 3

1. See, for instance, O'Dwyer, "The Metaphysics of Existence Rehabilitated," 711–30; Myers and Pappas, "Dewey's Metaphysics," 679–700; Gale, "The Metaphysics of John Dewey," 477–519; and Bernstein, "John Dewey's Metaphysics of Experience," 5–14. See also Boisvert, *Dewey's Metaphysics*.
2. Johnston, "Reflections on Richard Shusterman's Dewey," 106.
3. Shusterman, "Complexities of Aesthetic Experience," 110.
4. Johnston, "Reflections on Shusterman's Dewey," 106.
5. Ibid.
6. Shusterman, *Performing Live*, 115–36.
7. Shusterman, "Complexities of Aesthetic Experience," 110.
8. Ibid.

9. Dewey, *Experience and Nature*, 30.
10. Shusterman, "Complexities of Aesthetic Experience," 109. For more on the problems with ignoring the aesthetic's linkage to cultural forces, see Shusterman, *Surface and Depth*, 91–107.
11. Note how this differs from the account offered by Walton, "How Marvelous!," which replaces the immediacy of such an account. For instance, he states that "one *appreciates* the work. One does not merely enjoy it; one takes pleasure or delight in judging it to be good" (504).
12. Dewey, "The Logic of Judgments of Practice," 242.
13. For more on Moore's approach, see his *Principia Ethica*.
14. Dewey, "Ambiguity of 'Intrinsic Good,'" 43.
15. Ibid., 44.
16. Dewey, "Valuation and Experimental Knowledge," 5.
17. Dewey, *Democracy and Education*, 113.
18. Another way of getting at such a point is to highlight the process as being the product desired. This is the approach taken by Sawyer, "Improvisation and the Creative Process," 149–61.
19. Dewey, *Art as Experience*, 285.
20. Ibid., 201.
21. Gouinlock, *John Dewey's Philosophy of Value*, 131.
22. Dewey, *Human Nature and Conduct*, 182.
23. Ibid., 184
24. Ibid.

Chapter 4

1. One possible exception would be some of the authors in or around the eighteenth century, such as Kant and Schiller.
2. Ivanhoe, *Confucian Moral Self-Cultivation*.
3. For example, think of Immanuel Kant's employment of the *"summum bonum,"* the highest good composed of the most perfect union of virtue and happiness that can be imagined. This good, according to his moral thought of the 1780s, was an unreachable ideal that we merely approximated in our earthly activities. For his description of this ideal, see *Kritik der praktischen Vernunft* (1788), "Critique of Practical Reason," in Kant, *Practical Philosophy*, especially around 5:123.
4. A similar pragmatist reading of morality as being without foundations and without certain ending principles is given in Margolis, *Moral Philosophy After 9/11*.
5. Alexander, *John Dewey's Theory of Art, Experience, and Nature*.
6. Dewey, "From Absolutism to Experimentalism," 147–60.
7. Welchman, *Dewey's Ethical Thought*.
8. Dewey, *The Study of Ethics*, 241.
9. Ibid.
10. Welchman, *Dewey's Ethical Thought*, 99.
11. Ibid., 100.
12. Dewey, *The Study of Ethics*, 244.
13. Dewey, *Outlines of a Critical Theory of Ethics*, 378.
14. Dewey, *Human Nature and Conduct*, 182.
15. Dewey, *Ethics*, 227, 298.
16. Fesmire, *John Dewey and Moral Imagination*, 99.
17. Boisvert, *John Dewey*, 60.
18. Dewey, *Outlines of a Critical Theory of Ethics*, 322 (capitalization altered).
19. Dewey, *Human Nature and Conduct*, 182.
20. Dewey, *Experience and Nature*, 291.
21. Dickie, "Beardsley's Phantom Aesthetic Experience," 129–36.

22. Beardsley, "Aesthetic Experience Regained," 3–11.
23. See, for instance, Taylor, "The Two-Dewey Thesis, Continued," 17–25, and Shusterman, "Home Alone?," 102–15.
24. Alexander, *John Dewey's Theory of Art*, 203.
25. Habit and attention are interrelated concepts. For instance, Dewey notes that "attention is simply the conscious use of habit" in his lectures on social ethics (from the spring quarter of 1901), 280.
26. Dewey, *Art as Experience*, 177.
27. Ibid., 187.
28. Sawyer, "Improvisation and the Creative Process," 149–61.
29. Dewey, *Art as Experience*, 181.
30. Ibid., 189.
31. Petts, "Aesthetic Experience and the Revelation of Value," 69.
32. Dewey, "The Lost Individual," 66–76.
33. Sartwell, *The Art of Living*.
34. For a variety of creative attempts to define art, see Carroll, ed., *Theories of Art Today*. One interesting feature about all of these theories is that they try to describe what art actually *is*, not how art *can be*. Notice that pragmatist aesthetics, starting with Dewey, tethers an account of art to what it can and should be like—a very normative approach to thinking about art, but one that is much more sophisticated than those whose theories entail simple judgments of some works as good and others as bad (Tolstoy, perhaps). For more on Dewey's take on defining art, see Shusterman, *Pragmatist Aesthetics*, 34–61.
35. Sartwell, *The Art of Living*, xi.
36. Ibid., 13–14.
37. Ibid., 97.
38. Ibid., 97–98.
39. For alternative accounts of Deweyan pragmatism and the *Bhagavad Gītā*, see Stroud, "Orientational Meliorism, Pragmatist Aesthetics, and the *Bhagavad Gītā*," 1–17, and Alexander, "The Music in the Heart, the Way of Water, and the Light of a Thousand Suns," 41–58.
40. Nussbaum, *Love's Knowledge*, 156.
41. Dewey, *Experience and Education*, 29–30.
42. Carroll, *Philosophy of Art*, 174.

Chapter 5

1. Eames, *Experience and Value*, 85.
2. See Margolis, *Selves and Other Texts*.
3. For detailed argumentation on this point, consult Margolis, "One and Only One Correct Interpretation," 26–44.
4. For one such account of intention, see Stecker, *Interpretation and Construction*.
5. Shusterman, *Surface and Depth*, 226–38.
6. For instance, Seel, "On the Scope of Aesthetic Experience," 101, emphasizes works of art as "presentation events" to an audience, and Crowther, "The Aesthetic," 41, argues that the artist's experience is embodied in the work of art. These are helpful readings, of course, but I believe they do not entail the same transactive emphasis that accompanies Dewey's pragmatist account.
7. Note that Dewey is not giving a definition of art, conceived of in terms of covering the extension of the term "art." For an analysis of why Dewey does not attempt this, see Shusterman, *Pragmatist Aesthetics*, 34–61.
8. Dewey, *Art as Experience*, 53.
9. Tormey, *The Concept of Expression*, 104.

10. See the discussion of Dewey's aesthetics in Shusterman, *Pragmatist Aesthetics*, as well as in Alexander, *John Dewey's Theory of Art, Experience, and Nature*.

11. Dewey, *Art as Experience*, 60.

12. Ibid.

13. Of course, this does not mean art is to be totally disconnected from everyday life or use. Dewey rails against such a museum conception of art in the first chapter of *Art as Experience*. What I mean to exclude are merely those forms of experiencing art that do not allow it to evoke an experience different in degree from seeing a valuable plumbing wrench, for instance.

14. Rader and Jessup, *Art and Human Values*, 59–60.

15. This point is emphasized by Fenner, *The Aesthetic Attitude*, 120.

16. Langsdorf, "Reconstructing the Fourth Dimension."

17. By now it should be evident that I have adopted Dewey's convention of referring to art *objects*. Not all of art is constituted by a physical object, and I believe that this is one point about which Dewey could be more explicit. He does discuss ritual and ceremonial activity (briefly), but the majority of his analysis in *Art as Experience* centers on objects. I will attempt to extend his analysis to a more process-based one in the final half of this section.

18. I will not rehearse the intentionalist debate here. I merely assume that there are significant cases of art where one cannot know what the author actually intended (even if intentionalists are correct in their postulation of a monolithic and determinative "intent" behind the creation of each work).

19. Taylor, "The Two-Dewey Thesis, Continued," 17–25.

20. Shusterman, "Pragmatism and Criticism," 32–33.

21. Shusterman, *Practicing Philosophy*, 157–77. For Rorty's critique, see Rorty, "Dewey Between Hegel and Darwin," 54–68, and *Consequences of Pragmatism*.

22. *Lao-Tzu*, trans. Henricks, 53.

23. For such a reading of the *Tao-Te Ching*, see Mou, "Ultimate Concern and Language Engagement," 429–39.

24. *Lao-Tzu*, trans. Henricks, 56.

25. Spielberg, quoted in Hertzberg, "Theatre of War," 31.

26. For a further analysis of vicarious audience involvement in war films, as well as their ability to argue by mood, see Nelson, "Argument by Mood in War Movies," 262–69.

27. Indeed, Spielberg was so successful at evoking such experiences that he was awarded the Distinguished Civilian Service Award from the U.S. Army, the Distinguished Public Service Award from the U.S. Navy, and the Department of Defense Medal for Distinguished Public Service for the public service his film did for simulating the horrors of war and for showcasing the bravery of American soldiers. For more on these awards, see Sheftick, "Army Awards Spielberg for Telling Soldiers' Story," "Navy Honors Spielberg and Hanks for Film *Saving Private Ryan*," and Kozaryn, "DoD Honors *Private Ryan* Director Spielberg."

28. Kivy, *Philosophies of Arts*, 132.

29. Richard Serra, from a transcript quoted in Battin and others, *Puzzles About Art*, 182.

30. Suzuki, *Zen and Japanese Culture*, 220. For discussion of Suzuki's general take on Zen and its connection to aesthetics, see Odin, *Artistic Detachment in Japan and the West*, 141–56.

31. For my analysis of *kōans* as evocative art objects, see Stroud, "How to Do Things with Art," 341–64.

32. Hoover, *Zen Culture*, 204, 206–7.

33. Translated in Beilenson, *Japanese Haiku*, 42. Also, see the alternate translation in Hoover, *Zen Culture*, 206.

34. Hoover, *Zen Culture*, 206.

35. Suzuki, *Zen and Japanese Culture*, 241.

36. This point is emphasized in the reading of the power of *haiku* in Higginson, *The Haiku Handbook*, 5.

37. Jackson, *John Dewey and the Lessons of Art*, 119–20.

38. The related division between product-centered and process-centered notions of art and creativity are discussed by Sawyer, "Improvisation and the Creative Process," 149–61. While Sawyer argues that Dewey is focused on the process-centered approached, he does note product-centered deviations in *Art as Experience.*
39. Sartwell, *The Art of Living.*
40. Shusterman, *Pragmatist Aesthetics,* 56.
41. Shusterman, "Pragmatism and Criticism," 31.
42. Shusterman, *Body Consciousness,* 180–216.
43. Think here of art objects with unknown authors, or authors who are shrouded in the mists of time and distant history.
44. Shusterman, *Pragmatist Aesthetics,* 84–114. See also the arguments given against elitism in traditional theories of criticism, in Shusterman, *Surface and Depth,* 91–107; Stroud, "Pragmatism and the Methodology of Comparative Rhetoric," 353–79; and Stroud, "John Dewey and the Question of Artful Criticism," 27–51.
45. Shusterman, "Home Alone?," 102–15.
46. Shusterman, *Pragmatist Aesthetics,* 92.
47. Alexander, *John Dewey's Theory of Art,* 232.
48. Dewey, *Art as Experience,* 110.
49. Stecker, *Interpretation and Construction.*
50. See Dewey, *Construction and Criticism,* 125–44.
51. For example, the epic *Mahabharata* affects millions of people in India today, even though its author(s) and their actual intentions are unknown or uncertain. "Vyasa" is said to have written it, but he is also said to have written many other important philosophical/religious texts in the Hindu tradition. He also appears in the storyline as a character, further confusing fact and fiction. See Katz, *Arjuna in the Mahabharata,* and Minor, *Bhagavad Gita.*
52. Dewey, *Art as Experience,* 325.
53. Jhanji, *The Sensuous in Art,* 7.
54. Stroud, "Multivalent Narratives," 42–71.
55. Peirce, "The Fixation of Belief," 5–22.
56. See for instance, the disagreement between Fesmire, *John Dewey and Moral Imagination,* and Tiles, "Steven Fesmire, *John Dewey and Moral Imagination,*" 378–83.
57. Fesmire, *John Dewey and Moral Imagination,* 93.
58. Carroll, *A Philosophy of Mass Art* and *The Philosophy of Horror.*
59. Fisher, *Human Communication as Narration,* 194.
60. For more on my approach to this issue, see Stroud, "Simulation, Subjective Knowledge, and the Cognitive Value of Literary Narrative," 19–41.
61. For discussion of how self-realization fits into Dewey's later ethical thought, consult Roth, *John Dewey and Self-Realization.*
62. Dewey, *Human Nature and Conduct,* 196.
63. Ibid., 144.
64. Ibid.
65. Langsdorf, "Reconstructing the Fourth Dimension," 141–64.
66. Shusterman, *Surface and Depth,* 237.
67. Odin, *Artistic Detachment,* 256–57.
68. Dewey, *Art as Experience,* 274.
69. Shusterman, *Surface and Depth,* 238.

Chapter 6

1. Shusterman, *Surface and Depth,* 191.
2. Dewey, *Reconstruction in Philosophy,* 181–82.

3. For further accounts of meliorism, see Ruetenik, "Social Meliorism in the Religious Pragmatism of William James," 238–49, and Stroud, "What Does Pragmatic Meliorism Mean for Rhetoric?," 43–60.

4. Seligman and others, "Positive Psychology Progress," 410–21. See also Pawelski, "William James, Positive Psychology, and Healthy-Mindedness," 53–67, and Seligman, *Authentic Happiness.* See also the anthology edited by Aspinwall and Staudinger, *A Psychology of Human Strengths.*

5. I have explored issues of orientation and orientational meliorism elsewhere. See Stroud, "Pragmatist Aesthetics and Film," 67–83, "Ontological Orientation and the Practice of Rhetoric," 146–60, and "Orientational Meliorism in Dewey and Dōgen," 185–215.

6. Paraplegics, while not as extremely incapacitated physically as quadriplegics, provide a similar case study in the limits of growth. Mihaly Csikszentmihalyi points out that paraplegics listed the accident that robbed them of their mobility as both the most negative *and* most positive event in their lives. Such individuals attend to the challenges of physical and mental life, and meet them with a renewed vigor. It would be hard to say that their growth is limited with their physical mobility; instead, such a case study highlights my general point—growth is largely a factor of the orientation and expectations of the agent in the situation, and such individuals find wonderful ways to adapt to their tragic situation. See Csikszentmihalyi, *Flow*, 193–96.

7. Of course, not all habits in such a Deweyan account will be mental. Habits are very often of the body—say, habits of smoking, piano playing, and softball hitting. The point I am emphasizing here is that there is a certain (very important) set of habits that reside in the mental functioning of humans that shape the ways that they think about and engage with the world. These mental habits marshal and organize other, subordinate habits, including those of the body.

8. This division is also evident in *Democracy and Education*, 52–53, although there it is discussed as habituation versus adaptation.

9. Lachs, "Stoic Pragmatism," 105.

10. Dewey, *A Common Faith*, 17–18.

11. Lachs, "Stoic Pragmatism," 105.

12. Dewey, *How We Think*, 286–87.

13. Dewey, *Democracy and Education*, 212.

14. For more on a Deweyan account of argument, see Stroud, "Mindful Argument, Deweyan Pragmatism, and the Ideal of Democracy."

15. John Dewey, as recorded in *John Dewey: Lectures in China, 1919–1920*, trans. Clopton and Ou, 206.

16. For the shortcomings of the example provided by the robber, see Hook, "John Dewey," 1010–18, as well as Dewey, *The Public and Its Problems*, 327–28. One could also think of the cocaine addict here—one who focuses so much on the object of one specific desire that he or she fails to adapt and grow in the face of other desires, needs, and expectations resident in the situation (including those from other individuals or groups).

17. Dewey, *How We Think*, 348.

18. Dewey, *Outlines of a Critical Theory of Ethics*, 316.

19. Dewey, *Democracy and Education*, 326–27.

20. Ibid., 326.

21. Portions of Dewey's religious works do point to such a change, but deny its voluntary nature. I believe Dewey is right on the difficulty of changing such habits due to their deep-seated nature, but I also believe that he is wrong to cast such a change as totally separate from will. This is the insight that one sees as evident in many cultivation practices, especially from the East. Meditation, *kōan* practice, and the varieties of yoga are all initiated by a student when he or she sees clearly enough to know that change is needed. For Dewey's perfunctory comments about religious change and will, see *A Common Faith*, 13.

22. Wrzesniewski and Dutton, "Crafting a Job," 179–201. See also Wrzesniewski and others, "Jobs, Careers, and Callings," 21–33.

23. Seligman, *Authentic Happiness*, 165–84.

24. Wrzesniewski and Dutton, "Crafting a Job," 191.
25. Dewey, *How We Think*, 329.
26. Seligman and others, "Positive Psychology Progress."
27. These details, as well as the story that follows, comes from Frankl, *Man's Search for Meaning*. Page numbers of quotations are cited parenthetically in the text.

Chapter 7

1. Important studies of communication that incorporate Dewey's thought have included Carey, "A Cultural Approach to Communication," 11–28; Belman, "John Dewey's Concept of Communication," 29–37; and Jensen, *Is Art Good for Us?*
2. Crick, "John Dewey's Aesthetics of Communication," 303.
3. Ibid., 314.
4. Ibid., 317.
5. Crick, *Democracy and Rhetoric*, 168–86. Danisch's analysis of Dewey in *Pragmatism, Democracy, and the Necessity of Rhetoric*, 41–64, also seems to follow a similar path. While interesting for a formal conception of rhetoric in situations of public address or debate, they both leave open the possibility of further analysis of Dewey on everyday communication.
6. Dewey, *The Public and Its Problems*, 350.
7. Belman, "John Dewey's Concept of Communication," 36–37.
8. For more on the differences between such ways of defining art, see Shusterman, *Pragmatist Aesthetics*, 34–61.
9. One must not think I am *defining* art in terms of aesthetic experience—that was the project that so troubled Beardsley in *Aesthetics*. Instead, I (along with Dewey) want to maintain that truly moving and powerful art will be correlated with aesthetic experience. Indeed, that is why we are drawn to say it is powerful—it has such a rapturous and absorptive effect on us.
10. Dewey, *Experience and Nature*, chap. 5.
11. Sartwell, *The Art of Living*, 97.
12. Dewey, *Art as Experience*, 110.
13. Habermas, "Philosophy and Science as Literature?," 223.
14. See, for instance, the analysis of jazz and improvisational drama given by Sawyer, "Improvisation and the Creative Process," 149–61.
15. Dewey, *Art as Experience*, 202.
16. Dewey, *How We Think*, 346–47.
17. Dewey, *Art as Experience*, 219.
18. For more on the relation of Deweyan aesthetics to communicative mindfulness, consult Stroud, "Toward a Deweyan Theory of Communicative Mindfulness," 57–75. The concept of Deweyan mindfulness I defend there is functionally equivalent to the notion of artful activity I elucidate here. Both feature the same sort of absorptive engagement with one's present activity.
19. Dewey, *Human Nature and Conduct*, 184–85.
20. Dewey, *Experience and Nature*, 144–45.
21. Dewey, *Democracy and Education*, 7.
22. Tannen, *The Argument Culture*; Stroud, "Ontological Orientation and the Practice of Rhetoric," 146–60; Foss and Foss, *Inviting Transformation*; Foss and Griffin, "Beyond Persuasion," 2–18.
23. Dewey, *Art as Experience*, 109–10.
24. Ibid., 262.
25. Sartwell, *Art of Living*, 97–98.
26. See, for instance, Dewey's early critique of such remote ideals of conduct in "Green's Theory of the Moral Motive," 155–73.

Notes to Pages 188–205

27. These details and others can be found in the introduction to *The Practice of the Presence of God,* trans. Sciurba. Quotes from or references to this source will be given parenthetically in the text.
28. For more on imagined interactions, see Honeycutt, *Imagined Interactions.*

Chapter 8

1. Lippmann, *Public Opinion,* 220.
2. Interestingly enough, a similar critique of pragmatic meliorism, albeit in the form of William James's writings, was given as early as 1943, but from a proponent of *Deweyan* pragmatism. See Otto, "On a Certain Blindness in William James," 184–91.
3. Wrzesniewski and others, "Jobs, Careers, and Callings," 179–201, and Seligman, *Authentic Happiness,* 165–84.
4. See, for example, Margolis, "One and Only One Correct Interpretation," 26–44, *Selves and Other Texts,* and *Historied Thought, Constructed World.*
5. Dewey, *Art as Experience,* 223.
6. Seligman and others, "Positive Psychology Progress," 410–21.
7. Greene, "Holocaust Survivors," 3–18.
8. Dewey, "Individuality in Our Day," 122–23.
9. Dewey, "Contribution to *Encyclopaedia and Dictionary of Education,*" 401.

Bibliography

Aldrich, Virgil C. "Back to Aesthetic Experience." *Journal of Aesthetics and Art Criticism* 24 (1966): 365–71.
Alexander, Thomas M. *John Dewey's Theory of Art, Experience, and Nature: The Horizons of Feeling*. Albany: State University of New York Press, 1987.
———. "The Music in the Heart, the Way of Water, and the Light of a Thousand Suns: A Response to Richard Shusterman, Crispin Sartwell, and Scott Stroud." *Journal of Aesthetic Education* 43 (2009): 41–58.
Aspinwall, Lisa G., and Ursula M. Staudinger, eds. *A Psychology of Human Strengths: Fundamental Questions and Future Directions for a Positive Psychology*. Washington, D.C.: American Psychological Association, 2003.
Bahm, Archie. "Aesthetic Experience and Moral Experience." *Journal of Philosophy* 55 (1958): 837–46.
Battin, Margaret P., John Fisher, Ronald Moore, and Anita Silvers. *Puzzles About Art: An Aesthetics Casebook*. New York: Bedford St. Martin's, 1989.
Beardsley, Monroe C. "Aesthetic Experience Regained." *Journal of Aesthetics and Art Criticism* 28 (1969): 3–11.
———. *Aesthetics: Problems in the Philosophy of Criticism*. Indianapolis: Hackett, 1981.
———. "Intrinsic Value." *Philosophy and Phenomenological Research* 26 (1965): 1–17.
Beilenson, Peter. *Japanese Haiku*. Mount Vernon: Pauper Press, 1955.
Bell, Clive. *Art*. 9th ed. New York: Capricorn, 1958.
Belman, Lary. "John Dewey's Concept of Communication." *Journal of Communication* 27 (1977): 29–37.
Bernstein, Richard. "John Dewey's Metaphysics of Experience." *Journal of Philosophy* 58 (1961): 5–14.
Boisvert, Raymond D. *Dewey's Metaphysics*. New York: Fordham University Press, 1988.
———. *John Dewey: Rethinking Our Time*. Albany: State University of New York Press, 1998.
Budd, Malcolm. "Aesthetic Essence." In Shusterman and Tomlin, *Aesthetic Experience*, 17–30.
———. *Values of Art: Pictures, Poetry, and Music*. London: Penguin Press, 1995.
Bullough, Edward. "'Psychical Distance' as a Factor in Art and an Aesthetic Principle." In Levich, *Aesthetics and the Philosophy of Criticism*, 233–54.
Carey, James W. "A Cultural Approach to Communication." In *Communication as Culture: Essays on Media and Society*, 11–28. New York: Routledge, 1992.

Carroll, Noël. "Aesthetic Experience, Art, and Artists." In Shusterman and Tomlin, *Aesthetic Experience*, 145–65.
———. *Beyond Aesthetics: Philosophical Essays*. New York: Cambridge University Press, 2001.
———. *Philosophy of Art: A Contemporary Introduction*. London: Routledge, 1999.
———. *The Philosophy of Horror: Or, Paradoxes of the Heart*. New York: Routledge, 1990.
———. *A Philosophy of Mass Art*. Oxford: Clarendon Press, 1998.
———. "The Wheel of Virtue: Art, Literature, and Moral Knowledge." *Journal of Aesthetics and Art Criticism* 60 (2002): 3–26.
———, ed. *Theories of Art Today*. Madison: University of Wisconsin Press, 2000.
Crick, Nathan. *Democracy and Rhetoric: John Dewey on the Arts of Becoming*. Columbia: University of South Carolina Press, 2010.
———. "John Dewey's Aesthetics of Communication." *Southern Communication Journal* 69 (2004): 303–19.
Crowther, Paul. "The Aesthetic: From Experience to Art." In Shusterman and Tomlin, *Aesthetic Experience*, 31–44.
Csikszentmihalyi, Mihaly. *Flow: The Psychology of Optimal Experience*. New York: Harper Perennial, 1990.
Danisch, Robert. *Pragmatism, Democracy, and the Necessity of Rhetoric*. Columbia: University of South Carolina Press, 2007.
Danto, Arthur C. *The Philosophical Disenfranchisement of Art*. New York: Columbia University Press, 1986.
Davies, Stephen, ed. *Art and Its Messages: Meaning, Morality, and Society*. University Park: The Pennsylvania State University Press, 1997.
Dewey, John. "The Ambiguity of 'Intrinsic Good.'" In *Later Works of John Dewey*, 15:42–45.
———. *Art as Experience*. In *Later Works of John Dewey*, vol. 10.
———. *A Common Faith*. In *Later Works of John Dewey*, 9:1–58.
———. *Construction and Criticism*. In *Later Works of John Dewey*, 5:125–44.
———. "Contribution to *Encyclopaedia and Dictionary of Education*." In *Middle Works of John Dewey*, 13:397–406.
———. *Democracy and Education*. In *Middle Works of John Dewey*, vol. 9.
———. "Democratic Ends Need Democratic Methods for Their Realization." In *Later Works of John Dewey*, 14:367–68.
———. *The Early Works of John Dewey*. Edited by Jo Ann Boydston. 5 vols. Carbondale: Southern Illinois University Press, 1969–1972.
———. *Ethics*. In *Later Works of John Dewey*, vol. 7.
———. *Experience and Education*. In *Later Works of John Dewey*, 13:1–188.
———. *Experience and Nature*. In *Later Works of John Dewey*, vol. 1.
———. "From Absolutism to Experimentalism." In *Later Works of John Dewey*, 5:147–60.
———. "Green's Theory of the Moral Motive." In *Early Works of John Dewey*, 3:155–73.
———. *How We Think*. In *Later Works of John Dewey*, 8:105–352.
———. *Human Nature and Conduct*. In *Middle Works of John Dewey*, vol. 14.
———. "Individuality in Our Day." In *Later Works of John Dewey*, 5:111–24.
———. "In Reply to Some Criticisms." In *Later Works of John Dewey*, 5:210–17.
———. *John Dewey: Lectures in China, 1919–1920*. Translated by Robert W. Clopton and Tsuin-Chen Ou. Honolulu: University of Hawaii Press, 1973.

Bibliography

———. *The Later Works of John Dewey.* Edited by Jo Ann Boydston. 17 vols. Carbondale: Southern Illinois University Press, 1981–1990.
———. Lectures on Social Ethics. In *John Dewey, Lectures on Ethics, 1900–1901*, edited and with an introduction by Donald F. Koch, 267–448. Carbondale: Southern Illinois University Press, 1991.
———. "The Logic of Judgments of Practice." In *Middle Works of John Dewey*, 8:14–82.
———. "The Lost Individual." In *Later Works of John Dewey*, 5:66–76.
———. *The Middle Works of John Dewey.* Edited by Jo Ann Boydston. 15 vols. Carbondale: Southern Illinois University Press, 1976–1983.
———. Outlines of a Critical Theory of Ethics. In *Early Works of John Dewey*, 3:239–388.
———. "The Postulate of Immediate Empiricism." In *Middle Works of John Dewey*, 3:158–67.
———. Psychology. In *Early Works of John Dewey*, vol. 2.
———. The Public and Its Problems. In *Later Works of John Dewey*, 2:235–372.
———. Reconstruction in Philosophy. In *Middle Works of John Dewey*, 12:77–202.
———. The Study of Ethics. In *Early Works of John Dewey*, 4:221–364.
———. "Valuation and Experimental Knowledge." In *Middle Works of John Dewey*, 13:3–28.
Dickie, George. "Beardsley's Phantom Aesthetic Experience." *Journal of Aesthetics and Art Criticism* 62 (1965): 129–36.
———. "The Myth of the Aesthetic Attitude." *American Philosophical Quarterly* 1 (1964): 56–65.
Diffey, T. J. "What Can We Learn from Art?" In Davies, *Art and Its Messages*, 26–33.
Eames, S. Morris. *Experience and Value: Essays on John Dewey and Pragmatic Naturalism.* Carbondale: Southern Illinois University Press, 2003.
Fenner, David E. W. *The Aesthetic Attitude.* Atlantic Highlands, N.J.: Humanities Press, 1996.
Fesmire, Steven. *John Dewey and Moral Imagination: Pragmatism in Ethics.* Bloomington: Indiana University Press, 2003.
Fisher, Walter R. *Human Communication as Narration: Toward a Philosophy of Reason, Value, and Action.* Columbia: University of South Carolina Press, 1987.
Foss, Sonja K., and Karen A. Foss. *Inviting Transformation: Presentational Speaking for a Changing World.* Prospect Heights, Ill.: Waveland Press, 2003.
Foss, Sonja K., and Cindy L. Griffin. "Beyond Persuasion: A Proposal for an Invitational Rhetoric." *Communication Monographs* 62 (1995): 2–18.
Frankl, Viktor. *Man's Search for Meaning: An Introduction to Logotherapy.* Boston: Beacon Press, 2006.
Gale, Richard M. "The Metaphysics of John Dewey." *Transactions of the Charles S. Peirce Society* 38 (2002): 477–519.
Gaut, Berys. *Art, Emotion, and Ethics.* New York: Oxford University Press, 2007.
Gouinlock, James. *John Dewey's Philosophy of Value.* New York: Humanities Press, 1972.
Greene, Roberta R. "Holocaust Survivors: A Study in Resilience." *Journal of Gerontological Social Work* 37 (2002): 3–18.
Habermas, Jürgen. "Philosophy and Science as Literature?" In *Postmetaphysical Thinking: Philosophical Essays*, translated by William Mark Hohengarten, 205–28. Cambridge: MIT Press, 1996.
Hertzberg, Hendrik. "Theatre of War." *New Yorker*, July 27, 1998, 30–33.

Higginson, William J. *The Haiku Handbook*. Tokyo: Kodansha International, 1985.
Honeycutt, James M. *Imagined Interactions: Daydreaming About Communication*. Cresskill, N.J.: Hampton Press, 2003.
Hook, Sidney. "John Dewey—Philosopher of Growth." *Journal of Philosophy* 56 (1959): 1010–18.
Hoover, Thomas. *Zen Culture*. New York: Random House, 1977.
Iseminger, Gary. "Experiential Theories of Aesthetic Value." In Shusterman and Tomlin, *Aesthetic Experience*, 45–58.
Ivanhoe, Philip J. *Confucian Moral Self-Cultivation*. 2nd ed. Indianapolis: Hackett, 2000.
Jackson, Philip W. *John Dewey and the Lessons of Art*. New Haven: Yale University Press, 1998.
James, William. "The Will to Believe." In *The Writings of William James: A Comprehensive Edition*, edited by John J. McDermott, 717–35. Chicago: University of Chicago Press, 1977.
Jensen, Joli. *Is Art Good for Us? Beliefs About High Culture in American Life*. New York: Rowman & Littlefield, 2002.
Jhanji, Rekha. *The Sensuous in Art: Reflections on Indian Aesthetics*. New Delhi: Motilal Banarsidass, 1989.
Johnston, James Scott. "Reflections on Richard Shusterman's Dewey." *Journal of Aesthetic Education* 38 (2004): 99–108.
Kant, Immanuel. "Critique of Practical Reason." In *Practical Philosophy*, translated and edited by Mary J. Gregor, 133–272. Cambridge: Cambridge University Press, 1996.
———. *Critique of the Power of Judgment*. Edited by Paul Guyer. Translated by Paul Guyer and Eric Matthews. Cambridge: Cambridge University Press, 2001.
Katz, R. C. *Arjuna in the Mahabharata: Where Krishna Is, There Is Victory*. New Delhi: Motilal Banarsidass, 1990.
Kivy, Peter. *Philosophies of Arts: An Essay in Differences*. New York: Cambridge University Press, 1997.
Kozaryn, Linda D. "DoD Honors *Private Ryan* Director Spielberg." *American Forces Press Service*, August 1999.
Lachs, John. "Stoic Pragmatism." *Journal of Speculative Philosophy* 19 (2005): 95–106.
Lamarque, Peter. "Tragedy and Moral Value." In Davies, *Art and Its Messages*, 59–69.
———. "The Uselessness of Art." *Journal of Aesthetics and Art Criticism* 68 (2010): 205–14.
Lamarque, Peter, and Stein Haugom Olsen. *Truth, Fiction, and Literature: A Philosophical Perspective*. Oxford: Clarendon Press, 1994.
Langsdorf, Lenore. "Reconstructing the Fourth Dimension: A Deweyan Critique of Habermas's Conception of Communicative Action." In *Habermas and Pragmatism*, edited by Mitchell Aboulafia, Myra Bookman, and Catherine Kemp, 141–64. London: Routledge, 2002.
Lao-Tzu: Te-Tao Ching. Translated, with an introduction and commentary, by Robert G. Henricks. New York: Ballantine Books, 1989.
Lawrence of the Resurrection. *The Practice of the Presence of God: Writings and Conversations*. Translated by Salvatore Sciurba. Washington, D.C.: ICS, 1994.
Lee, Morgan. "Subway Books Give Mexico a Novel Way to Fight Crime." *Seattle Times*, January 24, 2004, A8.

Levich, Marvin, ed. *Aesthetics and the Philosophy of Criticism*. New York: Random House, 1963.
Levinson, Jerrold. "Intrinsic Value and the Notion of a Life." *Journal of Aesthetics and Art Criticism* 62 (2004): 319–29.
Lippmann, Walter. *Public Opinion*. New York: Dover Publications, 2004.
Margolis, Joseph. "The Deviant Ontology of Artworks." In Carroll, *Theories of Art Today*, 109–29.
———. *Historied Thought, Constructed World: A Conceptual Primer for the Turn of the Millennium*. Berkeley and Los Angeles: University of California Press, 1995.
———. *Moral Philosophy After 9/11*. University Park: The Pennsylvania State University Press, 2004.
———. "One and Only One Correct Interpretation." In *Is There a Single Right Interpretation?*, edited by Michael Krausz, 26–44. University Park: The Pennsylvania State University Press, 2002.
———. *Selves and Other Texts: The Case for Cultural Realism*. University Park: The Pennsylvania State University Press, 2001.
Minor, Robert N. *Bhagavad Gita: An Exegetical Commentary*. New Delhi: Heritage Publishers, 1982.
Moore, G. E. *Principia Ethica*. New York: Prometheus Books, 1988.
Mothersill, Mary. "Beauty and the Critic's Judgment: Remapping Aesthetics." In *The Blackwell Guide to Aesthetics*, edited by Peter Kivy, 152–66. Oxford: Blackwell, 2004.
Mou, Bo. "Ultimate Concern and Language Engagement: A Reexamination of the Opening Message of the *Dao-De-Jing*." *Journal of Chinese Philosophy* 27 (2000): 429–39.
Myers, William T., and Gregory F. Pappas, "Dewey's Metaphysics: A Response to Richard Gale." *Transactions of the Charles S. Peirce Society* 40 (2004): 679–700.
"Navy Honors Spielberg and Hanks for Film *Saving Private Ryan*." *U.S. Navy Press Releases*, November 1999.
Nelson, John S. "Argument by Mood in War Movies: Postmodern Ethos in Electronic Media." In *Argument at Century's End: Reflecting on the Past and Envisioning the Future*, edited by Thomas A. Hollihan, 262–69. Annandale: National Communication Association, 2000.
Novitz, David. "Messages 'In' and Messages 'Through' Art." In Davies, *Art and Its Messages*, 84–88.
Nussbaum, Martha C. *Love's Knowledge: Essays on Philosophy and Literature*. New York: Oxford University Press, 1990.
Odin, Steve. *Artistic Detachment in Japan and the West: Psychic Distance in Comparative Aesthetics*. Honolulu: University of Hawaii Press, 2001.
O'Dwyer, Shaun. "The Metaphysics of Existence Rehabilitated." *Transactions of the Charles S. Peirce Society* 40 (2004): 711–30.
Otto, Max C. "On a Certain Blindness in William James." *Ethics* 53 (1943): 184–91.
Pawelski, James O. "William James, Positive Psychology, and Healthy-Mindedness." *Journal of Speculative Philosophy* 17 (2003): 53–67.
Peirce, Charles S. "The Fixation of Belief." In *Philosophical Writings of Peirce*, edited by Justus Buchler, 5–22. New York: Dover, 1955.
Petts, Jeffrey. "Aesthetic Experience and the Revelation of Value." *Journal of Aesthetics and Art Criticism* 58 (2000): 61–71.

Rader, Melvin, and Bertram Jessup. *Art and Human Values*. Englewood Cliffs: Prentice Hall, 1976.
Rorty, Richard. *Consequences of Pragmatism*. Minneapolis: University of Minnesota Press, 1982.
———. "Dewey Between Hegel and Darwin." In *Modernist Impulses in the Human Sciences*, edited by Dorothy Ross, 54–68. Baltimore: Johns Hopkins University Press, 1994.
Roth, Robert J. *John Dewey and Self-Realization*. Englewood Cliffs: Prentice Hall, 1962.
Ruetenik, Tadd L. "Social Meliorism in the Religious Pragmatism of William James." *Journal of Speculative Philosophy* 19 (2005): 238–49.
Sartwell, Crispin. *The Art of Living: Aesthetics of the Ordinary in World Spiritual Traditions*. Albany: State University of New York Press, 1995.
Sawyer, R. Keith. "Improvisation and the Creative Process: Dewey, Collingwood, and the Aesthetics of Spontaneity." *Journal of Aesthetics and Art Criticism* 58 (2000): 149–61.
Seel, Martin. "On the Scope of Aesthetic Experience." In Shusterman and Tomlin, *Aesthetic Experience*, 98–105.
Seligman, Martin E. P. *Authentic Happiness*. New York: Free Press, 2002.
Seligman, Martin E. P., Tracy A. Steen, Nansook Park, and Christopher Peterson. "Positive Psychology Progress: Empirical Validation of Interventions." *American Psychologist* 60 (2005): 410–21.
Sheftick, Gary. "Army Awards Spielberg for Telling Soldiers' Story." *Army News Service*, September 18, 1998.
Shusterman, Richard. "Aesthetic Experience: From Analysis to Eros." In Shusterman and Tomlin, *Aesthetic Experience*, 79–97.
———. *Body Consciousness: A Philosophy of Mindfulness and Somaesthetics*. Cambridge: Cambridge University Press, 2008.
———. "Complexities of Aesthetic Experience: Response to Johnston." *Journal of Aesthetic Education* 38 (2004): 109–12.
———. "Home Alone? Self and Other in Somaesthetics and *Performing Live*." *Journal of Aesthetic Education* 36 (2002): 102–15.
———. *Performing Live: Aesthetic Alternatives to the Ends of Art*. Ithaca: Cornell University Press, 2000.
———. *Practicing Philosophy: Pragmatism and the Philosophical Life*. New York: Routledge, 1997.
———. *Pragmatist Aesthetics: Living Beauty, Rethinking Art*. 2nd ed. New York: Rowman & Littlefield, 2000.
———. "Pragmatism and Criticism: A Response to Three Critics of *Pragmatist Aesthetics*." *Journal of Speculative Philosophy* 16 (2002): 26–38.
———. *Surface and Depth: Dialectics of Criticism and Culture*. Ithaca: Cornell University Press, 2002.
Shusterman, Richard, and Adele Tomlin, eds. *Aesthetic Experience*. New York: Routledge, 2008.
Stecker, Robert. *Interpretation and Construction: Art, Speech, and the Law*. Oxford: Blackwell, 2003.
Stolnitz, Jerome. *Aesthetics and Philosophy of Art Criticism: A Critical Introduction*. Boston: Houghton Mifflin, 1960.

———. "On the Cognitive Triviality of Art." *British Journal of Aesthetics* 32 (1992): 191–200.
Stroud, Scott R. "How to Do Things with Art." *Southern Journal of Philosophy* 44 (2006): 341–64.
———. "John Dewey and the Question of Artful Criticism." *Philosophy and Rhetoric* 44 (2011): 27–51.
———. "Mindful Argument, Deweyan Pragmatism, and the Ideal of Democracy." *Controversia* 7 (2011, in press).
———. "Multivalent Narratives: Extending the Narrative Paradigm with Insights from Ancient Indian Philosophical Texts." *Western Journal of Communication* 66 (2002): 369–93.
———. "Narrative as Argument in Indian Philosophy: The *Astāvakra Gītā* as Multivalent Narrative." *Philosophy and Rhetoric* 37 (2004): 42–71.
———. "Ontological Orientation and the Practice of Rhetoric: A Perspective from the *Bhagavad Gītā*." *Southern Communication Journal* 70 (2005): 146–60.
———. "Orientational Meliorism in Dewey and Dōgen." *Transactions of the Charles S. Peirce Society* 43 (2007): 185–215.
———. "Orientational Meliorism, Pragmatist Aesthetics, and the *Bhagavad Gītā*." *Journal of Aesthetic Education* 43 (2009): 1–17.
———. "Pragmatism and the Methodology of Comparative Rhetoric." *Rhetoric Society Quarterly* 39 (2009): 353–79.
———. "Pragmatist Aesthetics and Film: *The Thin Red Line* and Orientational Meliorism." *Film and Philosophy* 10 (2006): 67–83.
———. "Simulation, Subjective Knowledge, and the Cognitive Value of Literary Narrative." *Journal of Aesthetic Education* 42 (2008): 19–41.
———. "Toward a Deweyan Theory of Communicative Mindfulness." *Imagination, Cognition, and Personality* 30, no. 1 (2010–2011): 57–75.
———. "What Does Pragmatic Meliorism Mean for Rhetoric?" *Western Journal of Communication* 74 (2010): 43–60.
Suzuki, Daisetz T. *Zen and Japanese Culture*. Princeton: Princeton University Press, 1973.
Tannen, Deborah. *The Argument Culture: Stopping America's War of Words*. New York: Ballantine, 1999.
Taylor, Paul C. "The Two-Dewey Thesis, Continued: Shusterman's *Pragmatist Aesthetics*." *Journal of Speculative Philosophy* 16 (2002): 17–25.
Tiles, J. E. "Steven Fesmire, *John Dewey and Moral Imagination: Pragmatism in Ethics*." *Transactions of the Charles S. Peirce Society* 40 (2004): 378–83.
Tormey, Alan. *The Concept of Expression: A Study in Philosophical Psychology and Aesthetics*. Princeton: Princeton University Press, 1971.
Walton, Kendall L. "How Marvelous! Toward a Theory of Aesthetic Value." *Journal of Aesthetics and Art Criticism* 51 (1993): 499–510.
Weingarten, Gene. "Pearls Before Breakfast." *Washington Post*, April 8, 2007, W10.
Welchman, Jennifer. *Dewey's Ethical Thought*. Ithaca: Cornell University Press, 1995.
Wrzesniewski, Amy, and Jane Dutton. "Crafting a Job: Revisioning Employees as Active Crafters of Their Work." *Academy of Management Review* 26 (2001): 179–201.
Wrzesniewski, Amy, Clark McCauley, Paul Rozin, and Barry Schwartz. "Jobs, Careers, and Callings: People's Relations to Their Work." *Journal of Research in Personality* 31 (1997): 21–33.

Index

absorption. *See* attention
accommodation, 147–48, 152, 166
adaptation, 147–48, 151–52, 166
adjustment, 147–48, 151–52, 164. *See also* progressive adjustment
aesthetic attitude
   aesthetic experience, relation to, 18, 28–29, 185
   aspects of, 17, 18
   criticisms of, 19–21, 194
   internal/external aspects of, 25
aesthetic experience
   artistic value, and, 25–28
   attention and, 9, 30
   communication and, 105, 112–16, 171
   conceptions of, 5, 7, 13–14, 30, 73–87
   concepts and, 19, 28, 168
   criticism of, 21
   distance and, 15
   experiential reading of, 10, 34, 36, 50–60
   expression and, 174–78
   intrinsic value and, 42–47
   media and, 52
   morality and, 2–3, 6, 8, 137, 200–202
   orientation and, 6
   process as, 114
   reflection, connection to, 9, 40
   rhythm, connection to, 80–87
   work and, 159
aesthetic properties, 21, 25, 31
Aesthetics and Philosophy of Art Criticism, 15
Aldrich, Virgil, 21, 29
Alexander technique, 10, 116
Alexander, Thomas, 82–83
analysis, 119, 121–22, 125
appreciation. *See* immediate experience
art
   aesthetic experience and, 73, 77, 93
   avant-garde, 29–30
   characteristics of, 2, 5, 7, 84
   communication and, 104–5, 109
   dramatic rehearsal and, 130–35
   effects of, 13, 26–27, 33–34
   ends and means and, 51–57, 89
   everyday experience and, 4
   internal/external aspects to, 21, 31–32
   interpretation of, 9, 31
   intrinsic interest in, 16
   objects of, 9–10
   theorizing about, 5, 172
   value of, 3, 5, 14, 25–28
Art as Experience
   aesthetic experience, on, 59–60, 75, 79, 83, 129, 150, 171, 183, 195
   art, analysis of, 8, 172–74, 203
   on communication, 97, 101, 106, 115, 176
   criticism and, 104, 123
   ends and means and, 50–51
   experience and, 39
   growth and, 146, 151–52, 157
   moral cultivation and, 61, 73
artful activity, 3, 75, 161, 167, 169–70, 190
artful living, 6, 87–92, 137, 151, 158, 183–84, 193–94, 200–206
artful communication, 168, 171, 179, 185, 188
artistic value, 25, 178. *See also* art
attention
   absorption and, 11, 52–57, 88–89
   aesthetic attitude and, 15, 19, 20
   aesthetic experience and, 30, 59, 103, 185
   art and, 95, 133, 192
   desire and, 148–51, 153, 158, 161
   means and ends and, 55–57, 180–81

attention (*continued*)
  as mindful, 10
  moral cultivation and, 61–62, 68–72, 74, 200–202
  to situations, 8, 79, 83–85, 92, 137, 162
attitude
  aesthetic, 16, 86
  communication and, 171
  ends and means and, 50
  experience of art objects and, 28–29
  growth and, 152
  play and work and, 154–58
  power of, 28
  See also aesthetic attitude
auditor
  aesthetic response of, 19, 26, 108
  identification and, 131–32
  interpretation and, 31–32, 121, 129
  value of art and, 25, 134
Austria, 163
authorial intention, 117, 123
Avadhoota Gītā, 127

Bahm, Archie, 14–15, 32
Barrie, J. M., 85
Basho, 111–12, 114
Beardsley, Monroe, 34, 77
belief, 28
Bell, Clive, 14
Bell, Joshua, 1, 4
Belman, Lary, 170–71
Bhagavad Gītā, 88–89, 91, 186
Biosvert, Raymond D., 70
Brother Lawrence of the Resurrection, 188–91
Budd, Malcolm, 7, 25–28, 33
Buddhism, 187, 197
Bullough, Edward, 13, 15, 18–20

capacity. *See* specific capacity
Carroll, Noël, 20–21, 28–30, 91, 103
causal account, 34, 36, 49–50
Chan Buddhism. *See* Zen Buddhism
character, 61–62, 64–65, 67–70, 140, 201
China, 60, 111, 156
cognition. *See* reflection
cognitive therapy, 10, 143
cognitive value, 24, 27, 41
Coleridge, Samuel Taylor, 33
A Common Faith, 147, 151
communication
  as aesthetic, 179–88, 190

art and, 27, 94–95, 97–98, 101–17, 124–25, 134–35
  empirical method and, 98–100
  everyday experience and, 6, 10, 169–71
  expression and, 173–78
community, 11, 71, 140, 183, 205
Confucius, 60
consummatory end, 52, 54, 83, 150
craft, 74–75
Crick, Nathan, 169–70
criticism, 41, 98, 104, 116–26, 135, 137, 157
Critique of the Power of Judgment, 18
Croce, Benedetto, 61

deflationary account, 20, 31
deliberation, 43–44, 53–54, 94–95, 127–35
Democracy and Education, 46, 140
democracy, 46, 90, 170
descriptive pragmatism, 138
design appreciation, 20
desire, 137, 149–50, 152–54, 158–59, 161–67, 177, 180–81, 186, 192
Dewey, John
  aesthetic theory, 5, 7, 13, 28–29, 32, 35
  artful living and, 6
  avant-garde art and, 29–30
  on criticism, 117–26
  ends and means and, 6–8, 51–57
  on happiness, 70
  on intrinsic value, 8, 42–47
  on meliorism, 138–39
  on play and work, 154–58
  on primary and secondary experience, 36–39, 98–99
  on process/product distinction, 113–16
  self-cultivation and, 60–72
dialectic, 113, 115
Dickie, George, 20–21, 28–31, 77, 103
Diffey, T. J., 24–25
Dirty Harry, 131
discharge, 104
discursivity, 106
disinterested attention, 17–19, 29–32
distance. *See* psychical distance
Dostoevsky, Fyodor, 165
drama, 134
dramatic rehearsal, 130, 132–33, 135
drudgery, 10, 59, 150–52, 154, 158–61, 169, 180, 195, 197–98, 204
dualism, 7, 30–31, 36–39, 203

Eames, S. Morris, 94
Eastman, Max, 59

education, 85, 90, 142, 159, 201, 205
empirical method, 98–101, 107–8, 112. *See also* reflection
ends. *See* means and ends
enlightenment, 111–12
environment, 63–69, 75, 79, 81, 86, 96, 118, 120, 140–42, 145, 147–48, 150, 152, 166–67, 172, 183, 185
Ethics, 65
evaluation. *See* judgment
existential psychotherapy. *See* logotherapy
experience
   as aesthetic, 21, 30–31, 49, 195
   art and, 112–16, 127
   communication and, 107
   expression and, 175–79
   growth and, 198
   identification, 131–32
   meliorism and, 138–39, 205
   rhythm and, 80–87
   and subjects, 8, 98–99
   types of, 36–39
Experience and Nature, 4, 36, 43, 47–48, 54, 78, 98–99, 104, 106, 169, 176
experiential account, 34, 36, 47, 50–57, 82–87, 90
expression, 10, 68, 96–98, 104, 107–9, 112–16, 174–78
extrinsic value. *See* instrumental value

Fesmire, Steven, 70, 130–31
Finding Neverland, 85
Fisher, Walter, 131
formalism, 14
France, 178, 188
Frankl, Viktor, 163–67, 188, 199
function, 63, 96

Gaut, Berys, 4, 26
genealogical analysis, 47
Gouinlock, James, 53
great community, the, 170–71
Green, Thomas H., 61
Greene, Roberta R., 199
growth, 8, 59, 72–73, 89, 137, 139, 143–68, 180, 192, 198–99, 205

Habermas, Jürgen, 178
habit
   art and, 93–94, 104, 109–10
   attention and, 83, 137
   communication and, 103, 177, 180, 184

criticism and, 117, 127
   deliberation and, 127–29, 133–34
   ethics and, 65–66, 201–4
   growth and, 145, 147, 156, 168
   means and ends and, 50, 190
   meliorism and, 9–10, 116
   orientation and, 11, 140–41, 143
   the present and, 11
   reflection and, 38–40, 44, 127
   the self and, 194–98
haiku, 111–12, 135
Hamburger Hill, 113
Hamlet, 22, 124, 130
happiness, 70–73, 151
hedonistic paradox, 71–72
Hegelianism, 62
heresy of paraphrase, 51–52
Herman, Nicholas. *See* Brother Lawrence of the Resurrection
Hoover, Thomas, 111
How We Think, 154–56, 158
Human Nature and Conduct, 39, 54, 65, 127–28, 132, 141, 149–50, 194, 204
hypothetical intentionalism, 125

idealism, 61–62
identification, 131–34
imagination, 15, 128–29, 132, 152, 154, 158, 165, 169, 186, 190
imagined interaction, 189
immediate empiricism, 38
immediate experience, 7, 29, 36–40, 106, 203–4. *See also* primary experience
immediate value, 29, 33, 35, 42–47
impressionist criticism. *See* criticism
impulse, 37, 64, 76, 113, 128, 132, 134
India, 60, 126, 197
inquiry, 37–41, 171
instrumental value, 4, 7, 25–28, 33–34, 42–47, 193
intellectual fallacy, 38
intention, 94–98, 104–5, 125, 178
interpretation, 31, 39–40, 122–26
intrapersonal communication. *See* imagined interaction
intrinsic value, 3, 25–28, 33–34, 42–47, 50–57, 193
Ivanhoe, Philip J., 60

Jackson, Philip W., 114
James, William, 28
Japan, 60, 111

Jessup, Bertram, 103
Jhanji, Rekha, 126
Johnston, James Scott, 39–40
judgment, 42–47, 60, 107, 116–18, 120
judicial criticism. *See* criticism

kairos, 170
Kant, Immanuel, 3, 18, 186
karma yoga, 88
Kivy, Peter, 110

Lachs, John, 143–49, 157
Lamarque, Peter, 23–24
Langsdorf, Lenore, 134
language, 105–6, 120, 134, 175, 177
Lao Tzu, 106
Lippmann, Walter, 193
literature, 21–25
logotherapy, 163–64

Malick, Terrence, 120
Margolis, Joseph, 94
The Matrix, 84
meaning, 39–40, 155, 157–58, 165–66, 174–75, 177, 189–90
means and ends
  aesthetic experience and, 59
  art and, 109–10, 116, 158–59
  connection in experiential approach, 51–57
  expression and, 176–78, 181
  meliorism and, 139, 161, 167
  moral cultivation and, 63, 69–70, 72, 149
  orientation and, 180, 185, 191
  as process or product, 54–55, 90
  rhythm and, 82
  separation of, 4, 6, 47–50
measurement, 121
media, 52, 108, 113–14, 159, 171, 176–79
meditation, 10, 143
medium. *See* media
meliorism, 124, 137, 143–44, 170, 184, 194, 196–98, 199, 204
Mengzi (Mencius), 60
mindfulness, 112, 162, 181, 192
Moby Dick, 84
Mona Lisa, 74
Moore, G. E., 44
moral cultivation, 5, 8, 30, 50–51, 57, 59–73, 86–87, 93, 132, 138, 200–201, 205
moral fatalism, 61
moral improvement. *See* moral cultivation
moral theory, 24, 60, 137

moral value, 3, 13, 23, 33, 45, 68, 82–87, 132
museum conception of art, 5, 51, 179
mushin, 111
music, 2, 96, 113, 201

nature, 36–39, 48, 98
New Testament, 186
noncognitivism, 7
nondiscursivity, 106
Novitz, David, 25
Nussbaum, Martha, 24, 89

Odin, Steve, 134
Olsen, Stein, 23–24
ontology, 21, 205
openness, 102–3, 122–23
optimism, 138–39
orientation
  activity and, 137–43, 145, 189–91
  art and, 102–5, 116–17, 119, 121–22, 126, 135
  communication and, 98, 102, 114, 171, 178–79, 182, 184–85, 188
  defined, 136
  desire and, 149–52, 159
  growth and, 147–48, 153, 166–68, 204–5
  habit and, 6, 194
  means and ends and, 53–57
  mental aspects, 10
  play and work and, 155
  the self and, 194–97
  value and, 45–47
orientational meliorism
  communication and, 188, 191–92
  defined, 9, 137, 160–61, 168
  growth and, 89–90, 143
  mental means of, 143, 159–62, 186
  methods of, 10, 138–43, 197
  somatic means of, 143
Othello, 24, 51
Outlines of a Critical Theory of Ethics, 6, 63, 73

Peirce, Charles S., 127
Pepper, Stephen, 61
perception, 16–17, 84–85, 103
pessimism, 138–39
Peter Pan, or The Boy Who Wouldn't Grow Up, 85
Petts, Jeffrey, 86
play, 154–59
pluralism, 200
popular art, 115

present situation, 46, 51–57, 66, 68, 70, 72, 84, 157–58, 167, 183–85, 191–92, 195, 204–6
primary experience, 36–40, 78, 98–99, 120
progressive adaptation. *See* progressive adjustment
progressive adjustment, 6, 8, 62, 67, 69–70, 72, 75, 87, 91, 139, 143, 147, 192, 198
psychical distance, 15
psychology, 62
The Public and Its Problems, 141, 169
Putnam, Hilary, 24

qualities, 39–40, 44, 49, 78, 80, 82, 100, 105, 120–21, 173, 181, 205

Rader, Melvin, 103
reconstructive pragmatism, 138
reflection
  art objects and, 93–95, 98, 106, 108–13
  compared to immediate experience, 6–7, 203
  deliberation and, 128–30, 133
  empirical method and, 98–101
  interpretation and, 116–17, 119, 125–27, 137
  means and ends and, 51–57
  as a phase of experience, 9, 36–42, 78–79, 98–99, 112, 201
  value and, 43–45, 53
reflective activity. *See* reflection
reflective afterlife, 110
regulative principle, 124–25
relationships, 69–72, 81, 83, 100, 108, 145–46, 155–56, 161
rhythm, 8, 80–87, 107, 170
Rorty, Richard, 106, 115

Sartwell, Crispin, 8, 87, 91, 114, 177, 186
satori, 111–12
Saving Private Ryan, 109, 129
Sawyer, R. Keith, 85
science, 48–49, 51, 100, 107–8, 114, 139. *See also* inquiry
secondary experience. *See* reflection
self, 60, 62, 66–67, 69
self-cultivation. *See* moral cultivation
self-realization. *See* moral cultivation
Seligman, Martin, 160, 162

Serra, Richard, 110, 114
Shusterman, Richard, 5, 39–41, 95, 105–6, 114, 124, 134, 138
specific capacity, 63, 65, 76
specific environment, 63
Spielberg, Steven, 109, 114, 129
statement, 107, 175–79
Stecker, Robert, 125
stoic pragmatism, 144–48
Stolnitz, Jerome, 7, 13–14, 16, 19, 23–24, 28, 32
The Study of Ethics, 62, 64, 66–67, 69, 128
Suzuki, D. T., 111–12
synthesis, 122–23, 156

Tao Te Ching, 106–7
tao, 106–7
taste. *See* immediate experience
Taylor, Paul C., 105–6
technology, 48–50
The Thin Red Line, 120
Tilted Arc, 110, 135
Tormey, Alan, 96–97
truth, 22–24, 100

understanding. *See* reflection
unit of analysis, 140, 197

value
  art and, 121–22, 128, 134
  conceptions of, 8, 33, 66, 155
  experience and, 36–42
  identification and, 131–32
  intrinsic and instrument, 42–47
  means and ends and, 50–57
  orientation and, 136, 142, 160, 167, 179, 188, 194
Values of Art, 25, 27
Van Gogh, Vincent, 108
vector of change, 140, 197

Welchman, Jennifer, 62, 66
will, 62, 67
work, 10, 50, 154–63, 189–90, 199
Wrzesniewski, Amy, 160–61

Xunzi, 60

Zen Buddhism, 111–12

www.ingramcontent.com/pod-product-compliance
Lightning Source LLC
Chambersburg PA
CBHW021402290426
44108CB00010B/352